# WHO REALLY
# RULES?

# WHO REALLY RULES?

# New Haven and Community Power Reexamined

## G. WILLIAM DOMHOFF

Goodyear Publishing Company, Inc.
Santa Monica, California

Library of Congress Catalog Number: 76-58230
ISBN: 0-87855-228-6(cloth)
ISBN: 0-87620-965-7 (paper)
Y-9657-1
Printed in the United States of America.

Library of Congress Cataloging in Publication Data

Domhoff, G. William.
   Who really rules?

   Includes bibliographical references and index.
   1. New Haven—Politics and government. 2. Dahl,
Robert Alan, 1915-       Who governs? 3. Community
power—Case studies. I. Title.
JS1195.2.D65       320.9'746'804       76-58230
ISBN 0-87855-228-6 (cloth)
ISBN 0-87620-965-7 (paper)

Current Printing (last digit): 10 9 8 7 6 5 4 3 2

TO FLOYD HUNTER

# CONTENTS

# PREFACE

This book is a detailed study of the power structure and the policy-formation process in New Haven, Connecticut, during 1940-1960, but it is also much more than that. It presents a methodological statement on how power structures should be studied. It also provides a theoretical framework for understanding local power structures in general by showing how they function within the overall context of the national power structure. It is not possible to comprehend the operation of a community power structure without a conception of how any given city or community functions as part of the national corporate community and the national ruling class.[1]

A detailed study of any single city has little inherent interest in and of itself, for there are dozens of cities which could be studied with equal profit. What makes this investigation of New Haven of significance within the context of American social science is that previous research on this city provides one of the major bases for the widely accepted claim that power is diffused among several groups and classes in the United States. I am referring, of course, to Robert A. Dahl's *Who Governs?*, and to a lesser extent to companion volumes by his two former research assistants, Nelson W. Polsby's *Community Power and Political Theory* and Raymond E. Wolfinger's *The Politics of Progress.*[2] Together, this trilogy presents a theoretical, methodological, and empirical basis for the conclusion that there is no ruling elite or ruling class or covert oligarchy in either New Haven or the United States in general.

In Dahl's words, "an elite no longer rules New Haven" (p. 86). [3] Having disposed of the hypothesis that an upper-class elite rules in New Haven, Dahl asks: "Who, then, rules in a pluralist democracy?" His answer is that New Haven has a system "dominated by many different sets of leaders, each having access to a different combination of political resources," which is what is meant by the term *pluralist democracy* (p. 86).[4]

This book is meant as a challenge to the work on New Haven by Dahl, Polsby, and Wolfinger. It can be used as a companion piece to their work, and in particular to Dahl's *Who Governs?*, to suggest to students and scholars a very different picture of who really rules in New Haven.[5] The book begins with a statement of Dahl's view of New Haven, and then turns in chapter 2 to a mapping of the power structure of New Haven as it existed in the late 1950s, the same years Dahl and his associates used in their research. The second chapter can also be considered a practical demonstration of how a systematic study of a power structure should begin. The third chapter is a detailed study of the origins of urban renewal in New Haven, 1940-60, for urban renewal was the most important of three decisions Dahl studied and is the primary focus of Wolfinger's *The Politics of Progress.*[6]

Chapter 4 builds on the empirical work in chapters 2 and 3 to present a comprehensive rationale for power structure research in general, and also provides specific direction for those wishing to undertake such research on the local, state, or national level. It seeks to provide a direct challenge to what I see as the limited conception of power structure research presented by Dahl in *Who Governs?* and in two papers preliminary to his work on New Haven—papers that have generally been accepted as important statements on the proper approach to the study of power.[7]

The final chapter shows how New Haven is connected with the nationwide ruling class and the corporate business community upon which the national ruling class is based. It also outlines the several institutions and policy-influencing networks that link national and local power structures in general, and hopefully rescues community power structure studies from the sterile isolation which has led many social scientists to a considerable disinterest in community power studies because such studies do not seem to add up to a significant, generalizable body of knowledge.

In preparation for this study I have been collecting information on New Haven since the late 1960s, relying at first on the work of political activists in New Haven who published the alternative newspaper *Modern Times*. The impetus for undertaking in-depth research dates from 1972-73 when I came to know the founder of power-structure research in American sociology, Floyd Hunter. Hunter's unpublished preliminary work on New Haven, which gave every indication of a power hierarchy, and his theoretical savvy about the role of communities in the national power network, convinced me that such a study would be feasible as well as theoretically fruitful. It is with extreme pleasure that I am able to acknowledge his influence on this study by dedicating the book to him.

When I began my research I had a good idea of where and how to look for the information I needed, but I never would have reached the level of detail and complexity that is recounted in the chapter on urban renewal in New Haven without the friendly sharing of information by American studies scholar A. Tappan Wilder, who has been engaged for several years in a study of New Haven's changing physical fabric from an historical perspective and with an interest in the role of planners. Wilder, who is undoubtedly the outstanding authority on twentieth-century New Haven history, directed me to sources I otherwise would not have uncovered, and corrected and gave historical perspective to my earlier, tentative hypotheses. While we disagree in some of our emphases and interpretations, the benefit of our relationship has been all mine. I gratefully acknowledge his willingness to share his original research with me.[8]

In doing the empirical work that appears in chapters 2 and 3 I had the help of two fine research assistants, Deborah Samuels-Robinson and Susan Kay Sloan, and I am beholden to them for their tireless efforts with tedious material. I also want to express my thanks to Patricia Nelson, a former Santa Cruz student now in the American Studies Program at Yale University, for the many hours she spent in New Haven archives as my research assistant.

It is not possible to single out all of the many people who offered suggestions and criticism or consented to interviews—partly because many of them prefer to remain anonymous—but my collective debt to them is very great indeed. In particular I want to thank Harris and Joan Stone for giving me a basic orientation to the subject of urban renewal in New Haven.[9] For careful and critical readings of the entire manuscript, I am grateful to Harvey Molotch, Robert Alford, Roger Friedland, and Jonathan Turner. For comments on the chapters on New Haven, I thank Philip Burch, Jr., John Mollenkopf, and Marshall Pomer. For very helpful comments on the methodology chapter, I am indebted to Jefferson Livesay, Bill Friedland, Charles Kadushin, Thomas Koenig, David Bunting, and Peter Euben. Chester Hartman was kind enough to comment on the final chapter. My thanks also go to Charlotte Cassidy and Mark Mumper for undertaking the chore of typing the manuscript in their usual fine style.

This research was made possible by small grants from the Research Committee of the Academic Senate, University of California, Santa Cruz, and I extend my appreciation to that committee for supporting my efforts. My own field visits to New Haven—three in all—were made possible by speaking engagements at the University of Connecticut, Amherst College, Hampshire College, University of Hartford, Quinnipiac College, and Yale University, and I thank the various social science departments at those campuses for providing these lecture opportunities.

I want to thank Robert A. Dahl for giving me access to his original research materials and for other professional courtesies shown to me. I also am grateful to Raymond Wolfinger for providing me with his list of New Haven social notables.

*G. William Domhoff*
*Santa Cruz, California*
*February 1977*

## NOTES

1. The phrase *power structure* will be used as a generic term for all research that concerns the pattern and distribution of power in a given community, city, state, or nation. Although the phrase has a commonly understood meaning in American society that makes it possible to use it without precise definition, I will discuss the phrase in more detail in chapter 4. Similarly, other commonly understood phrases, such as *social class* and *ruling class*, will be defined at appropriate places in the text.

2. Robert A Dahl, *Who governs? Democracy and Power in an American City* (Yale University Press, 1961); Nelson W. Polsby, *Community Power and Political Theory* (Yale University Press. 1963); Raymond E. Wolfinger, *The Politics of Progress* (Prentice-Hall, 1974).

3. All page references in the main text of this book are taken from *Who Governs?* (Yale University Press, 1961).

4. In the first paragraph of *Who Governs?* Dahl poses his question in slightly different words: "In a political system where nearly every adult may vote but where knowledge, wealth, social position, access to officials, and other resources are unequally distributed, who actually governs?" (p. 1) As a close reading of the entire text makes clear, Dahl uses the terms *rule* and *govern* interchangeably. When he addresses the possibility that those who "rule" (dominate or control the governmental structure) do not "govern" in the sense of occupying the formal seats of political authority, he uses such phrases as "who actually governs" (pp. 1, 5), "who in fact does govern" (p. 3), "real decision-makers" (pp. 11, 63), "covert influence" (p. 66), and "indirect influence" (p. 89). In his methodological appendix, Dahl writes that one of his methods of studying power, reconstructing the decision-making process, "is intended to penetrate the veil of official position and overt participation in order to determine, as far as possible, who *really* influences decisions" (p. 332).

5. Dahl poses the question as "who rules in New Haven?" on page 165 of his text. Chapter 4 of Polsby's *Community Power and Political Theory* is entitled "Who Rules in New Haven? An Empirical Test of the Stratification Theory."

6. The other two decisions concerned public education on the one hand and nomination for political office on the other. I consider public education less important to the leaders of New Haven because, as Dahl himself states, they either live in the suburbs or send their children to expensive private schools (pp. 70-71, 144-45). Their only concern in this issue area is that public education be as inexpensive as possible and that it provide students with practical skills and good work habits. Nominations for political office are of less importance because leaders in New Haven tend to deal directly with whoever is the mayor, as we will see in the case of urban renewal. Their only concern here is that they have "access" to government officials, which is obtained through campaign donations and other favors.

7. Robert A. Dahl, "The Concept of Power," *Behavioral Science* 2 (1957); idem, "A Critique of the Ruling Elite Model," *American Political Science Review* (June 1958).

8. Wilder presented some of his research findings in a talk to the American Political Science Association meetings in San Francisco, September 4-7, 1975. For a detailed account of his findings, and a greater emphasis on the independent role of planners than in my theoretical perspective, see his forthcoming Yale University Ph.D. dissertation on the physical fabric of New Haven in the first half of the twentieth century.

9. For a unique and sensitive account of New Haven urban renewal by a radical architect, see Harris Stone, *Workbook of an Unsuccessful Architect* (Monthly Review Press, 1973).

Figure 1: New Haven and Nearby Cities

# 1
# DAHL'S VIEW
# OF NEW HAVEN

In an era of Watergate-type scandals, energy crises, runaway inflation, high unemployment, and the discovery of massive illegal corporate donations to both American and foreign political leaders, it may seem beside the point to focus attention on the little New England city of New Haven, Connecticut (population in 1960: 152,000 and falling). However, such a concern is more than justified because political scientist Robert A. Dahl's highly regarded book on New Haven, *Who Governs?*, is one of the major bulwarks of the "pluralistic" conception of America that makes it all but impossible to understand the larger ills of the society generated by the needs and policies of the corporation-based national ruling class.

Based on research conducted in 1957-59 and published in 1961, the book is considered a landmark in rigor and insight, and is the model for many other similar studies. It claims to show that there is no ruling elite or powerful upper class in New Haven which dominates the scene in the interest of big business and big property owners, but rather a variety of middle-class leadership groups influential in the different issue areas investigated—political nominations, public schooling, and urban renewal. Not only was the business community passive and divided, but elected officials, and particularly the mayor, provided the decisive initiative and leadership.

Despite the disclaimer that "explanations presented in this study are tested only against the evidence furnished in New Haven" (p. vi), it is also suggested that the book may help readers "gain a greater understanding of their own communities, American politics, or even democracy itself" (p. vii). The implication that the findings in New Haven may have relevance to the United States in general is also indicated in the claim that because of its "highly competitive two-party system" the city "offers analogies with national politics that few other cities could provide" (p. v).

The book was an immediate success in the academic community. It was greeted with generally enthusiastic reviews, hailed as "a landmark of American political science" and a "major break-through."[1] In 1962 it received the Woodrow Wilson Foundation Award because it "illuminated a central question in political science, the problem of how men can govern themselves in complex societies, through the close and exhaustive tracing of the rubric of power in an American city." The citation accompanying the award went on to say that the book "provides a dynamic, pluralist theory of local power structure," and that it "will become a classic reference for those seeking an understanding of political behavior in modern urban environments under democratic regimes."[2] In terms of classroom usage and frequency of citation, the predictions of reviewers and the Woodrow Wilson Foundation were completely vindicated, for the book remains today as one of the two or three research works most often referred to by social scientists who disagree with the growing body of research and argument which suggests that American society is dominated by a small ruling class rooted in the ownership and control of major financial and corporate institutions.

It would be wrong to imply that every reviewer was an un-qualified admirer of Who Governs? Several political activists and academics made cogent theoretical and methodological criticisms that would have considerably diminished the impact of the book had they been taken more seriously.[3] However, these critiques based upon alternative theoretical assumptions about the nature of power were not taken seriously by a majority of the social science community, and therefore had little effect upon the widespread acceptance of the pluralistic paradigm. One of the factors which made it possible to ignore these critiques was the lack of an empirical challenge to the adequacy of Dahl's analysis. By remain-ing at the level of "theory" and "method," the critics seemed as mere quibblers trying to explain away the hard-gained and unassailable "empirical facts" which Dahl and his associates had accumulated over a two-year period. Given the general ascendancy of pluralist assumptions and the degree of detail in Dahl's account, it was strictly no contest.

It is because the "evidence" presented in *Who Governs?* is one of the major empirical efforts held to contradict the ruling-class notion that this study was undertaken. It is based upon hundreds of hours of new research by myself and several research assistants, and by the historian A. Tappan Wilder. This research, by both myself and Wilder, includes a detailed searching of the minutes, memos, and letters in numerous historical archives as well as personal and telephone interviews with people all over the country. Thanks to the well-known and admirable openness of Robert A. Dahl, it incorporates much of the original research material collected by Dahl and his associates in the 1950s.[4]

My purpose will be to show that *Who Governs?* is wrong about who really rules in New Haven. Contrary to Dahl's belief, there is an active and organized business community in New Haven, and Yale University is a very important part of it. The "economic notables" (his term for the leaders of the business community) are in good measure part of the city's "social notables" (his term for the social upper class). Finally, the leaders of the business community, and not Mayor Richard C. Lee and his redevelopment assistants, urged and made possible the large federally and state-subsidized urban renewal program that helped make New Haven a focal point of research attention.

Before embarking upon an empirical refutation of the factual claims in *Who Governs?*, it is important to carefully state the view of New Haven I am challenging. First, I disagree with the proposition that the "economic notables" and "social notables" are two distinct sets of individuals in New Haven (p. 68). Second, I disagree that Yale University is "in fact" in a "weak political position" in New Haven (p. 138). Third, further analysis refutes the claim that urban renewal was not "produced by the wants and demands of the Economic Notables" (p. 115). Having stated Dahl's three major findings, it will be useful to look in turn at each of them a little more closely, and to examine the pluralistic inferences Dahl drew from them.

## SOCIAL NOTABLES AND ECONOMIC NOTABLES

Dahl arrived at his conclusion about the lack of overlap between social and economic notables by the following procedures. He began by defining social notables as all those invited to the New Haven debutante ball, called the Assembly, for the years 1951, 1958, and 1959; this produced a list of 231 different families (p. 64). Then he developed a list of economic notables for 1957-58 by including people in the following categories (pp. 67-68):

1. The president or chairman of the board of a corporation with property in New Haven assessed in any of the five years 1953-57 at a value placing it among the fifty highest assessments in the city.

2. Any individual or group of individuals with property in the city assessed in the years 1953-57 at a value of $250,000 or more.

3. President or chairman of the board of any bank or public utility in the city.

4. Any individual who was a director of three or more of the following: a firm with an assessed valuation of $250,000 or more; a manufacturing firm with fifty employees or more; a retailing firm with twenty-five employees or more; a bank.

5. All directors of New Haven banks.

After eliminating duplications, there were 238 economic notables. He then compared the two groups of notables and found only 24 overlappers, a finding that seems to contradict the notion that the upper social class in any large American city includes the biggest business people and property owners.[5]

### THE IMPOTENCE OF YALE UNIVERSITY

Dahl makes his assertions about Yale University in a discussion of how, in the case of urban renewal, "the organized interest groups are too weak and divided to carry on the task of initiating and coordinating redevelopment" (p. 137). He arrived at this judgement on the basis of interviews with leaders in all areas of New Haven life. His conclusion about Yale, which I hope to show totally misses the heart of the matter, will be quoted at length. It contradicts my belief that the most important institutions in a local economy are likely to have great political power, and thus helps to make clear the differences in our perspectives:

Although the university is sometimes regarded by suspicious citizens of New Haven as an obscurely powerful force in local politics, in fact it is in a weak political position. Like academic people everywhere, Yale faculty members are politically heterogenous and jealous of their individual autonomy; they can be counted on to raise a cry for academic freedom at the first suggestion from an incautious university administration that they are expected to hew a single political line on anything.

Certainly no administration in recent years has even hinted at the existence of a Yale party line. Although a few individual faculty members are involved in New Haven politics—the last three Democratic aldermen from the First Ward have been young Yale Faculty members—most Yale people are much less interested in the politics of New Haven than in the politics of Yale, their professional associations, the nation, or the international arena. And more of Yale's faculty and other employees live outside New Haven than in the city. Finally, although the university is one of the biggest property owners in New Haven, it also happens to be far and away the largest owner of tax-free property; hence Yale officials are highly sensitive to community hostility and fearful of any action that might embroil the university in local controversy [p. 138].[6]

## ORIGINS OF URBAN RENEWAL IN NEW HAVEN

Dahl's analysis of the origins of the urban renewal program, based in good part on interviews, encompasses an entire chapter. There is no one sentence or paragraph in the chapter itself which captures his conclusion that political leaders initiated the program and had to convince local businessmen to endorse the program—a conclusion diametrically opposite to that of my own research on the subject. A dramatic summary of his perspective can be found in an earlier chapter where he discusses the lack of "direct influence" on the part of economic notables. This summary sets the tone of his overall view of the power of businesspeople, and makes later qualifications on this statement seem like minor caveats:

Even on urban development, their record is a curious one. Few aspects of local policy could be more salient to the Notables than efforts to save downtown New Haven, yet the Economic Notables were able neither to agree on nor put through a program of urban redevelopment even under a Republican mayor anxious to retain their support. When redevelopment came to New Haven the leadership for it came less from the Notables than from a Democratic mayor, whom most of them originally opposed and who as mayor had to wheedle, cajole, recruit, organize, plan, negotiate, bargain, threaten, reward, and maneuver endlessly to get the support and participation needed from the Notables, the small businessmen, the developers (who came principally from outside New Haven), the federal authorities, and the electorate [p. 79].

Dahl's claims in the chapter itself are only slightly less straightforward. Early in the chapter he writes that "very little happened until redevelopment became attached to the political fortunes of an ambitious politician," that urban renewal was not "produced by the wants and demands of the Economic Notables, even though many of them believed that changes in the physical pattern of the city were necessary for their own goals"; that "aggressive action by city officials [was] required for comprehensive reshaping of the face of the city" (p. 115). Then, after several pages are given over to the energy and coalition-building efforts of the mayor and his aides, Dahl claims that the Citizens Action Commission, set up in 1954 to lead the urban renewal program and made up in good part of business and Yale leaders, "never directly initiated, opposed, vetoed, or altered any proposal brought before it by the Mayor and his Development Administrator" (p. 131). Finally, after a discussion of the mayor's skills (p. 137), there appears a discussion of the "weak and divided" interest groups, a category which includes the Chamber of Commerce and Yale University (pp. 137-38).[7]

## DAHL'S VIEW OF NEW HAVEN

In Dahl's view of New Haven the social upper class is not based in the business community, and the business community is passive and divided. It can block proposals it does not like that directly affect its economic interests, but it seldom takes an initiatory role in new programs. Yale University, the biggest and most prestigious institution in the city, is on the periphery of political activity, partly out of fear of local resentment toward it, partly because its faculty has more interest in activities outside New Haven. When it comes to power, the most important arena in New Haven is the political one.[8] It is the mayor and his aides who initiate new programs and forge new coalitions, selling their programs to the business community, Yale, and the general electorate. No one social class or interest group is able to dominate the political sector on a variety of issues. The restraining role of the electorate on politicians' programs is at least as important as the more focused pressures of specific interest groups—for the fear of losing an election is said to be a major factor in shaping the policies of ambitious politicians.

Dahl draws several general conclusions from his specific studies of social notables, economic notables, political nominations, public education, and urban renewal. The first is that there is inequality in New Haven, but it is not an inequality that favors one specific group or class, as it did in the past:

In the political system of the patrician oligarchy, political resources were marked by a cumulative inequality: when one individual was much better off than another in one resource, such as wealth, he was usually better off in almost every other resource—social standing, legitimacy, control over religious and educational institutions, knowledge, office. In the political system of today, inequalities in political resources remain, but they tend to be *noncumulative*. The political system of New Haven, then, is one of *dispersed inequalities* [p. 85].

A second major conclusion drawn by Dahl is that movement into the small stratum of individuals who are highly active in politics, a stratum he calls the political stratum, is relatively "easy" (pp. 91-93). Because of the "ease" with which this political stratum can be "penetrated," politicians will be alerted to citizen desires and will try to be responsive if they see an "electoral payoff" (p. 93). This point is closely related to a third general conclusion—that the effects of political competition in New Haven are quite significant (p. 228). Who holds elective office **does** have an effect on some policies. Moreover, "political competition and elections, at a minimum, lead to the rejection of a great range of possible policies" (p. 220).

The importance of competitive politics leads Dahl to one of his most important conclusions, that "numbers" (the majority of voters) would triumph over "Notability" if the goals of the majority were to become different from those of economic and social notables. This conclusion is part of an argument in which Dahl acknowledges the indirect or nondecisional power of social and economic notables to limit policy options entertained by politicians. This acknowledgement may seem to favor a ruling-class perspective, but that is only a surface appearance, for Dahl goes on to emphasize that politicians are ultimately responsible to the belief system and demands of the majority:

The Social and Economic Notables of today, then, are scarcely a ruling elite such as the patricians were. They are, however, frequently influential on specific decisions, particularly when these directly involve business prosperity. Moreover, politicians are wary of their potential influence and avoid policies that might unite the Notables in bitter opposition. Fortunately for the politician, it is easy to avoid the implacable hostility of the Notables, for living conditions and the belief system of the community have not—at least so far—generated demands for local policies markedly antagonistic to the goals of businessmen and Notables. What would happen if such demands ever developed is not easy to predict. But judging from the fate of the patricians, competitive politics would lead in the end to the triumph of numbers over Notability [p. 84].

Dahl does not make this prediction lightly, for he elsewhere describes the relative lack of political participation and political confidence in the working class as opposed to the "Better-Off" citizens with "middle-class" attributes (pp. 286-93). However, his ultimate emphasis is on dispersed inequalities, the openness of the political stratum, and the leverage provided by competitive politics in a society where every adult can vote. It is these emphases which focus his attention on governmental decision making on specific issues in order to understand power and democracy in New Haven.

Having stated Dahl's arguments and conclusions as clearly and fairly as I can, let me turn to a reanalysis of his basic empirical claims. In chapter 2 I will deal with the alleged division of social and economic notables into two separate categories. In chapter 3 I will discuss Yale's alleged impotence and the origins of New Haven's urban renewal program as a single problem, for Yale was in fact a major force behind the urban renewal program. The aim of these chapters is to show that detailed empirical analysis reveals the New Haven social structure and the origins of urban renewal in New Haven to be quite compatible with the theory that wealthy businessmen are at the center of the social upper class and are the rulers of New Haven—and America.

## NOTES

**1.** Duane Lockard, *The Annals of the American Academy of Political and Social Science (March 1962): 157;* Heinz Eulau, *American Political Science Review* (March 1962): 144. Excerpts from these reviews are quoted on the back cover of the paperback edition of *Who Governs?*

**2.** As quoted on the back cover of the paperback edition.

**3.** Todd Gitlin, "Local Pluralism as Theory and Ideology," *Studies on the Left* (Summer 1965); Shin'ya Ouo, "The Limits of Bourgeois Pluralism," *Studies on the Left* (Summer 1965); Thomas Anton, "Power, Pluralism, and Local Politics," *Administrative Science Quarterly* (March 1963); Peter Bachrach and Morton S. Baratz, "Two Faces of Power," *American Political Science Review* (December 1962). The Bachrach and Baratz critique is vastly overrated.

**4.** As per my agreement with Dahl, I have preserved the confidentiality in my writing that he promised to his interviewees and informants when he collected the original data.

**5.** For previous arguments for this position, see E. Digby Baltzell, *Philadelphia Gentlemen: The Making of a National Upper Class* (Free Press, 1958); G. William Domhoff, *The Higher Circles* (Random House, 1970); Paul M. Sweezy, "The American Ruling Class," in idem, *The Present as History* (Monthly Review Press, 1953).

**6.** Raymond Wolfinger, *The Politics of Progress* (Prentice-Hall, 1974), gives more attention to Yale, but also downplays its role (e.g., p.p. 26-28). At one point he adds that the New Haven mayor found Yale administrators to be "easy marks" (p. 179). In a discussion of downtown urban renewal he claims that Yale's "most important contribution to New Haven politics" is as "a focal point for fortuitous events" (p. 345n.).

7. Wolfinger's discussion of urban renewal in New Haven is considerably more detailed than Dahl's, as was planned to be the case when Dahl wrote *Who Governs?* (p. vi). Although he adds certain understandings that Dahl did not include, his basic concepts and conclusions do not differ from those put forth by Dahl.

8. Although the subtitle of *Who Governs?* is *Democracy and Power in an American City*, there is no explicit discussion of the concept of power. A reading of all relevant passages suggests that Dahl uses *power* and *influence* interchangeably, and that by *power* or *influence* he means success in shaping the nature and content of specific political and governmental decisions, whether directly or indirectly, overtly or covertly (e.g., p. 3). The best evidence for the interchangeability of *power* and *influence* in *Who Governs?* can be found in Appendix B, where Dahl writes that "one who wishes to consider more rigorous formulations of the concept of influence used in this volume and problems of measuring differences in the influence of different individuals or actors should consult my article, 'The Concept of Power,' *Behavioral Science*, 2, 1957" (p. 330). In that paper Dahl explicitly states that he is using the terms interchangeably.

# 2
# SOCIAL AND ECONOMIC NOTABLES OF NEW HAVEN

From the very beginning of the United States, Americans have resisted the notion of social class. Historian Jackson Turner Main, in a careful sifting of newspapers and letters from the late eighteenth century, has documented this popular denial, based upon a comparison with European countries, while at the same time presenting evidence that there were social classes in that era, including a clearly demarcated social upper class.[1] In more recent times sociologists have encountered this hesitancy to speak of social classes, although most people do believe that they exist. A study of social class in New Haven epitomizes the point. The investigators report that "a class I matron, who was startled by the questions but who identified herself as 'upper' class, provided insight into this facet of the social ethic with the acid comment, 'One does not speak of classes; they are felt.' "[2]

Social scientists have the same ambivalence toward the notion of social class as do other citizens. Some embrace the concept wholeheartedly, some see utility in the idea in modified form, and others reject the notion entirely. The result is a profusion of definitions, counterdefinitions, and polemics. The first task is to sort through the welter of arguments in order to determine if there are any agreed-upon definitions of "social class," "upper class," and "ruling class" upon which we can build an empirical argument.

The theory I work from, which is somewhat similar to the elite dominance theory which Dahl examines and rejects throughout *Who Governs?*, is that the owners and managers of major banks and corporations are the heart of an upper social class that can be considered a ruling class because it dominates all major aspects of American life. In order to develop and support such a theory in a systematic, step-by-step fashion, it is necessary to

1. define what is meant by "social class";

2. define what is meant by "upper class";

3. provide evidence that the owners and managers of large banks and corporations are part of this upper class;

4. define "ruling class" and provide evidence that the upper class is in fact a ruling class.

A "social class" is a network of interacting and intermarrying families who perceive each other as equals and have distinctive lifestyles and attitudes which differentiate them from other social classes. This is a generally accepted definition in the social sciences, although some pluralists prefer to speak of "social stratum," "status group," or "social standing" instead of social class.[3] Dahl adopts this definition of a social class in *Who Governs?*, although he usually prefers to use the term *social standing:*

> What I have in mind by referring to social standing in a given circle is the extent to which members of that circle would be willing—disregarding personal and idiosyncratic factors—to accord the conventional privileges of social intercourse and acceptance among equals; marks of social acceptability include willingness to dine together, to mingle freely in intimate social events, to accept membership in the same clubs, to use forms of courtesy considered appropriate among social equals, to intermarry, and so on. To the extent that individuals and groups accord one another these privileges, they may be said to enjoy equal social standing [p. 229].

Marxist social scientists also accept this definition of a social class, but add three crucial caveats which they believe to be lacking in other perspectives. First, a social class is based upon its relationship to the means of production in a given society. In the United States this means ownership versus nonownership of major income-producing property and two basic social classes, the ruling class and the working class. Second, Marxists would emphasize that the attitudes and values of members of a social class are determined in good part through conflicts with the other social classes in the society. Finally, Marxists would emphasize that class is a relational concept; classes are not layers of people along a continuum from top to bottom, but inextricably related categories of people.[4].

The Marxist view need not be taken as axiomatic. It is amenable to empirical test. For example, it is possible to determine whether there is a social class made up of owners and managers of major income-producing property. This is what Dahl attempted to do when he sought to determine the degree to which economic notables overlapped with social notables, and it is what I will try to do after I have defined "upper class" and developed indicators of upper-class membership.

"Upper class" means a clearly demarcated social class that can be reliably discriminated as having the highest social standing. Dahl adopts this type of definition in *Who Governs?* (pp. 63-64, 229), and it is used by most social scientists who accept the notion of social class. The idea of an upper class is generally foreign to Marxist scholars, however. From their perspective, there is a capitalist class or ruling class, but to speak of an upper class is to adopt the language and perspective of their theoretical antagonists.

It is self-evident or axiomatic from a Marxist perspective that if there is an upper class it must be a ruling class, because staying "upper" is what "ruling" is all about. But the point is not at all self-evident from a pluralist perspective, as Dahl's simultaneous acceptance of the existence of an upper class in New Haven and rejection of the idea that it rules or governs would indicate. Rather than end the argument with pluralists, as Marxists do, by immediately adopting opposing theoretical assumptions—which does little to resolve the conflict, as the acrimonious history of power structure research reveals—it seems more sensible to accept the analytical distinction between upper and ruling class and make explicit the kind of evidence which justifies thinking of an upper class as a ruling class. Indeed, this is another way of saying what this book is about.[5]

The problems of demonstrating to everyone's satisfaction that an upper class is a ruling class are several, and they will be dealt with throughout chapters 3, 4, and 5. In this chapter I will focus on the question of defining and demonstrating the existence of a social upper class in New Haven, and then determining whether or not leading business figures are part of that upper class. In Dahl's terms, I will be trying to determine the degree to which economic notables are also social notables.

The finding reported in *Who Governs?* of little overlap between social and economic notables in New Haven is flawed by the way in which both categories are conceptualized. The inadequate procedures by which social and economic notables are determined maximize the possibility of the two sets of individuals being distinct. It is thus necessary to develop a set of indicators of upper-class standing in New Haven, and then determine if there is a group of economic notables in New Haven whose class membership can be ascertained in terms of these indicators.

## UPPER-CLASS INDICATORS IN NEW HAVEN

The development of adequate indicators of upper-class membership is a difficult problem that requires considerable research effort, but it is basic to any discussion of who the "social notables" in New Haven might be. For purposes of my approach, the matter was first addressed in a systematic fashion by sociologist E. Digby Baltzell in *Philadelphia Gentlemen: The Making of a National Upper Class.*[6] Drawing upon his personal experience as a member of the upper class as a starting point, Baltzell began with the notion that the *Social Register* is an excellent indicator of upper-class standing in Philadelphia and several other major cities. However, he buttressed this claim in a variety of ways—by tracing the history of the *Social Register*, by showing how families are selected for inclusion in the listings, and by showing that the people who were listed were also the same people who were members of high-status social clubs, graduates of high-status private preparatory schools and universities, and residents of exclusive neighborhoods.

In my own work, building on Baltzell, I have been concerned to refine and extend upper-class indicators. In so doing, I have tried to use a variety of different methods so as to reduce the possibility that the biases of one or another method might be producing inaccurate indicators. I used a statistical method called "contingency analysis" to show that those people in *Who's Who in America* who list exclusive clubs and preparatory schools in their brief biographies are much more likely to be listed in the *Social Register* than those who do not list such schools and clubs. This finding supports the hypothesis that certain schools and clubs, as well as the *Social Register*, are good—but not perfect for a variety of reasons—indicators of upper-class membership.[7] Then I queried women's page editors in major cities as to which blue books, schools, and social clubs they believed to be of the highest social ranking. This "reputational" study led to the same indicators as the contingency analysis, thereby increasing our confidence in the validity of the indicators.[8]

Dahl uses a single indicator of upper-class standing in order to ascertain the social notables of New Haven. His treatment of the problem is relatively brief:

> However, one symbol—perhaps the best—of membership in upper-class New Haven society today is an invitation to the annual Assemblies held in the New Haven Lawn Club. There are more exclusive criteria, and those who meet together might look upon the Assemblies as a trifle undiscriminating. But the Assemblies are the closest approximation modern New Haven has to a list of families of highest social standing [pp. 63-64].

No systematic evidence is adduced to suggest that this debutante ball encompasses the social upper class in the New Haven area. And even if we were to accept the debutante ball as our single upper-class indicator, there are two problems with the debutante guest lists as Dahl uses them. First, there is no discussion of whether or not some people from the 1951 list may be deceased or living in another city by 1958, making it impossible for them to overlap with a 1957-58 list of local economic notables; thirty-three people—14 percent of his list—are in this category.[9] Second, there is no consideration of how many people from the lists may be from cities outside the New Haven area; such "outsiders" are sometimes present at these occasions, as my inquiries on the subject indicate.[10]

Aside from the problems inherent in the application of this particular indicator, there is the more important problem of whether or not it reflects the entire upper class in New Haven. Only 150 families attend the dance each year. In a county with 660,000 people in 1960, this would mean that the upper class includes about 600 people if we assume a family size of four. This is less than .1 percent of the population.[11] This figure is well below estimates of the size of the upper class—.5 percent to 1 percent—based upon *Social Register* listings, private school attendance, and exclusive club member-ships.[12]

As has been found in larger cities, social clubs are an accurate indicator of upper-class membership in New Haven. Hollingshead and Redlich report as follows on their detailed investigation of social status in New Haven:

> A family's class status can be determined most accurately by its club memberships because the private clubs of the area are graded according to the prestige of their members. Conversely, a man, woman, or a nuclear family is ranked by those conversant with the elite's system of values in terms of the clubs to which one belongs. Memberships in appropriate clubs

are evidence of validated status and they symbolize for the initiated "who one is." [13]

My own research suggests that membership in any one of three social clubs provides ·a reasonably accurate indicator of involvement in upper-class life in New Haven, thereby supplementing the cotillion list. These clubs are the New Haven Lawn Club, an in-town family club where the debutante ball is held; the New Haven Country Club, a nearby suburban country club with a golf course; and the Graduates Club, a men's club located in the heart of the downtown area. While I was led to examine these clubs by informants' suggestions, there are three empirical bases for this claim. First, the people who attend the debutante ball are in good measure members of these clubs. Of the 198 couples or individuals who attended the Assembly in 1958 and 1959, 70 percent are in at least one of the three clubs. Twenty-nine percent are in two or more of the three, and 4 percent—9 people—are in all three. This finding suggests that the dance group is really one part of the upper class in New Haven, and that the upper class as a whole has its social basis in these three clubs.

The second basis for believing that these clubs provide an operational definition of the actual upper class in New Haven is the considerable overlap in membership among them. The Lawn Club, with about 500 local members, and the Graduates, with a little over 400 local members, have 113 members in common. The country club, with some 650 local members, had 76 overlaps with the Lawn Club and 56 with the Graduates. In addition, there are 17 people who are in all three clubs.

The third piece of evidence that these clubs are accurate indicators of upper-class standing in New Haven is the fact that some members of these clubs, particularly out-of-town members, are also members of exclusive clubs in larger cities which our earlier investigations have shown to be indicators of upper-class standing.[14]

The membership lists of these three clubs, in conjunction with the cotillion attendance lists, provide an operational definition of the upper class in New Haven as a network of overlapping social circles consisting of about 1,350 families. If we again assume that the average family size is four, then by this definition the upper class comprises about .8 percent of the population in New Haven County. If the economic notables are part of the upper class in New Haven, they should be members in large numbers of these three social clubs and the debutante assembly.

## DEFINING ECONOMIC NOTABLES

There are problems with Dahl's previously listed procedures for designating the economic notables of New Haven (see chapter 1). The most basic problem is that these procedures do not demonstrate that these various arbitrary lists add up to a *group* of economic notables. This contradicts the concern in *Who Governs?* with the power of a group, elite, or class, and contrasts with Dahl's claim in an earlier methodological article that any test of the ruling elite model must provide evidence that it is dealing with a clearly defined group.[15]

A second, and related, problem with Dahl's list of economic notables is that it contains eight businesspeople whose resident location is in New York, Boston, Hartford, or other cities. It is not clear whether or not these people are to be considered part of a group of New Haven economic notables. Nor are we given any reason why we should expect these men to attend a local debutante ball. They may or may not be part of a group of local economic notables, but it is not likely that they would overlap with a list of local social notables defined by attendance at a local debutante ball. It seems more likely that their daughters would be part of debutante balls in their home cities.[16]

In order to determine the overall adequacy of Dahl's list of economic notables, we constructed our own list for 1959 by a method which insures that members are part of a relatively cohesive group of economic notables. This method involves compiling the names of those persons who were directors or partners in banks, corporations, or law firms within the New Haven area that were connected, through what are termed "interlocking directorates," with the largest bank in the city. We then compared our list with Dahl's, and with the more complete list of social notables. The results give quite a different picture than is presented in *Who Governs?*

The year 1959 was used in our study for two reasons. First, the Dun and Bradstreet *Million-Dollar Directory,* which lists all companies which do $1 million of business each year for each city in the United States, was first issued in 1959. This volume provides the most convenient and objective source of information on businesses in New Haven, although we consulted other sources as well. Second, we used 1959 because the earliest New Haven Lawn Club membership list available to us was for that year, and the earliest Graduates Club list we could obtain was for 1964. Since our major concern was to determine the degree to which economic notables are part of these upper-class indicators, it was important to have social and economic lists from the closest years possible. For these reasons, 1959 was the best year for which to do a detailed analysis, even though Dahl used 1957-58 for his list of economic notables. This small difference presents no problems, for most of the boards we have been able to check were virtually identical over the three-year period, and the overlap of our list with Dahl's is very considerable in the case of the most central businesspeople.

One aspect of an empirical demonstration of the validity of ruling-class theory is the necessity to show that owners and managers of banks and corporations form a cohesive group and are part of the upper class. This can be done in a variety of ways, but one of the best, because of the public availability of data and the inherent demonstration of face-to-face interaction, is to trace overlapping memberships—interlocks—among boards of directors. If there is a dominant social class in a city such as New Haven, according to this reasoning, it should form a network of interlocking directorships, as well as sharing common social club memberships and other social activities.

Since the claim is that the major economic institutions are all linked to each other by interlocking directorships, it is not important exactly where the analysis is begun, for any part of the network created by the interlocks should lead to all other parts if the hypothesis is correct. We could begin with any company, bank, or law firm, tracing its interlocks to see if they lead into a larger network which can be analyzed in terms of its size, density, and points of concentration. Even though we could have started any-where, we started our analysis with the First New Haven National Bank because two of Dahl's most important informants told him that this bank was the center of the power structure and that nothing could be done in New Haven without its agreement. In making this claim, these informants sounded like Floyd Hunter and his informants, which is of interest because Dahl believes Hunter is wrong in his contention that power in America is concentrated in small power structures dominated by big businessmen.[17] Indeed, Hunter is mentioned by the research assistant who recorded these revealing conversations:

First informant (as summarized by one of Dahl's assistants):

It would be very interesting to explore the question of just what merchants and bankers were first approached by Lee during the planning of the Church Street project before it was made public. As I indicated earlier today, they did contact some people in the area and perhaps outside the area, such as

Malley's and First National Bank. First Informant [my cover name for the person] said this was essential, that they had to deal with what he called the "power structure" if they wanted to accomplish anything. First Informant kept emphasizing the "power structure."

Second informant (as summarized by one of Dahl's assistants):

Second Informant [again, my cover name] says that generally in the South Central Project [the Church Street project again] the city will lease the land, not sell it, but in the case of the First National Bank, the First National Bank said it wanted to own the property in the South Central Project, so it will get it. According to Second Informant, nothing gets done without the First National Bank saying so. According to him, it is "at the top of the power structure." The First National Bank's building is in the area which will be covered by the South Central Project. I asked him why the First National was at the top of the power structure and he suggested it was perhaps because of its control of investment money for redevelopment. [Then] he said no, this was not the reason and said, "Just look at who's on its board of directors." "Oh," I said, "you have to get the bank's support." He said, "The bank's support is necessary for anything that is done in this town including redevelopment." (Sounds like a quote from Hunter.)

This does sound like a quote from Hunter. More important, it gives us an informed basis for starting from the board of directors of this $154 million bank. Only the 186th largest commercial bank in the country in 1964, the closest year to 1959 for which I have rankings that reach down that far, it had 47 percent of the $329.9 million in commercial bank assets in New Haven as of the late 1950s.

Starting with the board of directors of the First New Haven National Bank, we added new people and companies to the network by searching out every connection of every director or partner in every interconnected bank, corporation, and law firm in the New Haven area for which we could find information. We did not study further connections of directors of corporations or partners of law firms located outside the New Haven area.[18] Such an investigation, we knew from previous studies, would have encompassed the entire United States. As sociologists John Sonquist and Thomas Koenig report in their detailed computer analysis of interlocks among directors of the top 797 corporations for 1969, "the level of connectedness in the total group of 797 corporations was so high that defining a link between corporations as one or more overlapping board members" would lead to the result that "the data would show up as one big clique." [19]

The network generated from the interlocking directorships of the twenty-five member board of the First New Haven National Bank is as interconnected as the one Sonquist and Koenig discovered for the nation as a whole. It encompasses fifty-four of the sixty-nine New Haven banks and corporations listed in Dun and Bradstreet's *Million Dollar Directory* for 1959, as well as the five corporate law firms with four or more partners.

The network embraces 416 people, including 97 who live in Hartford, Boston, New York, Los Angeles, and other cities outside the greater New Haven area. Ninety-six of the 416 economic notables discovered by this method sit on two or more corporate boards. They are the people who link the businesses and law firms together. Well over half of the 96—56 men—sit on just two boards; 25 sit on three boards, 4 sit on four boards, 8 sit on five boards, 2 sit on six boards, and 1 sits on seven boards. Ninety-one of those who sit on two or more boards are local people.

It is a relatively easy task to pinpoint the central institutions in this network. The organizations with the most connections to other organizations are the "centers" of a network. Counting the number of connections of each organization to every other, we find that the following ten organizations are central points in the New Haven network. All are banks or utilities, except for the law firm of Gumbart, Corbin, Tyler and Cooper:

| | |
|---|---|
| *First New Haven National Bank* | 52 connections to 28 organizations |
| *Connecticut Savings Bank* | 43 connections to 22 organizations |
| *New Haven Water Co.* | 27 connections to 15 organizations |
| *New Haven Savings Bank* | 26 connections to 18 organizations |
| *National Savings Bank* | 24 connections to 22 organizations |
| *New Haven Gas Co.* | 22 connections to 17 organizations |
| *Second National Bank* | 20 connections to 15 organizations |
| *Union and New Haven Trust Bank* | 19 connections to 15 organizations |
| *Gumbart, Corbin, Tyler, and Cooper* | 17 connections to 14 organizations |
| *United Illuminating* | 17 connections to 9 organizations |

Each of these central organizations has numerous connections, directly and indirectly, to the other central organizations. We thus know that they form "the" center of the network, not two or three or four distinct clusters or cliques loosely connected to each other. This is demonstrated most clearly in Table 1, which presents the interlocks among all the major financial institutions and utilities of the New Haven area. Nine of the fifteen companies in this matrix were among the ten organizations with the most connections to other organizations.

Within the cluster of organizations that is at the center of the New Haven economic network, the most central organization is clearly the First New Haven National Bank. Not only does it have by far and away the most connections (fifty-two) to the most organizations (twenty-eight) in the network as a whole, but it has connections with eight of the ten financial institutions and utilities with which it can legally interlock. These connections include ten overlaps with the Connecticut Savings Bank, two with the New Haven Savings Bank, five with the New Haven Water Company, one with the National Savings Bank, four with the New Haven Gas Company, and three with United Illuminating; that is, it has twenty-five interlocks with six of the other nine business organizations which had the most connections with the network as a whole.

This finding is not an artifact of our choosing the First New Haven National Bank as our starting point. To the contrary, it is evidence which supports the Dahl informant who said the First New Haven National Bank is "at the top of the power structure." It does not prove conclusively that he is right, but our network finding certainly makes his hypothesis worthy of further investigation.

The core of the network centered around the First New Haven National Bank is filled out by the major corporate law firms in the city. One of these firms, Gumbart, Corbin, Tyler, and Cooper, was among the ten organizations with the most connections to other organizations in the overall network. It had seventeen connections to fourteen other organizations. More important, it had fourteen connections with eight of the core financials and utilities, including two each with the First New Haven National Bank, Connecticut Savings Bank, and the New Haven Water Company. Ranking second among the law firms was Wiggin and Dana, which had ten connections with nine other organizations in the network. These connections include two interlocks with the Union and New Haven Trust Bank and one interlock each with the First New Haven National Bank and the New Haven Savings Bank. The relatively few director connections of other law firms are primarily with other financial institutions:

*Chambers & Chambers*                    one interlock with *National Savings Bank*

**TABLE I**

**Network Connections Among 15 Financials and Utilities in New Haven**

| | Community Bank & Trust | First Haven National Bank | Second National Bank | Tradesmen's National Bank | Union & New Haven Trust | Connecticut Savings Bank | National Savings Bank | New Haven Savings Bank | First Federal Savings & Loan | Chas. W. Scranton Company | Security Insurance of New Haven | New Haven Gas Company | New Haven Water Company | Southern New England Telephone | United Illuminating |
|---|---|---|---|---|---|---|---|---|---|---|---|---|---|---|---|
| Community Bank & Trust (resources: $12.1 MM) | ■ | x | x | x | x | 1 | 0 | 0 | 0 | 0 | 0 | 0 | 0 | 0 | 0 |
| First New Haven National Bank (resources: $154.6 MM) | x | ■ | x | x | x | 10 | 1 | 2 | 0 | 0 | 1 | 4 | 5 | 1 | 3 |
| Second National Bank (resources: $53.5 MM) | x | x | ■ | x | x | 2 | 2 | 4 | 0 | 0 | 2 | 0 | 1 | 1 | 1 |
| Tradesmen's National Bank (resources: $16.7 MM) | x | x | x | ■ | x | 1 | 0 | 1 | 1 | 0 | 0 | 0 | 1 | 1 | 0 |
| Union & New Haven Trust (resources: $76.5 MM) | x | x | x | x | ■ | 2 | 1 | 2 | 0 | 0 | 0 | 1 | 0 | 0 | 2 |
| Connecticut Savings Bank (resources: $136.7 MM) | 0 | 10 | 2 | 1 | 2 | ■ | x | x | 0 | 0 | 1 | 2 | 5 | 1 | 4 |
| National Savings Bank (resources: $33.7 MM) | 0 | 1 | 2 | 0 | 1 | x | ■ | x | 0 | 1 | 1 | 1 | 2 | 1 | 1 |
| New Haven Savings Bank (resources: $161.1 MM) | 1 | 2 | 4 | 1 | 2 | x | x | ■ | 0 | 0 | 1 | 1 | 2 | 2 | 2 |
| First Federal Savings & Loan (resources: $59.9 MM) | 0 | 0 | 0 | 1 | 0 | 0 | 0 | 0 | ■ | 1 | 0 | 0 | 0 | 0 | 0 |
| Chas. W. Scranton Co. (resources: NA) | 0 | 0 | 0 | 0 | 0 | 0 | 1 | 0 | 1 | ■ | 0 | 0 | 0 | 0 | 0 |
| Security Insurance of New Haven (assets: $35.0 MM) | 0 | 1 | 2 | 0 | 0 | 1 | 1 | 1 | 0 | 0 | ■ | 1 | 1 | 0 | 0 |
| New Haven Gas Company (assets: $1.7 MM) | 0 | 4 | 0 | 0 | 1 | 2 | 1 | 1 | 0 | 0 | 1 | ■ | 2 | 0 | 1 |
| New Haven Water Company (assets: $30.3 MM) | 0 | 5 | 1 | 1 | 0 | 5 | 2 | 2 | 0 | 0 | 1 | 2 | ■ | 0 | 0 |
| Southern New England Telephone (assets: $361.5 MM) | 0 | 1 | 1 | 1 | 0 | 1 | 1 | 2 | 0 | 0 | 0 | 0 | 0 | ■ | 0 |
| United Illuminating (assets: $138.8 MM) | 0 | 3 | 1 | 0 | 2 | 4 | 1 | 2 | 0 | 0 | 0 | 1 | 0 | 0 | ■ |
| | | | | | | | | | | | | | | | |
| Actual Number of Company Interlocks | 1 | 8 | 7 | 5 | 5 | 9 | 9 | 10 | 2 | 2 | 7 | 8 | 8 | 6 | 7 |
| Possible Number of Interlocks | 10 | 10 | 10 | 10 | 10 | 12 | 12 | 12 | 14 | 14 | 14 | 14 | 14 | 14 | 14 |

* Note: An X means that it is illegal for these companies to have interlocks with each other.

MM = Million

NA = Not Available

| | |
|---|---|
| *Clark, Hall, & Peck* | one interlock with *Second National Bank*<br>one interlock with *First Federal Savings & Loan* |
| *Dagget, Colby, & Hooker* | one interlock with *Connecticut Savings Bank* |
| *David E. Fitzgerald* | one interlock with *Tradesmen's National Bank* |
| *Morgan, Morse, Wells, & Murphy* | one interlock with *Tradesmen's National Bank* |
| *Thompson, Weir, & Barclay* | one interlock with *Connecticut Savings Bank*<br>one interlock with *Union & New Haven Trust Bank* |

The cluster of banks, utilities, and law firms that form the center of the network are also interlocked with the major industrial firms of the New Haven area. The First New Haven National bank alone has one or more interlocks with ten of the twenty-six firms appearing on Dahl's list of companies in the New Haven area with 250 or more employees. More generally, thirty-one of the thirty-three largest industrial enterprises with headquarters in the New Haven area have at least one connection to the network. These companies and their connections to the network can be found in Table 2. Forty-six percent of the connections are with financial institutions, reflecting both the presence of bankers on industrial boards and the presence of chairpersons and presidents of industrial enterprises on bank boards.

The network of economic notables defined by connections among businesses and law firms has links to other organizations which are important in understanding the power structure in New Haven. Although I did not include these organizations in the network that defines economic notables because they are not businesses or corporate law firms, they are in practice part of the big business community. First, the network I have been describing in the last few pages has numerous common directors with the local Manufacturers' Association and the local Chamber of Commerce, a finding that will become important when it is shown how the economic notables in New Haven shaped and pushed for the urban renewal program. The Manufacturers' Association is made up of the largest industrial corporations and utilities in New Haven. It is an organization wherein the leaders of these companies meet to discuss common problems and develop new policies of mutual interest. While the association is formally separate from the Chamber of

**TABLE II**
**Network Connections of 34 New Haven Corporations**

| Company | Sales | Employees | Total Connections | First New Haven | Other Financials | Law Firms | Utilities | Other Local Companies |
|---|---|---|---|---|---|---|---|---|
| | | | | | | Connections to: | | |
| Acme Wire | NA | 250+ | 16 | 2 | 6 | 0 | 4 | 4 |
| American Tube Bending | 1MM | 200 | 11 | 1 | 3 | 1 | 3 | 3 |
| Armstrong Rubber | 76MM | 3000 | 1 | 0 | 0 | 1 | 0 | 0 |
| Associated Seed Growers | 12MM | 450 | 2 | 0 | 1 | 0 | 1 | 0 |
| Atlantic Wire | 4MM | 200 | 4 | 1 | 0 | 1 | 0 | 2 |
| Berger Brothers | 5MM | 600 | 2 | 1 | 0 | 1 | 0 | 0 |
| Brock-Hall Dairy | 9MM | 400 | 3 | 1 | 1 | 0 | 1 | 0 |
| Carwin Co. | 2MM | 110 | 5 | 1 | 3 | 1 | 0 | 0 |
| Connecticut Coke | 10MM | 300 | 1 | 1 | 0 | 0 | 0 | 0 |
| Connecticut Hard Rubber | NA | 250 | 0 | 0 | 0 | 0 | 0 | 0 |
| C. Cowles & Co. | 5MM | 200 | 8 | 1 | 2 | 1 | 0 | 4 |
| Eachlin Manufacturing | NA | 300 | 1 | 0 | 0 | 0 | 0 | 1 |
| Eastern Machine Screw | 1MM | 125 | 11 | 1 | 4 | 1 | 0 | 5 |
| G & O Manufacturing | NA | 400 | 6 | 0 | 3 | 0 | 1 | 2 |
| A. C. Gilbert | 16MM | 1300 | 5 | 1 | 0 | 1 | 1 | 2 |
| Greist Manufacturing | 10MM | 700 | 10 | 1 | 4 | 1 | 1 | 3 |
| High Standard Manufacturing | 8MM | 600 | 4 | 2 | 1 | 0 | 1 | 0 |
| T. A. D. Jones & Co. | 18MM | 105 | 3 | 0 | 1 | 0 | 0 | 2 |
| M. B. Manufacturing | NA | 700 | 2 | 0 | 1 | 1 | 0 | 0 |
| Malleable Iron Fittings | NA | 800 | 10 | 1 | 3 | 1 | 2 | 3 |
| Marlin Firearms | 5MM | 400 | 0 | 0 | 0 | 0 | 0 | 0 |
| C. S. Mersick & Co. | 5MM | 200 | 8 | 0 | 3 | 1 | 1 | 3 |
| New Haven Board & Carton | 17MM | 1100 | 9 | 2 | 1 | 1 | 2 | 3 |
| New Haven Register | NA | 250+ | 2 | 1 | 1 | 0 | 0 | 0 |
| Pond Lily Co. | 5MM | 200 | 5 | 1 | 1 | 0 | 1 | 1 |
| Rockbestos Products | 10MM | 500 | 3 | 1 | 0 | 0 | 0 | 2 |
| Safety Industries | 23MM | 700 | 1 | 0 | 1 | 0 | 0 | 0 |
| Sargent & Co. | 12MM | 1400 | 6 | 2 | 1 | 0 | 1 | 2 |
| Sarong Inc. | 6MM | 400 | 2 | 1 | 1 | 0 | 0 | 1 |
| Seamless Rubber | 13MM | 1400 | 3 | 0 | 0 | 0 | 1 | 1 |
| Henry G. Thompson, Co. | 4MM | 300 | 1 | 0 | 2 | 0 | 0 | 0 |
| Whitney-Blake Co. | 11MM | 600 | 4 | 0 | 2 | 1 | 0 | 1 |
| Wyatt, Inc. | 30MM | NA | 1 | 1 | 0 | 0 | 0 | 0 |
| | | | 150 | 24 | 45 | 14 | 22 | 45 |

Commerce, it shares common offices and staff with the chamber, and all members of the association are also in the chamber. The Manufacturers' Association is the core of the Chamber of Commerce, which is a larger and more heterogeneous group, encompassing companies from the retail and service sectors, and as many small businesses as possible.

The chamber is a meeting ground between big and small businesspeople, between the nationally and the locally oriented. If there are monopoly, competitive, and governmentally oriented sectors within the overall economy—which sometimes creates conflict among businesspeople, particularly between members of the monopoly and competitive sectors—it is in organizations such as the Chamber of Commerce that policies and compromises for dealing with these problems are worked out. The chamber is not merely an organization dominated by the economic notables who tend to come from the larger businesses, but it is a transmission belt through which the policies of the biggest businesspeople are thrashed out with, and sometimes modified by, the smaller and more local businesspeople.[20]

The network has several links to the New Haven Foundation, a city-oriented foundation which receives bequests from numerous individuals and businesses. In the mid-1950s the foundation had about $8.5 million in assets and a distributable income of about $275,000. The foundation provides funds for charitable, cultural, and service organizations within the community, and is one of the means by which the local economic notables are able to shape the social environment within which the business community must function. The existence of this foundation, and its inclusion in the network, is of special interest because it provided necessary seed money for the urban renewal program in 1954 ($5,000) and 1955 ($30,000), a fact which Dahl does not mention but is included in passing in Wolfinger's more detailed account.[21]

There are several ways in which Yale University connects to this network. As the largest landholder and employer in the city, with service and construction contracts to hand out to eager local businesses, Yale is the single most important institution in the city. Moreover, it has the essential national function of training executives, lawyers, scholars, and technical experts for the staffing of the major institutions of American society.[22] It would be quite surprising, if there is anything to the ruling-class hypothesis, if Yale's central role did not reflect itself in a series of personal interlocks with the rest of the major institutions of New Haven and, indeed, the nation.

An analysis of our list of economic notables reveals that there are eleven trustees, administrators, and professors from Yale who serve on boards of directors of local companies. These eleven men provide fifteen connections to thirteen organizations in the network, which would make Yale the twelfth most connected institution if it were to be formally included. More strikingly, eleven of those connections are with nine of the fifteen financials and utilities at the core of the network; seven are with five of the ten most connected organizations. In short, Yale's local interlocks place it very close to the center of the network. Since Yale's role will be a major issue in my reanalysis of the urban renewal program in New Haven, it is useful to look at those trustees, administrators, and professors who provide Yale with formal interlocks to the local business community:

*Charles O'Hearn,* assistant to the president of Yale, was a vice president of Firestone Tire and Rubber and a partner in the investment firm of Scudder, Stevens, and Clark before joining the university staff. He is on the board of the First New Haven Bank and Trust. (He is also in the New Haven Country Club and the Graduates Club.)

*Reuben Holden,* secretary of the university, is on the board of Connecticut Savings Bank. (Married to the daughter of a Yale trustee, he is in the Lawn Club and the Graduates.)

*Edwin Blair,* a Yale trustee and a partner in a large New York law firm, is on the board of Security Insurance Company of New Haven and T.A.D. Jones and Company, a producer of coal, coke, and petroleum products. (He is in the Lawn Club and Graduates.)

*Lucius F. Robinson, Jr.,* Yale trustee and a Hartford lawyer who sits on several corporate boards in that city, is a director of Southern New England Telephone.

*Horace F. Isleib,* an investment officer in the treasurer's office, is a director of Connecticut Savings Bank and C.S. Mersick and Company.

*Charles Seymour,* emeritus president of Yale, is on the board of New Haven Savings Bank. (He is in the Graduates Club.)

*Samuel W. Dudley,* emeritus dean of the engineering school, is on the board of the National Savings Bank.

*Ray B. Westerfield,* emeritus professor of political economy, is chairman of the First Federal Savings and Loan Association and a director of Tradesmen's National Bank. (He is in the Lawn and Graduates clubs.)

*Fred Fairchild,* emeritus professor of political economy, is on the boards of United Illuminating, and Connecticut Savings Bank. (He is a member of the Lawn Club and the Graduates.)

*Kent Healy,* professor of transportation, is on the board of the Connecticut Company, a bus company owned by the New York, New Haven, and Hartford Railroad, on whose board he formerly sat. (He is in the Graduates Club.)

*Henry A. Pfisterer,* professor of architectural engineering, is on the board of the New Haven Trap Rock Company. (He is a member of the Lawn Club.)

The national-level business and legal connections of ten of Yale's fifteen outside trustees as of 1958 are even more impressive, demonstrating the fact that Yale is one of the major institutions of the national ruling class:

*Dean Acheson,* secretary of state in the Truman administration, is a corporate lawyer with Covington and Burling in Washington, D.C.

*Edwin Blair,* a New York Corporation lawyer who makes his home in the New Haven area, is on the boards of Union Bag-Camp Paper, Canada Dry, and Holly Sugar in addition to his two board affiliations in New Haven (Security Insurance Company of New Haven and T.A.D. Jones and Company.)

*Charles D. Dickey,* chairman of the executive committee of J.P. Morgan and Company, is a director of General Electric, Kennecott Copper, New York Life Insurance, Panhandle Eastern Pipeline, and Merck and Company.

*Morris Hadley* is a partner in the New York law firm of Milbank, Tweed, Hadley and McCloy.

*B. Brewster Jennings* is a director of New York Trust Company and the Central Savings Bank of New York.

*Lucius F. Robinson, Jr.,* a partner in the Hartford law firm of Robinson, Robinson, and Cole, is a director of Hanover Bank, Connecticut General Life Insurance, Veeder-Root Incorporated and Mutual Insurance Company of Hartford, in addition to his one board affiliation in New Haven (Southern New England Telephone.)

*Charles M. Spofford,* a partner in the New York law firm of Davis, Polk, Wardwell, Sunderland, and Kiendl, is a director of Guaranty Trust Bank, Mutual Life Insurance Company of New York, Ciba Pharmaceutical Products, Incorporated, and Distillers Limited.

*Juan T. Trippe,* president of Pan American World Airways, is a director of Metropolitan Life and Chrysler.

*George H. Walker, Jr.,* a senior managing partner in the New York investment firm of G.H. Walker and Company, and the father-in-law of Yale secretary Reuben A. Holden, is a director of Zapata Off-Shore Oil, City Investing, and Westmoreland Coal.

*John Hay Whitney,* heir to a huge Standard Oil fortune, is the publisher of the New York *Herald Tribune.*

A great number of the people on our economic notables list are graduates of Yale, a fact worth noting in light of Wolfinger's surprising claim that Yale does not "have much of a local 'old boy net' " in New Haven.[23] While it is true that Yale does not enjoy great favor with the black, Puerto Rican, Irish, and Italian working-class populations in New Haven who are seldom able to avail themselves of the amenities of the university, this is not true within the confines of the economic inner circles. This is seen most dramatically in the case of the major law firms, where virtually every partner is a Yale graduate. At Wiggin and Dana, the firm which represents Yale and several major banks, among others, twelve of the fourteen partners are Yale graduates (the other two are from Harvard and Columbia law schools). At Gumbart, Corbin, Tyler, and Cooper, which has an equally impressive list of clients that overlaps in part with Wiggin and Dana's list, all ten partners are Yale Law School graduates. Similarly at Thompson, Weir, and Barclay, which has Armstrong Rubber Company as its major local client, all four partners are Yale graduates. At both Daggett, Colby, and Hooker and Morgan, Morse, Wells, and Murphy, three of the four partners are Yale alumni. (Daggett, Colby, and Hooker has one Harvard-trained partner; Morgan, Morse, Wells, and Murphy has one Michigan-trained partner.)

Considerable significance should be attached to these findings on the Yale connections of the partners in the largest law firms, for there is evidence that several of these men do important work for the university. They are a major liaison between Yale and the rest of the business community, perhaps even more important than the directorship links that I presented a moment ago.[24]

Starting with the board of directors of the First New Haven National Bank, we generated a network of people and institutions which includes the major banks, corporations, law firms, and general purpose business groups of New Haven, as well as the New Haven Foundation and Yale University. It is the people linking these institutions whom I would assume to be the economic notables of New Haven. The list consists of 416 people, including 97 who live in Hartford, Boston, New York, Los Angeles, and other cities outside the greater New Haven area. Dahl's list of economic notables, on the other hand, consists of 238 persons, at least 8 of whom are from outside the area. How do the two lists compare? The answer cannot be completely precise, for I had to reconstruct his list from raw data in files that were over fifteen years old when I used them. I was able to determine 230 of his original 238 names, and found that our two lists compared fairly well, with 139 names in common. In addition, there are 14 names on Dahl's list which would have been on our list if they had not died or left their directorships between 1958 and 1959. Thus, I am in agreement with two-thirds of the names on Dahl's list of economic notables.

It is worthwhile to focus for a moment on the people on Dahl's list on whom we disagree:

1. Twenty-two people on Dahl's list are directors of two small commercial banks in the area, banks with assets of only $12.9 million and $3.5 million. They appear because Dahl chose to include all bank directors, even though he did not choose to include all directors of industrial corporations. Dahl biased his list with bank directors without providing any rationale for this decision, and the result was a list of economic notables which included small bankers with no connections to the dominant economic institutions.

2. Eight people on Dahl's list are major executives with businesses whose headquarters are in other cities. They appeared on the list because their companies had real estate holdings, factories, or retail outlets in New Haven. While it might be possible to argue that these people have power in New Haven through their local managers, I do not think they belong on a list of local economic notables that is being compared with a list of local social notables.

3. Thirty people on the list are local property owners and small businesspeople. Not only are their holdings relatively small in relation to those of the major institutions in New Haven, but many of these men and women are of Italian or Jewish background, which means they are likely to be excluded by the dominant group of economic notables. In any case, I do not think that car dealers, motel owners, and apartment house owners should be considered

economic notables in an arbitrary fashion. They are not people whom any advocate of the ruling-class view would accept as part of the alleged ruling class without an explicit demonstration of their inclusion in such circles.

4. There are several people on whom we could find no information.

The deficiencies in Dahl's procedures for determining economic notables led him to include a significant minority of people who are not part of the network of economic notables in New Haven. However, there is a group of people who can be called the economic notables of New Haven, and they include most of the important businessmen on Dahl's list. It is these people, in addition to the ones discovered by our network analysis, that I would expect to be part of the upper class in New Haven.

## OVERLAP OF SOCIAL AND ECONOMIC NOTABLES
Now that we have an adequate conception of the economic notables of New Haven as the 416 people who are part of the corporate network of interlocking directorships radiating out from the board of the First New Haven National Bank, we can return to the question of whether or not the economic notables of New Haven are also its social notables. In so doing, we will focus on those 319 economic notables who live in the New Haven area, for they are the people who are in New Haven on a regular basis and are most likely to belong to the local social institutions we are using as indicators of upper-class standing in New Haven. While nonlocal economic notables sometimes belong to local social institutions, a fact which is one piece of evidence for the supralocal nature of the American upper class, our concern here is to answer a question posed by *Who Governs?*, the number of economic notables in New Haven who are also social notables.[25]

Using the three aforementioned clubs and the debutante assembly as indicators of upper-class membership, the findings are quite clear. Fifty-eight percent of the 319 people on our local list are social notables, which is a far greater percentage than the 10 percent of economic notables whom Dahl found to meet his social notable criterion. Ninety-three of the local economic notables are in the New Haven Country Club, 83 are in the Lawn Club, and 77 in the Graduates Club. Twenty-eight are in both the Lawn and Graduates, 15 are in the Lawn and country club, and 12 are in the Graduates and the Country Club. Seven are in all three clubs.

The debutante assembly list added little to the overall findings. Thirty-one of the thirty-six men on our economic notables list who attended this function also were members of one of the three clubs, and twenty were in two or more. Thus the most interesting finding concerning this cotillion list was reported by Wolfinger: one-third of the guests were Yale professors or administrators, suggesting that this dance (which disappeared in the 1960s in any case) served the function of a social meeting place for town and gown.[26]

The men who stand at the center of the network of economic notables were much more likely to be social notables than those who were on the periphery. This point is made most simply by a look at the board of the First New Haven National Bank; twenty-four of its twenty-five members were in at least one of the three social clubs. Thirteen of the twenty-five were in two of the three clubs, and two board members were among the seven economic notables who were in all three clubs. Of the ninety-one locally based economic notables on two or more boards in the network, seventy-three were in one of the clubs; thirty-six of these seventy-three were in two or more of the three. The overlap is even greater for those who sit on several boards. Of the twenty-five men who sit on three boards, nineteen are in at least one of the clubs. Of the fifteen men who sit on four or more boards, thirteen are in clubs.

Conversely, of the 132 persons meeting none of the upper-class criteria, 42 percent are treasurers, managers, and vice-presidents who sit on the boards of their respective companies. They are executives who are part of the local business establishment, but they are not members of the upper class as we have defined it. There are also small companies at the periphery of the network whose directors do not have upper-class standing. For example, Community Bank and Trust Company, with only $12 million in assets and all of its directors from the Italian community, has one director who is also a director of a savings bank, but none of its directors are members of any of the three social clubs.

The conclusion to be drawn from these general findings is that the most notable of economic notables in New Haven are overwhelmingly part of the small social upper class in that city. That is, those who sit on the boards of the central institutions in the economic network, or sit on several boards of directors, are very likely to be members of the upper class. On the other hand, the case is more spotty with the smaller and more peripheral businesses and with the middle-range executives of the larger corporations.

The same picture emerges from a comparison of Dahl's list of economic notables with the club lists we are using as upper-class indicators. Of the 139 local businesspeople on his list of 230 that are also on our list, 97 are in one or more of the three clubs. However, virtually none of the smaller business owners and property holders are in any of the three clubs.

This high degree of overlap between social and economic notables is crucial for a ruling-class perspective. The finding contradicts the idea that in the United States there has developed an economic managerial group separate from the social upper class. This view, of which Who Governs? is one example, has been expressed as follows by sociologist Daniel Bell:

> Today, there is an "upper class" and a "ruling group." Being a member of the "upper class" (i.e. having differential privileges and being able to pass those privileges along to one's designees) no longer means that one is a member of the ruling group, for rule is now based on other than the traditional criteria of property; the modern ruling groups are essentially coalitions.[27]

Contrary to this claim, our work at the national level and the present findings on New Haven support the idea that there remains a privileged class in America which also provides the economic leadership of society. This social upper class, not a separate stratum of economic managers, sets the dominant values and goals of the banks and corporations. Clubs such as those used as upper-class indicators in this study are one of the means by which these values are transmitted to the new rich and rising executives, as this summary statement from a study by sociologist Reed Powell reveals:

> The clubs are a repository of the values held by the upper-level prestige groups in the community and are a means by which these values are transferred to the business environment. . . . The clubs are places in which the beliefs, problems, and values of the industrial organization are discussed and related to the other elements in the larger community. Clubs, therefore, are not only effective vehicles of informal communication, but also valuable centers where views are presented, ideas are modified, and new ideas emerge. Those in the interview sample were appreciative of this asset: in addition, they considered the club as a valuable place to combine social and business contacts.[28]

I would not want to close this demonstration of the considerable overlap of social and economic notables in New Haven by leaving the impression that there are no social and economic tensions within and around the upper class as I conceive of it. Such an impression is possible because of the static, categorical nature of the data analyzed in this chapter. However, once lists are constructed and compared, it is important to recognize that there are "rising commoners" among the economic notables who are pushing their way into the upper class, as well as a few impoverished gentry among the social notables who are falling out. There are also various conflicts within the class based upon personal jealousies, business rivalries, and differences of opinion on political strategy. At the same time, the emphasis in a sociological analysis of the functioning of the class system has to be on the fact that these personal- and business-rivalry tensions are *within* the dominant social class, and that there are social processes which work to keep their effects at a minimum. These tensions are constantly being diminished by anticipatory socialization of rising commoners, skillful marriages of falling gentry, homogenizing pressures created through common private schools, clubs, resorts, and retreats, and most important, by the need for shared strategies against the demands of those Americans who would like to curtail the power, dividends, and privileges of the rich. While it is true that the upper class is never quite as cohesive and serene as it looks from the outside, it is neither quite as diffuse as it looks to insiders and academics who take the shared assumptions and socialization processes for granted and see only tensions and conflicts.

The subtle tensions of which I am speaking, and the way in which they are contained within the upper class, can be demonstrated through an analysis of the two quotes used in *Who Governs?* to provide qualitative interview evidence for the "slight discordance" (pp. 68-69) between economic and social notables.[29] The first quote, from an economic notable who supposedly feels excluded by the social notables, says that his family was not accepted in the "sanctorum" of New Haven society, that they were considered newcomers who were "trying to horn in" (p. 69). The second quote, from one of the few social notables who is also an economic notable according to Dahl, contains a mild denial that the respondent is part of the business community, along with a disquisition about how business has changed and how the perquisites of hired executives are foreign to him and his kind (p. 69).

However, the quote from the economic notable who felt like an outsider begins with the statement that the man's father rejected the city, rather than the social upper class rejecting the father and his family. This puts the comment in an entirely different light, as this more lengthy quotation of the dialogue reveals:

*Informant:* [As he is describing why his company does not partici-
pate more actively in local affairs, he says his father] cared less
than nothing about this city.

*Dahl:* Is that so?

*Informant:* And his influence.

*Dahl:* Why did he care so little about it? He lived here for a long time.

*Informant:* [The man goes on to say that his father never had a feeling for New Haven and that] his friends were associates from college and out of town. He never had a great raft of close friends. He had a few good friends, but not very widespread.

*Dahl assistant:* He went to Yale, though, didn't he?

*Informant:* Yes, he went to Yale.

*Dahl assistant:* But most of these were still out-of-towners?

*Informant:* And I think that in the beginning New Haven gave him a rough time.

*Dahl:* Could you tell us more about that?

*Informant:* [The man explains this to Dahl in terms of denial of bank loans. He goes on to note that now he, the son, gets pressure to do business in New Haven, and says that his company has good relations with one of the leading banks.] We have a line of credit with them.

*Dahl:* [Dahl then asks a question about the local bankers which turns the discussion back to business for a moment. Then he returns to ask about the father] To go back to your father, and then in a brief moment I'd like to hear more about your own experience, was there any other way, aside from the difficulty of dealing with the banks and their conservative attitude on credit, in which the New Haven community gave him a hard time? Did he ever, for example, feel any social difficulty or pressure? One of the interesting things, I must say, that we run across and we keep asking people about it, is the relatively small number (in fact, it's almost negligible) of old Yankee families who have any positions of influence, not only in politics, which is quite understandable given the change of the town, but even in leading business corporations of the town, and to some extent though less so, in the banks. It's kind of interesting the way they've been almost washed out entirely. I wondered if there had been any such thing.

*Informant:* Well, my father was never a social lion and never gave a damn about being in the social world or anything like that. My mother didn't do much either. Now, us kids—we noticed it.

*Dahl:* You did? In what way?

*Informant:* Well, we noticed that we weren't readily accepted into the inner circle, you might say, the sanctorum of New Haven society the way these old-multi-generation families were. We've only been here for forty years. We're newcomers. We're nouveau riche. We're trying to crash. I mean, the old long society crowd looks upon us as trying to horn in.

*Dahl:* What would be the kinds of places where they would look upon you as trying to horn in? The Lawn Club?

*Informant:* The Lawn Club, your cotillions, places like that.

The dialogue I have quoted raises the possibility that this man's father was responsible for the rejection the son thought he suffered. After all, the father never cared for the city, had only a few close friends, and was not a social lion. Thus, more should be known about this man before quoting his experience as representative. My suspicions having been raised by a reading of the passages I have just quoted, I asked the social and economic notable whom Dahl quotes on the same page to tell me what this man was like. He replied that this man was one of the most "antisocial" people he had ever known, "a real loner." In short, I believe Dahl is taking as representative the experiences of a son who had a very unusual father. The son may be blaming his problems on the "sanctorum" rather than considering the possibility that his father's personality kept the family estranged from their social equals.

There is an even more basic problem. It is hard to understand in what way this man and his father were excluded, for his father was a member, at the time Dahl interviewed the son, of the very Lawn Club used as an example of a place where people would think he was "horning in," and the son was to become a member shortly thereafter. The son also was a member of the New Haven Country Club, and one of his two sisters was in both the Lawn Club and the country club at the time of the interview. Moreover, the father had become a director of a local bank in the early 1920s, only thirteen years after he founded his company. It must have been a very subtle exclusion indeed. The man Dahl interviewed may have *felt* excluded, but he was not as excluded as he claimed, and probably not for the reasons he thought.

Consideration of the social and economic notable whom Dahl quotes on the same page by way of contrast can be briefer. In my interview with him, I found him to be a friendly and open person, but he also had a modesty about his role and position that can hardly be taken at face value. He may be a professional person, technically speaking, but he cannot be taken seriously when he insists that "I don't really think I rate being described as an Economic Notable" (p. 69). In fact, he is a wealthy man who is very much a central figure in the business community as a partner in one of the law firms which serves the leading banks and corporations in New Haven, and as a member of the board of a large bank.

It is a mistake, then, to say that there are separate categories of social and economic notables in New Haven, or anywhere else in the United States. The reality in New Haven, as elsewhere, is a distinctive upper class which includes the most important business executives, bankers, and corporate lawyers of the city. Through a study of overlapping club membership lists and interlocking boards of directors, we have been able to describe in considerable detail the New Haven upper class. It is now time to consider the problem of how this class functioned on a policy question of importance to it. That is, it is time to show how the upper class is a ruling class.

## NOTES

1. Jackson Turner Main, *The Social Structure of Revolutionary America* (Princeton University Press, 1965).

2. August B. Hollingshead and Frederick C. Redlich, *Social Class and Mental Illness: A Community Study* (Wiley, 1958), p. 69.

3. Joseph A Kahl, *The American Class Structure* (Rinehart, 1959), p. 12.

4. For good treatments of the Marxist view, see T.B. Bottomore, *Classes in Modern Society* (Random House, 1968); Bertell Ollman, "Marx's Use of Class," *American Journal of Sociology* (March 1968); James Stolzman and Herbert Gamberg, "Marxist Class Analysis versus Stratification Analysis as General Approaches to Social Inequality," *Berkeley Journal of Sociology* (1973-74).

5. For three useful discussions of the concept of ruling class, see Paul M. Sweezy, "The American Ruling Class," *The Present as History* (Monthly Review Press, 1953); idem, "Power Elite or Ruling Class?" *Monthly Review* (September 1956); Charles H. Anderson, *The Political Economy of Social Class* (Prentice-Hall, 1974).

6. (Free Press, 1958).

7. G. William Domhoff, *The Higher Circles* (Random House, 1970), ch. 1, for a discussion of contingency analysis and the strengths and weaknesses of the upper-class indicators used in our research.

8. Eugene J. Webb, Donald T. Campbell, Richard D. Schwartz, and Lee Sechrest, *Unobtrusive Measures: Nonreactive Research in the Social Sciences* (Rand McNally, 1966), p. 3, suggest the importance of using several widely different operations or indices: "Once a proposition has been confirmed by two or more independent measurement processes, the uncertainty of its interpretation is greatly reduced. The most persuasive evidence comes through a triangulation of measurement processes. If a proposition can survive the onslaught of a series of imperfect measures, with all their irrelevant error, confidence should be placed in it."

9. Raymond Wolfinger, *The Politics of Progress* (Prentice-Hall, 1974), p. 20, discards the 1951 list for purposes of his analysis.

10. According to my informants, these non–New Haven attendees are people whose family roots are in New Haven.

11. Many upper-class people of the New Haven area live in posh suburbs and developments outside the city boundaries. Most of these areas are inside the county, and within a 30-35 mile radius of the city.

12. Baltzell; G. William Domhoff, *Who Rules America?* (Prentice-Hall, 1967), p. 7n and ch. 1; Beth Mintz, "The President's Cabinet, 1897-1972: A Contribution to the Power Structure Debate," *The Insurgent Sociologist* (Spring 1975).

13. Hollingshead and Redlich, p. 81. While I accept this observation, I cannot follow Hollingshead and Redlich in their use of an index of social position to define upper-class status, for that index includes occupation as one of its three criteria. The use of such an index would answer by definition the question of whether or not major businesspeople are part of the upper class. Put another way, the index confounds social with occupational criteria. A further weakness of this index is that it does not demonstrate that the "social classes" it differentiates are in fact interacting social circles. Instead of using educational level and occupational role as parts of their index in conjunction with place of residence, it would have been better, in terms of differentiating the upper class, to use social clubs, private school attendance, and similar criteria which give evidence of social interaction.

14. Domhoff, *Higher Circles*, ch. 1.

15. Robert A. Dahl, "A Critique of the Ruling Elite Model," *American Political Science Review* (June 1958).

16. Wolfinger, p. 20, eliminated these outsiders in his comparison of social and economic notables.

17. Floyd Hunter, *Community Power Structure* (University of North Carolina Press, 1953); idem, *Top Leadership USA* (University of North Carolina Press, 1959). As will be seen in ch. 4, Dahl's "A Critique of the Ruling Elite Model" is a sharp criticism of Hunter's *Community Power Structure*. Dahl wrote an even more critical review of *Top Leadership USA* in *Journal of Politics* (February 1960).

18. The connections of New Haven businesses and businesspeople to the national corporate community will be discussed in the final chapter.

19. John A. Sonquist and Thomas Koenig, "Interlocking Directorates in the Top U.S. Corporations: A Graph Theory Approach," *The Insurgent Sociologist* (Spring 1975).

20. James O'Connor, *The Fiscal Crisis of the State* (St. Martin's Press, 1973), for the argument that there are different sectors to the economy which have different needs and problems.

21. Wolfinger, p. 245.

22. Detailed evidence on the enormous role played by Yale graduates in all aspects of American life can be found in George W. Pierson, *The Education of American Leaders: Comparative Contributions of U.S. Colleges and Universities* (Praeger, 1969).

23. Wolfinger, p. 28. Dahl, on the other hand, notes that "many leading citizens in business and the professions are old Blues" (p. 138).

24. Wiggin and Dana, the Yale law firm, also provides the university with administrative personnel from time to time. Former partner Katherine Tilson was an assistant to the president in the 1950s, and former partner John Ecklund became treasurer in the 1960s.

25. The non–New Haveners who appear on our list will be discussed in the final chapter as part of the evidence that New Haven business leaders are part of a national ruling class.

26. Wolfinger, p. 21.

27. Daniel Bell, *The End of Ideology* (Free Press, 1960), p. 45.

28. Reed M. Powell, *Race, Religion, and the Promotion of the American Executive* (Ohio State University, College of Administrative Science Monograph no. AA-3, 1969), p. 50.

29. Wolfinger, pp. 21-22, also uses these two quotes.

# 3
# ORIGINS OF
# URBAN RENEWAL IN
# NEW HAVEN

The previous chapter identified the social and economic institutions I believe to be the basis for the upper class in New Haven. It is the upper class rooted in these institutions which I would expect to dominate any policy decision of importance to it in the New Haven area. The decision I shall analyze to demonstrate how this class dominates policy concerns the large urban renewal program which began in New Haven in the 1950s and received national acclaim as a model of urban renewal's great potential for the rebuilding of cities.

Urban renewal in New Haven was a critical case study for the pluralist thesis because it allegedly showed that politicians and government officials were more central in initiating and carrying through the program than were business leaders. The pluralist view that government is relatively free of big-business dominance was supposedly sustained even on a policy question that directly affected the vital interests of major businesspeople. It is not essential, from a ruling-class perspective, that business leaders be directly involved in governmental decisions if it can be shown that they dominate the social context and shape governmental structures in which decisions are made, as will be demonstrated in the final chapter. It would nonetheless be surprising if they were not more directly involved in shaping the urban renewal program and overseeing its development than *Who Governs?* suggests. Putting aside theoretical arguments about whether or not it is necessary to study decision making to ascertain who rules, here is an opportunity for a direct confrontation between pluralist and ruling-class research on the same decision-making process, providing a comparison of the usefulness of the two perspectives in determining how a major policy is shaped and implemented.

There are so many dates, details, and interconnections in the urban renewal process as it unfolded in New Haven that it is hard to be sure that even a lengthy chapter can lead the reader new to the subject into the complexities of the matter without creating boredom or complete confusion. Let me therefore begin with a few general comments about Dahl's study that may provide some orientation to the detailed chronology about to unfold.

## WEAKNESSES OF DAHL'S METHODOLOGY

Dahl chose to rely almost exclusively on interviews in 1957-58 for his information on the important formative years of urban renewal in New Haven during 1949-55. By so doing he put himself at the mercy of the frailty of human memory and its tendency to personalize events. It is not safe to assume that what people say in 1957 and 1958 is an accurate description of events that took place several years earlier, even if there is considerable consensus among interviewees. This point about mistrusting even a consensus among interviewees is critical, for it alerts us to the fact that everyone interviewed may be a victim of the ideological consensus that has slowly formed over the intervening years and rearranged memories about what actually happened. It sensitizes us to the anthropologists' point that beliefs about the past must be considered as myths that have functional relevance for the present.

From my reading of organizational and committee minutes, position papers, letters written by important decision makers, secret memos, and other documents only recently available to researchers, and from my interviews with people Dahl never interviewed or did not quiz closely, I believe he was the unwitting victim of the ideological climate in New Haven in the late 1950s. He unknowingly accepted and sanctified the claim of local Democrats that they, not the business leaders and local planners, were responsible for the urban renewal program. It is just "natural" in the United States for politicians to take credit for anything seen as good, and to blame others for anything bad. At that time, urban renewal was seen as good. It was going to create a new city, increase the tax base, bring retail trade back downtown, and eliminate slums. Moreover, the Democratic mayor, Richard C. Lee, was widely known to be ambitious for higher office right about that time—he was hoping to run for the Senate in 1958, or for governor in 1962.

It was not only the local Democratic party that wanted to make hay with the New Haven urban renewal program. New Haven was also one of the key examples being used by ACTION (American Council to Improve Our Neighborhoods) and other national ruling-class groups to push the urban renewal program that members of the ruling class had slowly and gropingly developed as a response to a variety of problems.

Evidence for my claim that members of the ruling class—with the help of hired experts—created the urban renewal program will be presented when I get into the details of the actual policy-making process. For now I want to give small examples of how a ruling-class organization used New Haven in its national propaganda in order to demonstrate the ideological climate in which Dahl was interviewing.

In a December 1953 report to President Dwight D. Eisenhower, a specially appointed blue-ribbon panel of big businessmen, mortgage bankers, real estate developers, and experts on urban affairs suggested that implementation of the urban renewal program would be aided by "the formation outside of government of a broadly representative national organization to help promote and lead this dynamic program for renewal of the towns and cities of America." [1] This new group was formed as the aforementioned ACTION in November 1954, with a roster of officers and directors which made it clear that the heavyweights within the ruling class were squarely behind the program. The ambitious nature of ACTION's plans are clearly stated in a story in the magazine *American City* shortly after the founding:

> A new nationwide slum-prevention organization titled the "American Council to Improve Our Neighborhoods"—AC-TION for short—was launched November 15 at Washington's Mayflower Hotel with an address by President Eisenhower. This new privately financed citizens' organization is shooting for an eyebrow-raising budget of some $750,000 per year. It plans to spend this money on a three-pronged program of research, education, and technical assistance to individuals and community groups aimed at stopping the deterioration of buildings and neighborhoods throughout the country.

> This is how ACTION plans to carry out its program. First, its research division will mass together all available information

on techniques of rehabilitating and conserving individual homes and neighborhoods. Where no data is available, pilot research projects will be set up to get the answers. Based on this reservoir of facts, the education division, aided by top-flight advertising and promotion personnel, will then beam the message of what must and can be done to local governments and to organizations such as chambers of commerce, real estate boards, women's clubs, and to community service groups such as Kiwanis, Lions, and Exchange clubs.

National advertising campaigns will also be carried on to arouse individual action against the threat of home and neighborhood decay.

Finally, to help local groups carry out their own blight-prevention programs, ACTION's field service division will send trained personnel out to give technical assistance to both local citizen and governmental groups. It is planned to mesh blight-prevention attack with the federal government's program of encouraging urban and neighborhood renewal.

Backing the ACTION program are men and women prominent in civic affairs, banking, manufacturing, religion, building, labor, women's associations, and other groups.[2]

Four days after ACTION was announced, a more established ruling-class organization in the area of public relations, the Advertising Council, announced a new national campaign called "Action on Slums." Using the various free media sources available to this group which brings us Smokey the Bear and Keep America Beautiful messages through television, radio, and magazines, the aim of the campaign was to "stimulate the rehabilitation or rebuilding of depressed areas."[3] At the same time, various real estate and home-building associations were conducting their own campaigns under such slogans as "Build America Better," "New Face for America," and "Better America, Inc."[4]

As one small aspect of the ACTION program, which was primarily an attempt to give people the feeling that something was happening and that they should become involved, the organization hired Jeanne Lowe in 1957 to be its "public information officer." As she describes it:

This work took me to many cities that were just starting such programs, and brought me into contact with officials and professionals who were running these programs, advising local leaders and shaping new government policies. I also came to know a number of business, civic, and neighborhood leaders who were engaged in the new activity of urban renewal.[5]

Lowe was not with ACTION long before she had visited New Haven and written an article for the October 1957 *Harper's Magazine,* entitled "Lee of New Haven and his Political Jackpot." As might be expected, it was an enthusiastic endorsement of what was happening in New Haven, with an almost breathless excitement about the magic leadership qualities of Mayor Richard C. Lee. It began:

> Richard C. Lee of New Haven is the first city Mayor in the country to make urban renewal the cornerstone of his political career. Today, as a result, this twice-defeated candidate for a once semi-ceremonial job in a second rate city is apparently assured of re-election next month for his third term. . . . Mayor Lee has struck political pay dirt in an unpromising issue.[6]

Five paragraphs later, Lowe notes that "what redevelopment needed was an example like New Haven's, which other cities have watched with envy and which Housing Administrator Cole has called 'spectacular, imaginative, exciting, comprehensive—a model for urban renewal in the cities of America.' "

New Haven had become one of the "demonstration projects" which President Eisenhower's blue-ribbon committee had said would be "tremendously useful" in the same report in which it had called for an organization such as ACTION to "help promote and lead" the urban renewal program.

That article was only one of many. *Time* had opened the campaign with "Forward Look in Connecticut" on June 24. *Life* had followed with "City Clean-up Champion" on February 17, 1958, and *Saturday Evening Post* was in the picture with "He is Saving a Dead City" on April 19, 1958. What Dahl recorded in his interviews in 1957 and 1958—most of his interviews were held between July 16, 1957, and October 30, 1957—were the memories of the years 1949-55 as distilled through the ideological atmosphere created by ACTION, the Advertising Council, and popular magazines.

The fact that the titles of several of these articles emphasize the mayor's personal role points to the danger of retrospective interviews. Recalling events in terms of persons and personalities allows the collective nature of power and decision making to be ignored, as well as the greater importance of changes in the legislative and legal structure in bringing about new programs. Consider for example this piece of puffery that appeared in a February 1957 article in *American City,* an article on an urban renewal clinic sponsored by ACTION:

In New Haven, Conn., the mayor himself spearheaded the drive, according to H. Gordon Sweet, executive director of that city's Citizens' Action Commission. The mayor's decision came about during his election campaign when he campaigned in certain blighted areas so depressing that he felt sick from the effects. He appointed a carefully-selected bi-partisan Committee after the election and *personally induced* them [my emphasis] to take action.[7]

That the mayor personally induced "them" to take action is just about the opposite of the truth, as I will show when I quote documents from 1949-54. Dahl's account falls into this personalistic pattern. The fateful error is revealed in the second paragraph of his account of urban renewal when he makes the already-quoted assertion that "very little happened until redevelopment became attached to the political fortunes of an ambitious politician" (p. 115). As I will show in great detail, urban renewal was making just about as much progress as could be expected given the situation until 1954, when important legislative, legal, and administrative decisions at the national and state levels made it possible for urban renewal to move ahead, not only in New Haven, but in other cities as well. Mayor Lee was a dynamic and persuasive salesman, but he was also the right man at the right time, capitalizing politically on a ruling-class program whose time had come, making possible the enactment of the plans of the New Haven Chamber of Commerce and its closely allied friends in the city planning department.

The methodological approach necessary to avoid these pitfalls is best described by Daniel Ellsberg in his reanalysis of how the Indochina war really heated up in the early 1960s. It is presented as part of his analysis of the "quagmire" nonsense put forth by liberal apologists for the war on the basis of hearsay, interviews, and a reading of The New York Times. After acknowledging that documents are not perfect, Ellsberg goes on to say:

Yet the fact remains that documents, when available, are the best place to start. They define usefully *what is to be explained* by those same officials: why they wrote, predicted, recommended, reported just what they did at that particular moment in time, to that recipient. Most documents raise more questions than they answer, yet those questions are essential. Interviews without documents to prime the questioner, to check and jog the memory and candor of former officials, are as unreliable as their memoirs, which, as the Pentagon Papers incidentally reveal, are very unreliable. Thus, the Pentagon Papers are a beginning, a framework, the basis for new interviews, cross-checks of memoirs and other journalistic data, and other further exploration that can eventually approach an adequate understanding.[8]

Following Ellsberg, documents were my starting point, and I was often reminded of the truth of his warnings as I read standard accounts on New Haven and conducted interviews. I became convinced that the "decisional method" of studying power, which Dahl believes to be the one best way, is rarely possible to utilize, whatever its theoretical merits, unless enough time has passed for insider documents and organizational records to be available. It may be that the most serious methodological criticism I can make of Dahl is that he never should have done this particular study in the first place, for it was doomed from the start to fall victim, for sociopsychological reasons, to the ambitions and plans of the politicians, planners, lawyers, and businessmen that he was interviewing.

## DAHL'S LIMITED THEORETICAL FOCUS

Dahl's most serious theoretical error was to consider decision making in New Haven as totally divorced from the national and state governmental context. He does not stress theoretically that New Haven is one part of a national socioeconomic system with a major resource—Yale University—and a major national product—Yale graduates. When it comes to the national level, Dahl's only comments are that the urban redevelopment legislation of 1949 provided "a partial solution to the problem of money" (p. 116) and that Mayor Lee and his aides were very good at negotiating with the "Feds" (p. 130). But the urban redevelopment act was more than "a partial solution," it was an invitation, and an invitation that New Haven could capitalize on because of the local experts Yale provided and the national connections Yale maintained.

Let me give one example here of how important Yale's national connections were to the program by quoting from Dahl's interview with one of the redevelopment bureaucrats who was supposedly so good at using his knowledge to cut through red tape with the federal government. The subject of the interview is Connecticut senator Prescott Bush, a very rich investment banker who was also a trustee of Yale University and chairman of the committee which developed Yale's long-term growth plan in 1949-50. Bush's contribution to the urban redevelopment program is not even mentioned in Dahl's account.[9] Moreover, and I find this surprising in light of Dahl's claims about Yale's lack of political clout in New Haven, Dahl did not even know very much about Bush's central role at Yale. Here is the dialogue:

*Informant:* [The informant is explaining to Dahl that the Church Street project, which was the major project in the downtown retail area, was really a stretching of the original concept of urban renewal.] What we're doing is a land use concept. We had a helluva time. We had to put pressure on Bush who was most helpful in getting it out.

*Dahl:* This is one thing I didn't question [other informant] about last night and should have. I don't really understand why it is that Bush has been so helpful on this. [Dahl then goes on for a minute to allude to the other senator from Connecticut, but the tape apparently was garbled and the written transcript has several gaps which make his sentence unintelligible.]

*Informant:* [The informant replies with one sentence in reply to Dahl's allusion to the other senator. He then turns to the subject of Bush and his role.] Bush's connections, I've never asked [other informant] directly why, but my own interest from what I know goes back to the fact that Yale was to be the developer on the Oak St. Liner. [Here he is referring to Yale's tentative agreement to buy property for apartment housing in the first renewal area, Oak Street, a tentative agreement that was essential before New Haven could submit its plans to the federal government.] Bush is on the Yale Corporation and there is an.... [Here there is a blank in the transcript due to difficulties in understanding the tape.] Also Bush is on the Banking and Currency Committee, which handles redevelopment legislation. So that he has a logical interest. Also taking advantage of the Yale connection, Logue and Lee, whenever Bush comes to town, dealing with the Yale Corporation, manage to have lunch with him at Mory's. And I've gone to some of those luncheons. The preparations when we're putting on a show for Bush, preparation for this one man, is quite intensive. We put out publications limited to him.

*Dahl:* Is that so!

*Informant:* Explaining what the program was, what the answers were, answers to the problems, and *where he could help in getting those answers* [my emphasis].

*Dahl:* I suppose it is also true that most of the people who ordinarily support Bush are, after all, behind the program. [Here we see Dahl searching for a political explanation for Bush's role, but in the next reply you will see that the informant does not give this factor much weight.]

*Informant:* Well, this is the other phase of it. You could get Bush interested through Yale.... His general method of operation, Lee has come close to making this a non-partisan thing. This is not a product of demand of slum dwellers for better space. This is a *top-level thing* [my italics] handed down from a box, as far as the community is concerned. [The informant goes on to criticize the program slightly.]

Dahl is equally silent on the importance of the state government, which was quite essential in providing financial subsidies and in agreeing to New Haven's desire for a large expressway, the Oak Street Connector. This new roadway was cut through the heart of the Oak Street area, the first low-income area to be redeveloped in New Haven, requiring the clearing of many acres of land at state expense. Dahl's one serious allusion to the state government comes in a discussion in which he concedes that one member of the allegedly impotent Citizens' Action Commission made a "minor," "technical contribution" by discovering an aspect of existing state legislation that was inadequate for redevelopment purposes (p. 133).

Dahl overlooks a more important instance of where CAC might have played a key role in dealing with the state level, an instance that might have contradicted his claim that the "muscles" on CAC "never directly initiated, opposed, vetoed, or altered any proposal brought before them by the Mayor and his Development Administration" (p. 131). I do not quote this instance to dispute Dahl's notion that CAC was unimportant in shaping the program, for I will show later that most important decisions were made by the Chamber of Commerce and members of CAC long before CAC was formed. CAC always was conceived to serve only an ideological function, and Dahl went through a futile exercise in demonstrating lack of initiative on the part of a group that was never meant to take any initiative. Instead, I quote this exchange about the role of CAC at this point to show the way in which Dahl and one of his assistants who helped in most of the interviews were single-mindedly focused on local decision making to the point that they could not follow up on a suggestion by an interviewee that CAC had played an important role at the state level. The interview is with a Yale official who was an informal adviser to Mayor Lee. The exchange shows how the Dahl assistant rejected the answer provided to Dahl's question on the role of CAC. The dialogue begins with Dahl offering his view of CAC as a rather passive group. The interviewee replies that he agrees in general, but that some important suggestions and efforts were made by CAC members:

*Dahl:* Could you give us a concrete example of that?

*Informant:* Well, the discussion of the relocation of Route 5 [the expressway northward to Hartford], I remember was a fruitful discussion.

*Dahl assistant:* Well, those decisions aren't made in town; they're made in Hartford.

*Informant:* Oh well, but they're made in town very vitally in that New Haven more than any other community has brought the full weight of its own considered views to bear on Hartford. We fought steadily with Hartford to modify those programs.

*Dahl assistant:* Well I think something that would interest us even more would be an example of a decision that is made in New Haven.

In some ways this exchange is even more revealing than the previously quoted dialogue about Bush, for it shows the power of theory to deflect the interviewers away from what an informant is trying to tell them about how other levels of government are often essential to understanding power in a local community.

## CENTRAL QUESTIONS ABOUT NEW HAVEN URBAN RENEWAL

As I think Dahl recognizes, there are two important questions to be explained about the urban renewal program in New Haven:

1. Why did the program "take off" in 1955-56, when it had been in the planning stages since 1951-52 and even before?

2. Why had New Haven received, by the end of 1958, so much urban renewal money that only Washington, D.C., "had received more per person in capital grants, and no other city had so much reserved for its projects" (p. 122)?

Dahl's answer to *both* questions is Mayor Lee and his redevelopment aides. In Dahl's view, Lee was the dynamic personality who sold redevelopment to reluctant businessmen and put together an executive-centered coalition; his aides were the tireless young action-oriented experts able to pull plans together and negotiate with the bureaucracy in Washington. My own answers to these questions are very different. First, the program got under way in 1955-56 because of three legislative, legal, and administrative decisions at the national and state level in 1954. Second, the program was so large because of Yale's resources and connections. Moreover, the program was shaped by the very eager—not at all reluctant or passive—local business leaders through the Chamber of Commerce and the Manufacturers' Association, groups dominated by the ruling class analyzed in the previous chapter. Mayor Lee carried out these plans because he was eager to further his career and be in the good graces of his friends and former employers at the Chamber of Commerce (1940-42) and Yale (1944 until he became mayor in 1954). As a Chamber of Commerce executive of the 1950s nicely summarized the relationship after noting his bemusement to me over the way in which Lee took all the credit for the program: "Lee was the right man at the right time. He knew Yale and he knew the businessmen." Or, as an important business leader said in this exchange with Dahl:

*Dahl:* You suggested this [program] to the city, did you?

*Business leader:* Yes, we [the Chamber of Commerce] had our own ten-point program which was incorporated in this phase of it. Finally we got approval of the plan by the city and Mayor Lee took the ball and has been throwing it ever since.

It is only in this limited sense of "ball thrower" that I see merit in the emphasis Dahl gives to the idea of an executive-centered coalition. Lee had to take the ball and throw it, that is, sell the idea to the populace. That he was a very good and hard-working salesman in no way contradicts the ruling-class view, for what he was selling, as will be shown, was a ruling-class program. Such is the traditional role of successful politicians in America. The trick is to "throw the ball" for the ruling class while receiving votes from ordinary citizens. Given this problem, it is not surprising that many politicians worry about being reelected.

I now turn to a detailed documentation of my argument. The story will be told in chronological order, with a weaving back and forth among national, state, and New Haven developments. I shall also explicitly compare Dahl's assertions on various aspects of the process with the understanding gained from a more in-depth and holistic analysis.

## IDEAS AND TENSIONS IN URBAN RENEWAL AND URBAN REDEVELOPMENT, 1937-1949

Beginning in the late nineteenth century, with the increase in inner-city problems due to industrialization and its attendant mass immigration from Europe and from rural areas, there were sporadic efforts by various groups to deal with slum conditions in many major Eastern cities. But it was not until the late 1930s that ruling-class groups, white-collar liberals, organized labor, and the national government began to give much serious attention to the physical structures of urban areas. From that time on urban redevelopment has to be seen in terms of two conflicting perspectives which battled each other vigorously. It is important to have these two perspectives clearly distinguished in order to understand one of the reasons for the tensions, delays, and compromises that persisted until 1954-55, when the federal program finally began to make drastic changes in the face of the city.

The first perspective was a concern for more and decent housing for the poor. It manifested itself in terms of programs for public housing, subsidized housing, and the rehabilitation of slums. It was termed *urban redevelopment,* and the forces behind it were primarily liberals of varying social and economic backgrounds, and representatives of organized labor and minority groups. The second perspective was a concern for real estate values, business buildings, universities, and hospitals of the inner city. This was primarily the concern of the business-financial community, and it manifested itself in a desire to remove slum housing from the cities in order to protect the values of existent nonhousing structures and to provide more land for the expansion of office buildings, retail centers, universities, hospitals, and cultural centers. It is to this concern that the term *urban renewal* was later applied, although the term is now used as a general designation encompassing both foci.

Many of those in the prohousing camp also shared some of the business perspective, and there were some far-sighted big businessmen who saw the need for some housing programs if they were considered within an overall urban renewal program. However, the groups behind the two perspectives had derogatory names for each other. Those with a primary concern for housing saw the business interests as "the reactionary real estate lobby" which manifested itself through the U.S. Chamber of Commerce, the U.S. Savings and Loan League, the Mortgage Bankers Association, and the National Association of Real Estate Boards.[10] Those in the "real estate lobby" called the public housing advocates "the housers," and often claimed their programs were "socialistic" and/or "communistic."

The first federal legislation aimed at urban problems in a serious way was the Housing Act of 1937, a redevelopment program for low-income housing providing federal aid to municipal housing authorities. By 1941, there were 200,000 people living in these federally aided projects, some of which were quite successful and aesthetically pleasing. However, the Act did not speak to the needs of the business community. More directly there was vigorous resistance to the program by the real estate sector because the National Housing Authority's desire to build public housing on *vacant* land was a serious threat to the value of slum property. The value of this property depended at least in part upon a limited housing supply in order to extract its profits from the poor people who were forced by circumstance to rent overcrowded and over-priced living quarters. Nathan Straus, the first administrator of the United States Housing Authority, put the matter this way:

> It would indeed have been a betrayal of a public trust to allow the USHA program to become a means of bailing out owners of slums at "values" of three, five, or ten dollars per square foot when such fictitious values arose out of use of property in a manner which was dangerous to the health of tenants and detrimental to the well-being of the community. The USHA program accordingly was planned to enable local authorities to build some of their projects on low cost land outside of slum areas.[11]

It was at this point that leaders within the ruling class, with the aid of economists and planners, began to involve themselves in urban problems in a serious way. As Lowe says:

> Business interests, particularly downtown property owners and realtors, wanted a clearance and rebuilding program that would be on a more "economic" basis—that would allow private entrepreneurs to participate as developers; permit re-uses other than public housing, especially in centrally located slum areas; and let cities reap the higher tax returns which private developers promised. Equally important, these inter-ests had come to accept the fact that in order to assemble land for feasible rebuilding, local government's power of eminent domain would be required to eliminate hold-out prices.[12]

The first organizational manifestation of this greater interest in urban redevelopment on the part of downtown business interests was the revitalization of the Urban Land Institute, an organization which had been founded by the National Association of Real Estate Boards in 1936. A March 1940, article in *The New York Times* reported that five New York businessmen had joined in sponsoring the institute, which was going to turn its attention to the "study of trends affecting real property uses and values and to provide an advisory service for cities interested in replanning and rebuilding their blighted and poorly planned central business districts." The five men were Rolland J. Hamilton, president of the American Radiator Company, Charles G. Edwards, president of Central Savings Bank of New York, Edward A. MacDougall, president of the Queensboro Transportation Company, George McAneny, president of Title Guarantee and Trust Company, and Sidney Weinberg, the lead partner in the investment banking firm of Goldman, Sachs, and Company.[13]

There was one major stumbling block faced by those who wished to renew the downtown areas, and that was the high cost of slum land. With a few notable exceptions, such as Indianapolis, Chicago, and Pittsburgh, it was too expensive for private groups, state governments, or cities to acquire large areas of slum housing for clearing and rebuilding. The answer to this financial problem was provided in the early 1940s by two economists, Alvin Hansen and Guy Greer. Their work was part of the large-scale postwar planning that was already taking place in 1940-42 under the auspices of three major policy-planning organizations of the big-business community—the Council on Foreign Relations, the Committee for Economic Development, and the National Planning Association.[14]

The general Greer-Hansen proposal for redeveloping the cities was very similar to one developed independently by the Urban Land Institute, the only difference being that Hansen and Greer suggested that the federal government might have to pay much of the cost for buying and clearing the land instead of merely granting long-term loans. Local government was to pay the remainder of the cost. The land would then be either leased (under the Greer-Hansen plan) or leased or sold (under the Urban Land Institute plan) to private developers at a lower price than the government had paid, a lower price which supposedly reflected the true earning power of the land when redeveloped. In other words, small property owners, mortgage holders, and slumlords would be bought out by the government, and the bigger businessmen and developers would be able to obtain the land at a reduced price that would allow them to make a profit with nonslum structures. The difference was to be absorbed by the ordinary taxpayer. Conflicts among small and large capitalists were to be ameliorated—as we will see, the attempt was not always successful—at the expense of the general taxpayer.

Greer and Hansen realized that the new plan might be viewed as I just have, "as a bail-out of the owners of slum properties and the lending institutions that held the mortgages." [15] So they argued that "this was not the issue, that the social and economic mess in American cities was the fault of so many public and private groups—indeed, of society as a whole—that society should pay the price of cleaning it up." [16] This weak argument was countered as follows by former U.S. Housing Authority administrator Straus:

> The high profits obtained from slum properties, the dogged insistence of slum-owners on their right to maintain housing

which flagrantly violates human decencies, the high returns derived from this method of operation, and the high capitalized value placed on the properties—these are typical conditions throughout the country. In view of the facts, the thesis that society is to blame for slum conditions and that there is moral justification for using the taxpayer's funds to bail out owners of the slums is hardly tenable.[17]

However, as Straus was well aware, the problem was not moral but financial, and his plan to lower downtown values and eliminate slums by building public housing on vacant or low-cost land was swept by the wayside. His approach was a challenge to city finances as well as business interests, as Greer made clear in a statement on the problems of allowing inner-city values to fall: "The consequences to the mortgages held by banks and other institutions that have thus invested the people's money, to the small businessmen and others who have put their life's savings into real estate, and to the city's finances, would not be pleasant to contemplate." [18]

The Hansen-Greer proposal was included in new legislation introduced into the Senate in 1943 by Senator Elbert Thomas of Utah. The bill was shaped in good part by Hansen and Alfred Bettman, a Harvard-trained corporation lawyer from Cincinnati, Ohio, who had been extremely active in local and national planning efforts, and was chairman of both the Legislative Committee of the American Institute of Planners and the Committee on Planning Law and Legislation of the American Bar Association.[19] A slightly different bill written by the Urban Land Institute was introduced the same year as a courtesy by Senator Robert Wagner of New York. Hearings on the ideas contained in the two bills were first held in 1944-45 before Senator Robert A. Taft's Special Subcommittee on Post-War Economic Policy and Planning. Among the most important witnesses for the legislation were Bettman and Seward Mott, director of the Urban Land Institute.

Bettman was in no way solely concerned with housing. As he said in his testimony, "serious warning needs to be issued against conceiving urban redevelopment as a subject identical with housing or just housing with little variations, housing the theme, urban redevelopment the variations." [20] He then went on to give examples of where housing might be removed from an area. This emphasis on housing as but one form of redevelopment also was "forcefully presented" by Mott as a representative of the Urban Land Institute.[21]

It would seem that the story from this point should be very straightforward, but the plans of the interests symbolized by the

Urban Land Institute were thwarted by the fact that the "housers" were able to mount a very convincing argument that public housing was a desperate need and that administration of the new program should be under the auspices of the newly named National Housing Authority, which had performed well during the war.[22] The emphasis on housing and the placement of the program under the housing authority were vehemently criticized by the real estate and banking groups, leading them to oppose a program they had helped create.

The story is also complicated by the fact that Taft was a very unusual conservative in that he believed the government was responsible for public welfare in the area of housing, and for the most part sided with the "housers" in formulating the bill he would support. He also surprised people by disagreeing with the idea "that the federal government was responsible for helping cities rebuild their economic base or readjust poor urban land uses with the proposed 'write-down,' as planners and some business groups were arguing it should." [23] One of the most detailed tracings of the origins of federal urban renewal legislation makes the same point, noting further that Bettman was not able "to persuade Senator Taft, that the economic deterioration of cities affects the national economy, thereby justifying federal aid." [24] The authors of this detailed account quote the following exchange between Taft and Bettman, which they see as the origin of the concern with the use of the phrase "predominantly residential" in the legislation:

*Senator Taft:* You tried to separate it [urban redevelopment] very clearly from housing. I wonder if there is not an intermediate step, an intermediate possibility? That is, that the federal government might finance the acquisition where, by doing so, they eliminate a comparatively large amount of slum housing, *where two-thirds of the place is residential.*

*Mr. Bettman:* That is right.

*Senator Taft:* In order to do that, you might have to help the city finance a somewhat larger development plan. That seems to me a possible approach to it. I would regard that more favorably than a wide open plan.

*Mr. Bettman:* It would be *predominantly* housing, because all urban development is predominantly housing.[25]

After lengthy hearings, the Taft committee supported a bill roughly as written by Hansen-Bettman, but including a "predominantly residential" requirement: "The Subcommittee is not convinced that the federal government should embark upon a general program of aid to cities looking to their rebuilding in more attractive and economical patterns." [26] As Lowe rightly observes, this "narrow construction of the new federal urban aid program as incorporated in the Housing Act, proved to be one of the big stumbling blocks to redevelopment." [27]

The formal struggle for enactment of new urban redevelopment legislation began in August 1945, when a bill was introduced which "very closely followed the recommendations of the Taft Subcommittee report, which was dated the same day." [28] A few months later, on November 14, a similar bill was again introduced, this time with Senator Taft as one of its sponsors. The bill then faced hearings before the Banking and Currency Committee of the Senate. Despite vigorous opposition by home-building, mortgage-lending, and real estate associations, it was reported out of the committee and passed by an overwhelming bipartisan majority. The bill was killed in the House by the usual tactics of the conservative coalition, "where opponents of the more controversial features were able to gain the support of many representatives from rural districts." [29]

Opponents of the bill were able to force two important changes before it was finally passed in 1949. They were introduced as amendments early in 1948 by a moderate Republican, Senator Ralph Flanders of Vermont, a manufacturer who was also one of the top leaders of the Committee for Economic Development. The first change made it mandatory that federal money be given to the local community in one lump sum, making it more difficult for the federal agency in charge of the program to monitor the local program:

> The most noteworthy from a long-range point of view was the change from a system of federal annual contributions for slum clearance to a system of capital grants. This change had been recommended during the hearings in the Seventy-ninth Congress by the National Association of Real Estate Boards and the United States Savings and Loan League. [30]

Another important change in the urban redevelopment provisions as a concession to conservative businessmen in the Urban Land Institute and the real estate lobby was the decision that city-cleared land could be sold as well as leased to private developers. This concession, as Foard and Fefferman note, made it possible for private entrepreneurs, rather than the city, to realize the gains from long-term increases in land values. [31] The emphasis on leases had been suggested by the moderates Hansen and Bettman, but they did not have a strong opposition to selling the land, as Bettman made clear at the 1945 Taft hearings. [32]

Congress passed the bill on July 8, 1949. Title I, which contained the all-important redevelopment provisions, was "essentially the same as proposals made in 1941" by Greer and Hansen, except for changes in the type of federal subsidy.[33] Despite these concessions that made the act even more attractive to conservative business interests, there was opposition by "every national trade organization whose members were primarily engaged in producing, financing, or dealing with residential property."[34] Furthermore, they had "substantial support" from several rural congressmen and from the U.S. Chamber of Commerce and the National Association of Manufacturers.[35]

This conservative business opposition was directed at the public housing provisions of the Act, not the redevelopment aspects, although the Chamber of Commerce did object to the commitment of federal funds as well. The opposition did not involve the Committee for Economic Development, the Business Council, or other organizations of the biggest of big businessmen. The equation of "business community" and "U.S. Chamber of Commerce-National Association of Manufacturers" is one of the major mistakes constantly made by pluralists.[36] In making this equation, they overlook the decisive role played by the "corporate liberals" or sophisticated conservatives in shaping social legislation of all types in the twentieth century.[37]

The attitude of the U.S. Chamber of Commerce changed after enactment of the program. It is essential to make this point in considerable detail because of Wolfinger's claim that "Most businessmen have been hostile or indifferent to the concept of urban renewal. The Chamber of Commerce of the United States strongly opposed adoption of Title I and has consistently maintained that the program is a failure and should be terminated."[38] This belief may have been one of the factors which led Wolfinger—and Dahl—to assume that business played very little role in New Haven's urban renewal program. As will be shown, though, the national chamber was very positive toward the urban renewal program during the years of the Eisenhower administration, when the New Haven urban renewal program was being studied by Dahl, Wolfinger, and Polsby.

The chamber's position in 1948, as recommended by its Construction and Urban Redevelopment Committee, was that

Chambers of Commerce should avail themselves of the unparalleled opportunity to urge state and local governments to take vigorous measures to encourage the redevelopment through private activity of slum and blighted areas. Urban redevelopment laws should be enacted by states to empower cities to take the necessary steps to clear slum areas and blighted areas and to encourage their rebuilding by private initiative and private investment.[39]

While this statement shows that the Chamber of Commerce had a definite interest in redevelopment, this interest clearly did not envisage a federal role. The chamber's attitude toward public housing, which appeared below its statement about urban redevelopment, explicitly called for the federal government to get out of that area: "There should be no further federal appropriation or participation in the financing of public subsidized or welfare housing."

Following passage of the Housing Act of 1949, the chamber policy position was slightly modified by adding a sentence to the 1948 declaration quoted above: "Activities of the federal government in this field should not extend to or include any types of subsidized government development." [40] In other words, if the federal government had to be involved, it should be restricted to preparing the land for private construction. The chamber then moved in a more positive direction by calling a Businessmen's Conference on Urban Problems for November 20-21, 1950, in Washington, D.C. The conference was summarized in a 200-page chamber book, *Creating Better Cities*.

The 1950 conference was concerned with several urban problems of interest to businessmen, including the financing of off-street parking and the improvement of traffic flow in downtown areas. For our purposes the most important session was entitled "Urban Redevelopment Today," featuring Paul L. McCord, a real estate man who was president of the Redevelopment Commission in Indianapolis and a director of the Urban Land Institute; General Otto L. Nelson, Jr., a vice-president from New York Life Insurance Company who was heading that company's urban redevelopment project in Chicago; Charles W. Hawkins, director of redevelopment in Nashville; Park H. Martin, executive director of the Allegheny Conference on Community Development that was sparking redevelopment in Pittsburgh; Seward H. Mott, executive director of the Urban Land Institute, who had testified so vigorously for the urban redevelopment proposals that transcended housing in 1944-45; and Nathaniel S. Keith, director of Slum Clearance and Urban Redevelopment for the Housing and Home Finance Agency in Washington, D.C. Max S. Wehrly, assistant director of the Urban Land Institute, served as secretary to the panel.

The panelists dealt with the many problems of carrying out

redevelopment programs, which they favored for their stimulating effects on the downtown business area and surrounding property values: Among these problems were litigation by small landholders, protests by the slum dwellers who would be relocated, and difficulties in coordinating the several city agencies that had to be involved in the program.

Equal stress was put on the fact that a redevelopment program does not mean public housing, or even housing of any type. McCord, in his opening talk on "Experience in Indianapolis," very quickly came to this point when he said:

> I should like to emphasize at this point that redevelopment does not necessarily mean clearing slums for housing. Proper land use should be the keynote of any redevelopment program. I cannot emphasize that too much. It seems to be the general concept around over the country that urban redevelopment means housing. It certainly does not. More often it means anything but housing.[41]

Hawkins, in recounting the story of "Redevelopment in Nashville," summarized his first major project as follows:

> In other words, in exchange for this ugly and distasteful slum which, for many years, has been a burden and eyesore in the heart of the city, we will have a logical and adequate system of streets and utilities complementing the city system as a whole, and approximately 45 acres of desirable property for private enterprise development—stores, wholesale houses, office buildings, hotels, and possibly downtown apartment houses.[42]

Mott of the Urban Land Institute was equally direct. He said that blighted areas near downtowns were ideal places for an "inner loop highway system," for parking garages, and for other uses that benefit the downtown business area. Proper land use, not housing, was his concern: "Under a well conceived redevelopment program, the highest and best use of the land must be the first consideration. Emphasis on housing, due to federal government subsidy, has blinded many to the more important and appropriate uses to which the redeveloped area should often be put." [43]

The director of Slum Clearance and Urban Redevelopment, Nathaniel Keith, after saying that housing for the poor would receive its due as required by law, then proceeded to remind the chamber leaders that housing was not his only concern either:

But in the course of doing the job, private enterprise will be given many opportunities in redevelopment beyond supplying housing alone. There will be, in redevelopment, all the many facets that go to make up a community—commercial, industrial, and mixed uses of all sorts, depending on the type of redevelopment admissible in areas selected.[44]

The way in which chamber-oriented business leaders intended to put housing in a secondary place came through even more clearly in the question and answer session following the panel presentations. At one point a question from the floor was directed to Martin of Pittsburgh, asking whether he thought it better for a "separate redevelopment authority" or the housing authority to act as the redevelopment agency. Martin answered directly that "the redevelopment authority is for that purpose."[45] McCord of Indianapolis then asked the other panelists what they thought. Government official Keith waffled a bit, saying it was hard to generalize and that his agency recommended that this be left a matter of local option.

Martin obviously did not like Keith's answer. He asked if he might "interject a remark":

Take a commercial redevelopment; by what right would a public housing agency be charged with the job of redeveloping a commercial area? I am like Mr. Mott; I think, in the first place, it belongs to the city planning commission, and in the second place with the urban redevelopment authority, to do the job of redeveloping a city.[46]

General Nelson of New York Life Insurance spoke next, agreeing with Martin: "I would favor very much the redevelopment authority being separate and distinct from the housing authority."[47] He was followed by Hawkins of Nashville, whose comments are especially interesting because redevelopment in Nashville seemed to be nominally under the Housing Authority: "In our situation, the Housing Authority is so organized that it makes very little difference. It has a Redevelopment Division that operates almost entirely separately, except for the matter of information, from the Management Division."[48]

Mott of the Urban Land Institute then spoke, presenting the position which the Institute had long favored and which had been built into a "model bill" for state legislatures that the institute had written in 1944-45 as part of its reaction to the housing emphasis of the contemplated urban renewal legislation. The bill was later adopted in many states:

I am in full accord with General Nelson and with Mr. Martin. I feel that there must be an absolutely objective approach to this problem of redevelopment and I think it will be extremely difficult for a housing agency (although apparently in Mr. Hawkins' case they are a fortunate exception), to be objective and to develop a plan that would be for the benefit of the city as a whole rather than for a particular objective, which is rehousing a group living in the area.

We find so many cases where the redevelopment area is not suitable for homes. It is much more suitable for industrial use, for commercial use, for parks, for highways, for parking facilities; and I feel very strongly that it would be much more desirable to have an entirely separate authority.[49]

McCord of Indianapolis, who was chairing the session, closed this part of the questioning with the comment: "I will content myself by saying that I concur." [50]

Clearly, then, the strategy of chamber businessmen and the planners was to ensure that urban redevelopment would take precedence over public housing. Their strategy was to turn the federal legislation to their advantage by setting up separate redevelopment agencies which would not be dominated by housing authorities. This strategy can be traced back to the early work of the Urban Land Institute and even to the original Greer-Hansen pamphlet published by the National Planning Association, and it had successful precedents in Pittsburgh, Chicago, and Indianapolis, among other cities.[51] And, as we will see shortly, it was the strategy adopted by the New Haven Chamber of Commerce when it began to make plans in 1950 to take advantage of the Title I provisions of the overall housing act.

An insight into how conservative businessmen would react to federal subsidies of land acquisition, which they had opposed in the 1949 Act, was also revealed during the question and answer session. A question from the floor was addressed to McCord, asking him if the Indianapolis program, which previously had footed its own bill through taxes, would now take advantage of the new write-down provisions. McCord replied that there had been much discussion of this in Indianapolis, with the end result that "a representative group of people" decided "that we could not justify not taking federal funds in our redevelopment program." Some of this federal money came "out of the city of Indianapolis in taxes of one kind and another." Even more important, McCord articulated a rationale for accepting the money which once again made clear the way in which the fear of public housing had clouded the issue:

I want to make one point: that, in my humble opinion, there is a vast difference between taking federal funds for assistance in redevelopment and taking federal funds for public housing. In one instance, the federal government becomes the landlord to its people, and that is an entirely different thing than making federal funds available for federal assistance in the acquisition of land which is ultimately put back in the hands of private enterprise for redevelopment, to pay taxes. We have gone along with federal assistance to road programs for many years and I think the redevelopment federal assistance plan is something of that nature.[52]

In short, as the discussions in *Creating Better Cities* make clear, Urban Land Institute and chamber leaders had developed both a strategy for isolating public housing through separate redevelopment agencies and a rationale for accepting federal subsidies of land acquisition through emphasizing the tax-creating benefits of private redevelopment and comparing such assistance to federal aid to road programs.

That the national chamber's attitude changed in the early 1950s is further evidenced by its appointment in 1952 of a special committee made up of six members of the American Institute of Planners to provide chamber members with a small pamphlet on the ins and outs of *City Planning and Urban Development*. Among the six members were committee chairman Seward H. Mott, executive director of the Urban Land Institute and an active participant in the 1950 conference just summarized. The pamphlet set out the rationale for federal involvement in the purchase of slum land and outlined the Urban Land Institute's fourteen principles for sound redevelopment, including the need for a separate redevelopment agency. It also suggested that cities form citizens' or mayor's committees to oversee the work and to ensure that "the interest of the citizen at large can be aroused and maintained." [53]

The chamber pamphlet on *Planning Urban Renewal Projects* for 1960 proclaimed that "urban renewal is probably the most creative and constructive tool with which to attack problems of community deterioration," noting further that a redevelopment project "generally results in completely new buildings on the land and, in some cases, in completely new land uses. It displaces most of the families living in the area. It is likely to effect a complete change of ownership of much of the property." [54]

Election of a Democratic president in 1960, which led to renewed emphasis on public housing, coupled with growing difficulties in the federal urban renewal program, led the national chamber to become once again highly critical of the federal role. By the mid-1960s its publications were critical of the urban renewal program and it was sponsoring regional conferences that criticized the program. At the same time, as Keith notes, "a survey of local chambers of commerce in cities with active urban renewal programs, made by the American Municipal Association, disclosed that a large majority opposed the position taken by the Chamber." [55]

"Business" at the national level, then, was hardly hesitant about the urban redevelopment program when it could be used for the purposes of clearing land, building parking structures, creating new expressways, and erecting new buildings suited to business interests. This was especially the case during the 1950s, the years during which New Haven became proof that urban renewal "worked."

## THE PITTSBURGH EXPERIENCE

Despite delays at the national level during the 1940s in obtaining urban redevelopment legislation, dominant businessmen in several large cities in the country—Chicago, Pittsburgh, Indianapolis, and Nashville, among others—were moving ahead with their downtown renewal plans on the basis of state and local laws, using municipal, state, and private financing. It is important to consider briefly the Pittsburgh experience in this regard, for it provided a model for some of the developments that were to occur in New Haven in the 1950s, particularly the formation of a Citizens Action Commission to oversee the program. One of the persons most responsible for the urban renewal program in Pittsburgh, lawyer Arthur Van Buskirk, was brought to New Haven in early 1954 for the annual Chamber of Commerce dinner to sing the praises of urban renewal and give his advice to local leaders.

The Pittsburgh strategy for revitalizing the downtown was relatively straightforward, according to Lowe: "The Pittsburgh formula seemed simple enough: first, bring together the top industrial-business leaders of the community in an organization to support a general program for overall community improvement; second, establish a cooperative working relationship between them and the political leaders to advance specific projects." [56] In this case, the top industrial-business leaders meant the superrich Mellon family. It was Richard King Mellon who founded the Allegheny Conference on Community Development in 1945 and put his lawyer, Arthur Van Buskirk, the man who was later to advise New Haven, in charge of carrying through the program.

Because the Mellon interests had the money and connections to create financing for the projects, Van Buskirk's only major task was to bring the Democratic machine into a coalition with the Allegheny Conference. So Van Buskirk "went to Mayor [David] Lawrence and proposed that the city establish a redevelopment agency that could exercise eminent domain for redevelopment under the new state law, and that he appoint to its board leading citizens, naming himself, Lawrence, as the chairman." [57] Lawrence reportedly balked at the idea at first, saying that if he were chairman the lesser local businessmen would call the program "socialistic" and state Republicans would block the needed legislation. He suggested that Van Buskirk chair the new agency.

"But Van Buskirk reasoned differently," writes Lowe, and she quotes him as saying that "if we condemned people's properties, it was better for the mayor *with his popular following* [my italics] to be responsible, rather than someone with the Mellon or U.S. Steel nameplate." [58] This is a remarkable degree of foresight indeed, an excellent instance of the mentality that has dominated the United States in the twentieth century. Moreover, Van Buskirk promised the mayor the support of the local Chamber of Commerce and the newspapers, and had the Allegheny Conference pass a resolution urging the mayor to appoint himself. The upshot of this meeting was that the mayor did appoint himself head of the new agency, with Van Buskirk as his vice-chairman, and if this is not using politicians as front men, I don't know what is. The other members of the Urban Redevelopment Authority when it was christened in 1946 were a soon-to-retire U.S. Steel executive, the president of the city's leading department store, and a Democratic city councilman.

Ensuing details of urban renewal in Pittsburgh need not concern us here. For our purposes, the only aspects worthy of further note are that: (1) the first attempt to build new housing was rejected in favor of high-rise office buildings by the insurance company brought in to finance the project; (2) the largest slum was replaced by a tax-free civic auditorium complex and a luxury-type housing development; and (3) very little was done in the way of providing new housing for low-income people.[59] What happened in Pittsburgh is additional evidence that business interests in inner cities wanted to replace low-income housing with city development programs and luxury apartments.

## PARALLEL DEVELOPMENTS IN NEW HAVEN, 1937-49

Events on the national level during 1937–49 were reflected in intertwined developments in two different aspects of New Haven—Yale and the downtown business community. These events show how important Yale was in making it possible for New Haven to receive an early and large share of urban renewal funds in the 1950s. They also show that the plans carried out in the 1950s by Mayor Lee had essentially been formulated by Yale-connected planners and architects by 1944.

The first local effects of the federal housing act of 1937 are evidenced in the files of Yale University president Charles Seymour on September 8, 1937, in a letter about the bill from a wealthy New York architect, Grosvenor Atterbury, to the head of the Yale Medical School. The letter was referred to Seymour, who then queried the Institute of Human Relations, the Department of Public Health, and the Architecture School about the idea of Yale involvement in housing research with the aid of foundation funding. The results of various memos and discussion are reflected in a memo from Dean E. V. Meeks of the Architecture School to Seymour on April 15, 1938: "It appears that almost simultaneously several of us in the University, in one way or another became rather actively interested in the matter of housing. This may be a natural result of the extensive program which the government is planning to undertake." [60]

Interest in public housing at Yale had two outcomes. First, the university became more involved in housing research. This was particularly the case in regard to Professor C. E. A. Winslow of the Department of Public Health, who had earlier shown an interest in public housing with the formation of the Committee on Mental Hygiene of the American Health Association.[61] Winslow's department was located in the Medical School, which was in the heart of the Oak Street slum, the slum which was the first to be eradicated by the urban renewal program in 1955-57. The area was an ideal "laboratory," and Winslow and his students did several studies of the area over the next decade. One of these studies was the basis for the criteria used in the 1950 U.S. census to determine whether a housing structure was inadequate. In other words, the unique resource of Yale University provided New Haven with the information and trained personnel to respond to the later governmental guidelines that had to be met in order to qualify for federal monies.

The second outcome of this interest was an increased concern with planning in the Architecture School. This led to a course in city planning that came to be taught by a city planner named Maurice Rotival, a Frenchman referred to by Dahl only as a "well-known city planner" (p. 116). It is important to realize—Wolfinger records the fact—that Rotival was a visiting Yale professor who had been urged upon the Architecture School by its chief design critic at the time, Wallace K. Harrison, a designer of Rockefeller Center, on the basis of his experience with Rotival in the redesigning of downtown Caracas, Venezuela. Rotival was also relatively well-connected socially. In addition to being from the French upper class, he was married to the daughter of Hamilton Holt, a Yale alumnus who was the president of Rollins College. The in-law relationship to Holt put him on a personal basis with Yale president Seymour, as the correspondence in the Seymour papers reveals.

Rotival's arrival was greeted with enthusiasm by several of the advanced students who had been urging greater emphasis on city planning in the Yale curriculum. Most prominent among them were George W. Dudley, son of the dean of the Yale Engineering School, and Maynard Mayer; they had developed the planning course which Rotival was asked to teach when a regular Yale professor went on sabbatical leave. These students, along with a young engineer, Charles Downe, were to help Rotival in developing a new master plan for the city of New Haven in 1941-42.

At the same time as these events were unfolding at Yale, several businessmen in the downtown area, working through the recently revitalized Chamber of Commerce, were pressing for the development of citywide plans by the City Plan Commission. The two most active leaders were Oscar Monrad, executive director of the local Chamber of Commerce, and Angus Fraser, an executive with Southern New England Telephone Company. Their interest, recalling the earlier quote from Lowe about how businessmen all over the country were realizing the need for downtown planning in this period, was not atypical. In 1941, after overcoming the initial reluctance of the cost-conscious mayor, the City Plan Commission, under the chairmanship of telephone executive Fraser, hired Rotival, Mayer, and Downe to develop a comprehensive plan for New Haven. Norris Andrews, a student of Rotival's at the time and later to be a key city planner in New Haven, recalls that the aforementioned Rotival student George Dudley introduced Rotival to Fraser and that the Rotival-Mayer-Downe team got the job because they submitted an exciting proposal and were willing to do the work at a very reasonable price. As Dudley remembers it, they merely submitted a proposal directly to the commission that was accepted. In any case, it is their plan which set the framework for later developments, so it is necessary to carefully consider the ideas behind it.

In order to grasp the implications of the redevelopment plan designed by Rotival and his students, it is first necessary to have an understanding of the physical layout of downtown New Haven. The center of New Haven, about a mile from the coastline of the Long Island Sound, is built around a large open square called "the green." On the southeast and southwest sides of the square area are the business and retail buildings of the downtown, along with the city hall. On the northeast and northwest sides of the square are Yale University, the city library, the court house, and, in a modest old New England house that has been refurbished and extended in the

Figure 2: The New Haven Area

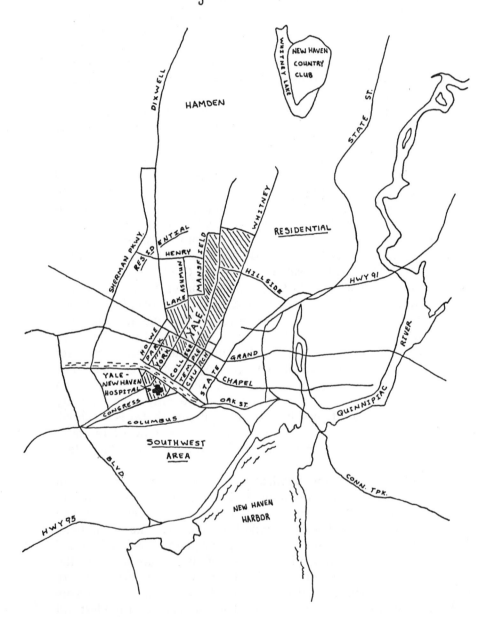

back, the exclusive Graduates Club. Two or three blocks beyond the southwest side of the green was the Oak Street slum, and on the west end of this slum was the Yale Medical School and the Grace-New Haven Hospital. The Oak Street area, then, stood between the medical school and the rest of the Yale campus, and was encroaching on the business district as well.

According to Rotival's 1960-61 outline for an overall appraisal of the urban renewal program, an appraisal that was never written, the objectives of his 1941 study were four: "(1) harbor (large)—and Quinnipiac Valley; (2) center of exchange; (3) save Yale from dirt disuse; (4) arterial system to have *sense* toward center." [62] Let me elaborate these cryptic points, which have little meaning for those not immersed in the geography and history of New Haven. By the point about the "harbor (large)," Rotival meant that New Haven must continue to develop, enlarge, and deepen its harbor, which was coming into growing use as an oil depot after a relative decline over the past decades of railroad preeminence. As Maynard Mayer put it to me independently in an interview, they wanted to emphasize that the town "should get back to the water." In regard to the mention of the Quinnipiac Valley, Rotival was referring to a relatively undeveloped area several miles to the northeast of the city, and he was suggesting that the area become the center for new industrial development in the New Haven region. Point (2), "center of exchange," meant that the downtown area must be reestablished as a commercial and retail center. Point (3), about saving Yale from "dirt disuse," was Rotival's peculiar phrase for emphasizing that Yale had become in the last few decades the central resource of the city, and that it must not be engulfed by slums. The final point, about the arterial system having a sense toward the center, meant that the highway system must bring cars into New Haven if it was to thrive as a center of exchange. As two different interviewees explained to me, and as Rotival's papers make clear, it was Rotival's strong belief that cities could be saved in the age of the automobile only if they were not by-passed by major highways, which many planners wanted to do. It was Rotival's assumption that the automobile was here to stay, and that it had to be planned for with good thruways and access roads if the inner city was to prosper.

Rotival's outline of the objectives of the 1941-42 planning squares with the memories of Dudley, Mayer, and Downe, the three people close to the study whom I was able to interview. Dudley, who did not have a formal role due to a growing interest in Latin America, recalls that the main thrust of the planning was to (1) anticipate major highways; (2) eliminate slums; and (3) consolidate Yale as a resource for the city. Mayer remembers, in addition to the concern

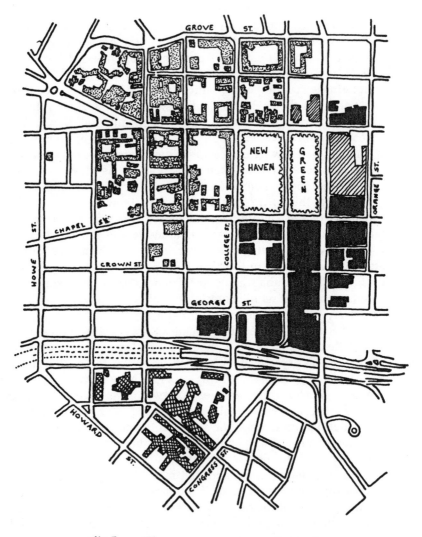

YALE 　▨
HOSPITAL 　▩

BUSINESS 　■
GOVERNMENT 　/////

with "getting back to the water," that there was talk about the Oak Street slum and the eventual unification of the Yale campus. Downe also mentioned the concern with slums and recalled "a lot of discussion of the Oak Street area as separating Yale."

It is within this context of concern for Yale and the business district that we must understand urban renewal in New Haven. However, there is no evidence that any high-level officials at Yale were greatly concerned at this time with the problems that exercised the planners. I looked long and hard for such evidence, but there simply is none—not in the files of key Yale administrators, not in the memories of any of those involved in the planning. Furthermore, as Dudley pointed out to me, no one really anticipated the large postwar growth of Yale or the metropolitan area population. When the City Plan Commission asked Yale about its growth plans in 1941, it replied that it had none.

What I have just said applies only to the concern with protecting Yale as the city's major resource. When it came to planning the highways, getting back to the harbor, and maintaining the downtown as a commercial and retail center, the business community, through the Chamber of Commerce, was actively involved.[63] All three planners whom I interviewed—Dudley, Mayer, and Downe— remember the Chamber of Commerce leaders as taking great interest in the planning. The minutes of the City Plan Commission also reveal this interest on the part of the business leaders, an interest that was shown by no other group in the community.

Among the Chamber-connected people who were active in the City Plan Commission sessions was a young Democratic alderman, Richard C. Lee, who was a Chamber of Commerce employee. Lee, originally a newspaper reporter with the local morning newspaper *Journal-Courier*, had been hired by the chamber in 1940 to do public relations and service-oriented work. Lee was with the chamber until 1942, when he left to serve in the army.[64] When ill health forced him to leave the army shortly thereafter, he was hired by Yale in 1944 to develop its public relations bureau, in good part through the auspices of Carl Lohmann, secretary of Yale, who served on the chamber's board of directors in the 1940s.[65]

The plan submitted by Rotival and his coworkers met with general approval by the City Plan Commission, which then hired them to make a more detailed study of the Southwest Area. The Southwest Area encompassed (1) the Oak Street slum; (2) the large residential area to the west of the medical-hospital complex; (3) the medical-hospital complex itself; (4) the food market area; and (5) the railroad terminal and related facilities. This second report appeared in 1943. For our purposes, the important proposals are the following, as summarized by Rotival in a 1951 document for the New Haven Redevelopment Agency. They presage much of what actually happened in the area:

> The proposals relative to thoroughfares and streets include the new Shoreline Parkway ... it was proposed to tie back the entire Southwest Area to the city center by boldly extending Church and College Streets directly across the Hill section to a new traffic circle at the junction of Howard and Columbus Avenues. This scheme, by eliminating the present jumble of streets, would permit the rebuilding along clean lines of this rundown area, and give new life to the residential areas beyond, which are gradually being strangled by the difficulties of movement from home to the downtown area.
>
> The redesign of the downtown area proper, in accordance with the general objectives outlined previously, provides for a main entrance diagonally from the new Shoreline Parkway to the foot of Chapel Street. The city is extended over the railway cut, thus reuniting the two severed parts of the city. . . .
>
> The existing arrangement around the Green is retained, including the administrative buildings on the southeast side and the churches on the Green itself, and Yale on the northwest side is preserved and protected. . . . Finally, the area between the Hospital and its related institutional establishments, and the University Campus on Chapel Street, an area which contains, as we have seen, some of the worst slums of the city, was allocated to future development of an institutional nature. A new building for the Hospital is at present being erected on a block adjoining this area.[66]

Once again, we see in this report the concern with expressways and local street patterns, and with revitalizing the downtown and protecting Yale and the medical complex. These objectives were finally to be realized in the 1950s.

Work on the general city plan was mostly suspended at this point, partly because it was essentially complete, partly because of World War II. Rotival left to serve in the French army, only to return to New Haven from his extensive consulting office in New York from time to time in the 1950s as a consultant and planner for the Redevelopment Agency. There were further developments in planning related to the anticipated postwar era, and this included many of the same people who had been involved with Rotival as coworkers and students. This work was part of the national postwar planning effort developed during the 1940s by the aforementioned national big-business Committee for Economic Development (CED).

The chairman of CED's committee in the state of Connecticut, which was called the Connecticut Postwar Planning Committee, was Yale president Charles Seymour. Although the committee did no specific planning for New Haven, it helped create the general mood which made city planning more acceptable, and it joined with the city of Hartford and others in working out a state-level redevelopment act in 1945, an act which incorporated the Urban Land Institute's suggestion of a separate redevelopment agency.

While the Connecticut Postwar Planning Committee was operating on the state level, the New Haven Chamber of Commerce had joined with the Committee for Economic Development in 1943-44 in creating a Postwar Council of the New Haven Chamber of Commerce. Chaired by Yale political economist Ray Westerfield, who was also an active leader in the business community, the concerns of that group mirrored exactly those of its national-level sponsor. The Postwar Council was broken down into several operating committees on different aspects of the economy. Among them was a City Development Committee, with subcommittees on harbor development, the airport, a trade school, taxation, new industries, public works, and city planning. One function of the City Development Committee was "reviewing the City Plan Commission's proposals and recommending changes in the plan." [67]

As part of this concern with planning for the postwar era, there appeared in 1944 a report on housing in New Haven from the office of Douglas Orr, a prominent local architect who was chairman of the Community Development and Housing Committee of CED's statewide Connecticut Postwar Planning Committee and a member of the local Postwar Council's City Development Committee. The report is of special interest because Orr is a central figure in the complex chain of events which finally led to urban renewal in New Haven. He was the architect for the university, the medical school, the hospital, and the telephone company, all of which were to figure prominently in New Haven's first redevelopment project, the Oak Street area. He thus was in a position to see and coordinate the overall picture quite clearly.

Orr's document, prepared for the Housing Authority, analyzed the housing situation in New Haven, suggesting the areas which should be developed, restored, or torn down. For our purposes, the important part of the document concerns the areas where housing should be eliminated, for Orr accepted Rotival's conclusion that housing should be eliminated from the Oak Street area. He suggested "redevelop[ing] this higher priced land in some other manner than with low-rent housing." [68] More specifically, his recommendations for the Oak Street area were that (1) part of it be put in the central business district; (2) part of it be utilized for highways; (3) part of it be used for professional buildings near the hospital; and (4) the northern part of it be used for housing professional persons in the hospital or university.[69] These proposals by Orr are central to an understanding of what happened in New Haven later, for they undoubtedly reflected—or helped shape—the general thinking of other members of the New Haven branch of the ruling class at that time. Indeed, what Orr proposed is exactly what eventually happened in the Oak Street area.[70]

Once the Rotival and Orr plans were completed, very little seemed to be done to implement them in New Haven in the postwar years. Dahl (p. 116) attributes this to three factors: (1) their great expense; (2) the lack of a "political process that would secure agreement on a strategic plan"; and (3) the presence of public officials "who saw no particular gain and much political loss if they were to push hard on city planning and development." While expense was certainly a major consideration, the lack of a political strategy and the absence of willing public officials were not the major problems at all. Those questions were not even addressed by New Haven leaders because they could not develop their plans further until decisions had been made at the national level about deepening the harbor and at the state level about determining the exact location of the new shoreline Connecticut Turnpike (Route 1) as it made its way through the New Haven area. The location of the turnpike had crucial consequences for future New Haven development in terms of how traffic would be routed into the downtown area. Its location would also determine where the large food market area would be relocated, a relocation that had to occur before the Southwest Area of which it was a part could be redeveloped. Thus, the logistics of redevelopment were closely connected to prior problems, as this account by the Union and New Haven Trust Bank makes clear:

This major project [harbor deepening] of the Chamber of Commerce was completed in 1948 by Army engineers at a cost of $3,750,000, giving the harbor a depth of thirty-five feet.... This deepening also yielded a by-product of great subsequent value—195 acres of new land along the western side of New Haven harbor east of the railroad station. This fill land provided a route for the relocation of U.S. Route 1.... Now under the market bill just passed by the Legislature, the city for $70,000 will acquire from the State Highway Department, for purposes of development, all of the harbor fill land not needed.[71]

Once the harbor was deepened and the new land was available, chamber committees devoted much of their attention to the exact location of the turnpike and to ensuring that the state would make adjacent lands available for parks, industrial development, and the new food market. These preliminary problems to further renewal and redevelopment were not finally resolved until the 1950s. At that point, the market's land near the Oak Street area was finally free to be redeveloped.

Now that we have seen how Yale and the business community reflected national developments in their own activities and how thoroughly New Haven renewal plans were developed by 1944, it is time to return to the national level to see what happened in urban renewal between the passage of the new Housing Act in 1949 and the amendments to it in 1954. This will set the stage for a fuller understanding of what was going on in New Haven in the four years before Lee became mayor in 1954.

## PROBLEMS AND DELAYS IN FEDERAL URBAN RENEWAL, 1949-1954

Dahl (pp. 116-18) emphasizes the fact that urban redevelopment plans did not move ahead rapidly in New Haven during 1949-54 despite the existence of the new Housing Act of 1949. Because he does not consider structural factors that led to this delay, he overemphasizes the election of Richard Lee as mayor in November 1953 in explaining the blossoming of the program in 1954-55. As we will see, the program was making as much progress as could be expected before he was elected, and was about to enter its action phase just as the new mayor took office.

Dahl's emphasis on Mayor Lee is muted considerably if we put the problem in a national context:

Redevelopment proved doggedly slow in getting started, in spite of the apparently attractive opportunity that Title I [of the Housing Act] presented to private enterprise and the cities themselves.... The pertinent fact here is that by 1954, few municipalities had been able to take a redevelopment project beyond its initial planning stage.[72]

There were several reasons for this nationwide delay. One is that most cities did not have technical experts who could prepare a program. Another is that private developers could make more money in other enterprises, or were leery of protests that might develop around tearing down people's houses. Still another is the curtailment of the federal program due to the emergency of the Korean War. However, the real sticking point was Senator Taft's provisions that redevelopment funds were to be used for neighborhoods that were predominantly residential to begin with or that were to be restored to predominantly residential uses—predominantly residential being administratively defined as over 50 percent. When that provision was loosened in 1954 by allowing 10 percent of federal urban renewal grants to be used for nonresidential uses, urban renewal moved ahead.[73]

This interpretation is supported by a consideration of the experience of New York City, which had made the greatest use of the new urban redevelopment act. In that city private investors began to steer clear of the federal government program because they found the provision of housing unprofitable and fraught with citizen protest. Moreover, and this is the central point, they wanted to use the land for other structures, as can be seen in this summary statement by Lowe following her account of how interest in Title I projects had declined in New York by the mid-1950s:

> However, individual Title I projects enjoyed the active, outspoken support of some of New York's most respected, powerful business figures. [Robert] Moses was helping to make land available to build things they, or the expanding private organizations and institutions they headed or supported— hospitals, universities, cultural and business promotional groups—wanted.[74]

Looking beyond New York, the long-standing desire of big business and real estate leaders for more commercial land can be demonstrated by the gradual enlargement of the "10 percent exception clause" to predominantly residential uses introduced in 1954. In 1959 the exception was enlarged to 20 percent, in 1961 to 30, and by 1967 it was 35 percent. Special laws passed by state legislatures also reveal this greater focus on commercial renewal. For example, in 1958 the Connecticut State Legislature, under the urging of New Haven leaders who feared the loss of two major manufacturers to Southern states, added its own wrinkle for getting around housing provisions. It passed an act setting up a separate state-local redevelopment program providing aid only for the renewal of blighted areas for predominantly commercial or industrial use. The legislature also passed a law which instructed the state to pay one-half of a Connecticut city's one-third federal share, thereby reducing New Haven's cost to one-sixth of any renewal program.[75]

The amount of money committed to different kinds of construction also suggests the primary reason that urban renewal grew after 1954:

> As of 1962, 492 projects had reached the stage where estimates could be made of costs of proposed construction. Commercial and industrial construction account for $1,824 million of a total estimated cost of $5,813 million. Another $1,806 million was estimated for public and semi-public uses [universities, stadia, etc.]. The bulk of the private residential construction through urban renewal, some $2,000 million, would be constructed for families with substantially higher incomes than those who had once inhabited the "blighted areas" for which urban renewal was designed. An obscenely small $83 million was estimated for public housing, which was one of the only places displaced residents could afford to live.[76]

The generalization about the national scene—and New Haven, for that matter—which seems to best capture the dynamic of the situation as of the early 1960s is that by urban sociologist Scott Greer: "In summary, the slum clearance provisions of the Housing Act of 1937 have been slowly transformed into a long-scale program to redevelop the central city." [77] In other words, during the Eisenhower years the urban renewal concerns of the big businessmen won out almost completely over the housing redevelopment and rehabilitation concerns of the "housers." [78]

The already-noted changes in the law in 1954 which led to the situation Greer summarizes were initiated by a blue-ribbon advisory panel set up by President Eisenhower in 1953. It was dominated by bankers, savings and loan officials, and real estate and development leaders. When their suggestions were brought to Congress there was little or no protest from any business groups, although conservative Southern congressmen registered their disagreement. It was at this time, too, that ACTION and the Advertising Council launched their nationwide publicity programs for the new approach to inner city problems. The stage was now set for cities like New Haven to renew their downtown areas. New Haven's second renewal project, known as the Church Street project, was the first city program to qualify under the new federal provisions.

## URBAN RENEWAL IN NEW HAVEN, 1949-1953
Dahl claims that the Redevelopment Agency in New Haven was created in 1950 in good part as a political strategy by Democrats to provide an issue with which "the Democratic majority [on the Board of Aldermen] might take the initiative away from the Republican

mayor for the next two years" (p. 117). Dahl emphasizes short-run political questions of who is elected or not in explaining events linked to a much deeper and more ongoing question, namely, the health and prosperity of the big-business community. As I will show in this section, leaders of the local Chamber of Commerce, who were overwhelmingly part of the ruling class identified in the previous chapter, were also involved in the origins of the agency, which is hardly surprising given the aforementioned evidence that the Urban Land Institute and the U.S. Chamber of Commerce had been working with local businessmen and planners to create such agencies.

In making this claim about the chamber's role, I am not denying Dahl's assertion that a young Yale political science professor, Henry Wells, who was serving on the Board of Aldermen at the time, was one of those who urged the Republican mayor, William Celentano, to set up a redevelopment agency. However, it was hardly he and his Democratic colleagues, Norton Levine and Richard C. Lee, who were alone in pushing for the necessary legislation, as Dahl implies. Equally active, if not more, were the leaders of the Chamber of Commerce, who were in regular contact with city planner Norris Andrews and Mayor Celentano, urging them to further action, a fact attested to independently by both Andrews and the retired executive director of the chamber, W. Adam Johnson.[79] Furthermore, the political scientist pegged as the originator by Dahl received his information from Andrews and acted in good part from a genuine interest in the program, according to interviews with him by myself and A. Tappan Wilder.

There were so many business leaders and planners in New Haven who had been waiting for redevelopment legislation to pass in Congress that it is really a futile exercise to try to trace the initiative to one individual, let alone a young political scientist who happened to be on the Board of Aldermen. Here we see the individualistic nature of Dahl's conception of power, not to mention his lack of deep concern for the way in which the structuring of the ideological atmosphere makes it beside the point as to which person actually made the specific proposal. Aside from his theoretical perspective, Dahl was steered in this individualistic direction in one of his interviews with a local politician of some prominence. The politician was explaining the origins of New Haven's urban renewal program in Rotival's 1942 master plan. Then he turned to more recent times:

*Informant:* Now the vehicle for doing it today is redevelopment. Now what happened? In 1949 the Federal Act was passed in redevelopment. And who is the father of redevelopment in New Haven? I'll tell you who the father is. Your old confrere, Henry Wells.

*Dahl:* Really?

*Informant:* Yes. Henry Wells came to me in 1950 as an enlightened political scientist, and he said to me, "there has been a great act which has been passed in Washington that *no one knows much about*" [my emphasis].

Unfortunately, this politician fails to recall New Haven's considerable interest in redevelopment in making his flattering remark to Dahl about "enlightened political scientists." Moreover, the July 21, 1950 minutes of the executive committee of the New Haven Chamber of Commerce show that the local chamber knew enough about the new law to send a letter to the mayor "urging him to set up an independent Redevelopment Agency" which would consider commercial and industrial questions as well as housing.[80] The chamber also made its desires known in a letter to the Board of Aldermen. While I do not think it possible to determine whether it was the chamber or the Democrats who most influenced the mayor and the Board of Aldermen, we can say at the very least that the chamber letters introduce a new element into the picture that Dahl did not even uncover because of his failure to take the chamber seriously enough to try to gain access to its minutes and records.[81] However, just as the Democrats took credit for themselves, so did the chamber think itself important, as evidenced by this note in its August 1950 *Newsletter:* "Shortly after this communique from the Chamber, the Board of Aldermen acted to establish such an independent Redevelopment Agency." [82]

Having introduced the chamber as a problem for Dahl's version of the story, let me move on to show how the chamber maintained constant contact with the agency itself and with its chief planner, Maurice Rotival.[83] There is no evidence in Redevelopment Agency minutes that any other group ever paid serious attention to the agency's plans. Nor was I able to turn up any evidence of interest on the part of other elements of the city when I asked former chamber officials and key planners whether there were "any other groups who showed an interest in urban renewal at this time."

On December 11, 1950, a five-member Redevelopment Agency board was announced after several months of discussion back and forth between the mayor and the Board of Aldermen. Appointed to the board were

1. Frank O'Brion (five-year term), executive vice-president,

Tradesmen's National Bank. O'Brion was a friend of Mayor Celentano's who had handled personal business transactions for him.

2. Myres McDougal (four-year term), Yale law professor with an interest at the time in property law and planning. He had been involved in planning studies since the early 1940s, when he had been greatly influenced by Rotival, with whom he became a friend and collaborator.[84] It was McDougal who insisted that Rotival be hired by the agency to do its planning. In fact, one interviewee very close to these matters at the time is sure that McDougal demanded the hiring of Rotival as his price for going on the agency, but McDougal recalls only that he had Rotival in mind from the beginning and urged his name at the earliest possible moment.

3. John M. Ingmanson (three-year term), vice-president, Whitney-Blake Company, a manufacturing firm in New Haven.

4. Richard Fletcher (two-year term), business manager for Douglas Orr's architecture firm.

5. Matthew Ruoppolo (one-year term), business agent for the Teamsters.

It takes only a cursory look at this line-up to see that it was dominated by the city's business interests. The second-string nature of most of these men is also readily apparent. Fletcher, who was elected chairman, was only a business manager for architect Douglas Orr. Ingmanson was only a vice-president at a company where two of the three local directors are social notables and cotillion guests. O'Brion, a member of the New Haven Country Club and later to be president of the bank, was at the time only a vice-president at the bank which is a distant fourth in assets to the First New Haven, the Union and New Haven Trust, and the Second National Bank.

As to McDougal, he was in no way "representing" Yale in any official sense, and he recalls, as do other interviewees, that Yale leaders took virtually no interest in the program in its early stages. McDougal, who was also a member of the Lawn and Graduates clubs, was very much a part of the Yale community and understood its needs and interests. He was a personal friend of the new Yale president, A. Whitney Griswold, who had been interested in planning throughout the 1940s as a Yale professor. When I asked McDougal who had represented Yale in an early meeting between Redevelopment Agency leaders and the Yale administration in 1951, he could not remember who had been officially present—after all, it had been twenty-four years hence—but he went on to say: "I more or less assumed that I was representing Yale. We were a pretty close-knit group that didn't have to make things explicit. Everybody knew everybody else."

Almost immediately, the new agency voted to ask the federal government for a project grant of $460,000. It had to act in haste to meet a December 29 deadline, and did so on the basis of the work that had been done by the staff of the City Plan Commission. Speaking for the City Plan Commission at the meeting were telephone executive Fraser, now its vice-chairman, and Andrews, planning director for the city.

The agency minutes reveal that the Chamber of Commerce almost immediately was in touch with it by means of a letter spelling out its own interests and plans. The chamber letter is referred to in a lengthy letter from the agency chairman to the other members, a letter which substituted for a January meeting. By February 1951, the agency had learned that the Housing and Home Finance Agency had earmarked $465,640 as New Haven's initial grant allocation for slum clearance. However, it was still awaiting confirmation of a planning advance of $16,000 to pay a professional staff for one year.

When that planning advance came through a month later, the agency agreed to approach Rotival about taking the job of planning consultant. Overtures were made to Rotival in early March, with an agreement being set on March 26. At the April 21 meeting the agency formally hired Rotival and announced that it had tentatively designated a portion of the Oak Street area as its first reclamation project. Rotival said he would work on the basis of his Southwest Area Plan from the early 1940s, but wanted to reconsider certain problems in light of developments concerning the harbor, placement of the Connecticut Turnpike, and expansion of the hospital. In addition to Rotival, the agency made one other major appointment, executive director Sam Spielvogel. Spielvogel was a young Yale professor in city planning who was recommended by McDougal.

The arrangement with Rotival was no sooner completed than the Chamber of Commerce was working with him closely, as evidenced by this story in the *Newsletter* for June 8, 1951:

Working closely with the City Plan Commission, the Chamber's Urban Redevelopment Committee has held several meetings with Mr. Maurice E. H. Rotival, Consultant to the New Haven Redevelopment Agency. The Agency has given favorable endorsement to the Chamber's plan to redevelop the public market as a central shopping area in conjunction with the development of the newly created land on the harbor front.[85]

By July 1951, Rotival had a draft of his report. After reexamining the various areas into which the city had been divided for planning purposes, he concluded once again that it was most important to start redevelopment in the Southwest Area in order to stop the drift of the city northeastward along Whitney Avenue, a mainly residential street of stately homes which connected to the suburban city of Hamden. To keep the city from "springing a leak," he suggested that expansion be encouraged in the opposite direction, into the Oak Street slum:

> This [the Oak Street area] also is the diseased area most closely adjoining the center of the city; it is part of the redevelopment area designated as No. 3, which extends along the entire southwestern border of the Nine Squares [i.e., the central green], and even penetrates within them. The rat's nest of small streets within this area, none of which line up in any way with the main downtown streets, is the barrier which has prevented healthy growth of this side, and is one of the causes of the creeping decay which has penetrated into the heart of the city. . . . The cleaning up of Area No. 3, desirable in itself, will be most effective, therefore, in rehabilitating the core of the city and beginning a realization of the objectives of the Master Plan.[86]

In this report Rotival made three major proposals:

1. The extension of one of the east-west downtown streets, College Street, through the Oak Street area into the "Hill" residential neighborhood to the west of the hospital. The concern here was to "reconnect" the Hill area to the downtown, an objective already expressed in the 1943 Southwest Area study.

2. A new retail center that would extend the Southwestern part of the downtown into part of the Oak Street area.

3. The development of the northern part of the area, between Yale University and Grace–New Haven Hospital, for residential purposes related to the university and the off-campus housing of some of its staff.

This third recommendation, housing for Yale, is of particular interest at this juncture, for it differs from the recommendation he had made eight years ago, when he had suggested that the section between Yale and the hospital be developed for "institutional use." There are two bases for this change. First, the Housing Act of 1949 was housing-oriented. It would not be possible to extend the retail area in the southern part of the region and also turn the northerly part to institutional use if the project was going to qualify for federal aid. Second, Rotival was well aware of Yale's own needs and interests, which had changed since the early 1940s. His suggestion for housing in the area dovetailed with new Yale plans presented in a special report, *Yale and Her Needs,* released on January 4, 1950. This report, based upon the realization that Yale was going to grow considerably during the 1950s, was the product of two years of committee work at the faculty, administration, and trustee levels. It is significant, considering my earlier discussion of how important Senator Prescott Bush was in pushing for the New Haven urban renewal program in Washington in 1955-57, that the chairman of the committee making the report was Prescott Bush.

The ambitious ten-year program called for in Bush's report would require $80 million in gifts—$60 million in new endowment and $20 million for buildings. Most of the many new buildings projected were to be placed within the framework of the existing campus or on readily accessible land. Most interesting in terms of the urban renewal program was a call for new married-student housing, particularly for medical students. Since the report lamented the fact that most housing for such students was far from the hospital, it was natural that Rotival would assume a university interest in the provision of housing. The exact words in the Yale report are as follows:

> Because of the shortage of all kinds of housing in the community, the students at the university's professional schools have to put up with some demoralizing makeshifts. This is particularly true of medical students, often housed far from the hospital where they have night duty. Other housing is also needed for student nurses, married divinity students and their families, and members of the student bodies of the Schools of Fine Arts and Music.[87]

Once again, it is clear from interviews and a search of relevant files that Rotival had no official contact with the university in making this proposal. The best evidence for his lack of consultation with Yale is found in the October 1951 minutes of the meeting of the Redevelopment Agency. When the proposals concerning Yale were discussed, McDougal suggested that "the Director start conferences with officials at Yale University in regard to their possible participation in the redevelopment area between Yale and the Hospital." The report from the informal meeting that ensued is as follows:

As suggested at the last meeting, the Director held an informal conference with representatives of the University, which was attended by Mr. McDougal, member of this agency, and Mr. Rotival, planning consultant. The general basis of redevelopment procedure was brought up in an attempt to ascertain what interest, if any, the University might have in participating in the redevelopment program which would (1) improve housing facilities in the city and (2) be of direct advantage to both the city, and perhaps the University, on a tax returning basis. The general conclusion which was drawn from that discussion was that some interest existed with the avenue left open for further discussion.[88]

There is no record of this meeting in any Yale file I was able to search in library archives, although it is possible that one may exist in the "Oak Street file" in the Treasurer's Office. However, agency director Spielvogel recalls that the principal Yale administrator present at the meeting was treasurer Laurence Tighe, and that interest was expressed in the Rotival proposal. There were two results from the meeting. First, Yale officials turned the idea over to a committee of the Alumni Council concerned with Yale's professional schools, as can be inferred from a 1953 report by that committee. Second, Richard C. Lee, head of Yale's News Bureau at the time, sent Spielvogel a breakdown of salary and residential information on Yale faculty and staff. According to Spielvogel, this May 1952 memorandum was the basis for a citywide housing-market analysis that was a documentation requirement that had to accompany any application for federal urban renewal money.

Although there was no great flurry of activity at Yale in the months after the meeting, Yale's expression of interest was absolutely essential from the point of view of the Redevelopment Agency, for major institutions would have to be interested in land acquisition if the program was to go anywhere at all. The importance of this fact, which shows how dominant institutions can have "power" even when they seem minimally involved in a "decision," can be seen in Dahl's 1957 interview with a highly placed Yale official who was well aware of the critical nature of the university's support of the urban renewal program.

The Mayor and [one of his aides] both testified publicly again and again at the Citizens Action Commission meetings and at luncheons and elsewhere that if it hadn't been for Yale's willingness to step up as original bidders on that property the whole Oak Street project would have died aborning . . . you know the rules, the laws, the policies in Washington that require a firm bid from some private agency in the community before contracts of this kind could be signed and the way cleared for the financing of the whole project. Well, anyhow, this is what we did. Now here again ... this was not sheer altruism on Yale's part. It was a case of, I think, truly enlightened self-interest. We were hard pressed, as we still are, for housing.

Similar discussions were undertaken with the hospital shortly after the meeting with Yale, with even more positive results: "The Grace–New Haven Hospital has indicated interest in redevelopment plans formulated by this Agency, following the example of Michael Reese Hospital in Chicago, which realized that it could not successfully think of its own future extension without fully cooperating with the city." [89] Spielvogel then hired two graduate students in the Art School to make a table-sized model of the plans for the medical-hospital complex, a model that was viewed by the Redevelopment Agency in February 1952.

With the assurance of cooperation from the Chamber of Commerce, the university, and the hospital, Spielvogel spent most of 1952 and 1953 doing the studies and gathering the statistics necessary to back up a final application to the federal government. However, a final application could not be made until an agreement had been reached between the city and the state on the location of major highways, on the basis of which commitments could be entertained from private developers. Delays at the city and state levels in making these decisions caused problems for the Redevelopment Agency, which had to adhere to federal guidelines.

The question of highways had been further complicated by a series of decisions which gradually moved the Connecticut Turnpike closer to the harbor so that land adjacent to the downtown could be used for other purposes. With this shift there arose the need for a major highway to bring fast traffic coming off the turnpike to the center of New Haven, for a mere exit from it would no longer do the job. Rotival had to return to the drawing boards to develop a supplementary report which was given to the agency in December 1951. The report called for a highway similar to one he had proposed in 1943 to serve the downtown area. This road, which came to be called the "Oak Street connector" in the planning discussions, would come off the turnpike and run parallel to the downtown retail area through the Oak Street neighborhood, allowing cars to exit at several different streets that ran east-west through the city. This connector, which seemed simple and was deemed absolutely necessary by the planners and business leaders, became a major basis for delay in the Oak Street project over the next several years, for the city and state were in a constant argument about its exact location, width, length, and who was going to pay for it. The Rotival report of December 1951 was only the first of many on this problem, which was not completely resolved until 1955.[90]

In addition to planning during the second half of 1951, Rotival also found time to give a speech to the Chamber of Commerce. On December 3, 1951, chamber executive W. Adam Johnson wrote to Rotival at his New York office, confirming the December 7 date of his noon-hour speech:

> It seems to us this is a great opportunity to sell the business- men in New Haven on the idea that redevelopment is the thing that makes any old city take a new lease on life so that it can compete with the more recently built cities. As you probably know, the Chamber has long been interested in the program to which you are giving so much of your time and effort. We are certainly grateful that we have a man of your vision guiding the way for us.[91]

Rotival replied in kind the next day, noting that "I only hope I can help the Chamber of Commerce in its effort to promote business and activity in New Haven which I consider a little bit like my hometown." [92]

During this 1950-53 period the Chamber of Commerce was slowly evolving its own "ten-point" program in conjunction with the work of Andrews and Rotival. The project began in January 1951, with a questionnaire to chamber members about what they saw as the most pressing needs of the city. The results, published in the June 1951 *Newsletter*, reveal the following concerns: (1) off-street parking; (2) completion of Route 1 (turnpike); (3) industrial and community development; (4) civic improvement and urban redevelopment; (5) civil defense; (6) a United Fund campaign.

Serious work on the ten-point plan was taken up in 1952 and 1953 by W. Ogden Ross, secretary of the chamber's Division of Manufac- turing and executive director of the Manufacturers Association. (The Manufacturers Association, as noted in the previous chapter, was an independent organization made up of the biggest industrials and utilities in the New Haven area. However, it used the same employees as the chamber, and for our purposes will be considered as part of the chamber group because of its complete overlap in members and employees.) Ross told me he talked to what he termed "influential people" in a number of sectors of the community to see "what was on their minds." This led to twenty points that were cut down to ten by the various divisions of the chamber. Among the people Ross consulted were city planners Downe and Andrews. When I asked if Downe and Andrews worked closely with the chamber, Ross replied, "they did indeed," and noted that both were in the junior chamber which had been formed by the chamber in the early 1940s. He also noted that both men were well trained and progressive. "They educated us," he said.[93]

The ten-point program was formally completed in June of 1953 and made public the following month. Six of the points concerned uses for the land in the harbor area, including the relocation of the New Haven market to the filled land near the harbor. Two other points concerned the Parking Authority and the need for the city to hire a full-time traffic engineer. A ninth point noted that the Quinnipiac Valley should continue to be developed as an industrial area, a point from the original Rotival proposal that was only later accepted by chamber leaders. A final point, and one of the most relevant to our consideration of the origins of urban renewal in New Haven, concerned the chamber's endorsement of the newly revised freeway plans that Rotival had developed in conjunction with traffic consultant and Urban Land Institute member Lloyd B. Reid:

> The proposed plan for routing of U.S. Route One, as developed by Mr. Reid and Mr. Rotival, and officially approved by the Chamber, must be promoted and put into effect as promptly as possible. In conjunction with the establishment of U.S. Route One, it is recommended that the State Highway Department, together with the city, provide a connector between the expressway and the central city. Access and egress from the connector shall be provided in the Oak Street area for Church, Temple, and College Streets. In conjunction with this connecting link, Parking Areas must be provided immediately adjoining these points so that the shopping public wishing to do business in the central city will be enabled to park immediately upon arrival.[94]

In April 1953, before the ten-point program was completed, the chamber moved to aid the city in carrying out those aspects of its plans related to urban redevelopment. It first of all formed a new committee on urban renewal to help the Redevelopment Agency. Its members were Leo F. Caproni, whose firm of Caproni Associates did consulting and engineering work; Allan R. Carmichael, a vice-president of Connecticut Savings Bank and a director of First New Haven National Bank and the New Haven Water Company; Dominic A. DeVito of the New Haven Market Exchange; Andrew F. Euston, a consulting architect; William Horowitz, vice-president of the manufacturing firm of Botwinik Brothers and local treasurer of the Democratic party; Roy E. Norcross, head of the New Haven County Farm Bureau; and Henry A. Pfisterer, a Yale architecture professor who was on the board of the New Haven Trap Rock Company.

The chamber then formed a special committee to work with the city and state in settling the issues around placement of the turnpike and the Oak Street connector. The members of this second committee were Charles H. Costello, president of the large local manufacturing firm of C. Cowles and Company; William J. Falsey, a municipal bonds specialist in the investment firm of Scranton and Company and a member of the city's Board of Finance; and Henry B. Brightwell, a vice-president at the First New Haven National Bank who had married into one of the "oldest" and richest of New Haven families.

Such was the situation, then, when interest in the forthcoming mayoralty election developed in the fall of 1953. The Redevelopment Agency was working on plans which the Chamber of Commerce actively supported and aided. The university and the hospital had shown interest in the program. The program was being delayed by problems with the placement of highways. It is within this framework that we must consider Richard C. Lee's campaign for mayor in that year.

## THE 1953 MAYORALTY CAMPAIGN

The events of late 1953 in New Haven must be considered in the context of the mayoralty campaign of September, October, and early November to provide stark contrast to the claim that Lee had to start from scratch with the urban renewal program when he took office in early 1954. A close reading of what happened in the month of September, before Lee revealed his program on October 5, shows that the mayor and the Redevelopment Agency were moving ahead on the basic problems facing the program. As for the remainder of the campaign, it will be seen that Lee said very little about urban renewal or slum clearance until November 2, after a month in which the Republican candidate, incumbent mayor William Celentano, was talking about the master plan that had been developed by Rotival and Reid for the Redevelopment Agency.

Data for this section are taken from the news pages of the New Haven *Journal-Courier,* one of the city's two daily newspapers, both of which are owned by the superwealthy Jackson family whose aged patriarch was later to be a major opponent of urban renewal. This newspaper was chosen because it had the reputation of being slightly more enlightening on local politics than the New Haven *Register* (see *Who Governs?*, p. 257), and because Lee had worked as one of its reporters in 1935-40 and knew many of its staff.

According to *Journal-Courier* accounts, Lee announced on August 26 that he would shortly decide whether or not to run for mayor for a third time, having been defeated by 714 votes in 1949 and just 2 votes in 1951. The account noted that Lee was being urged to try again by the Political Committee of Greater New Haven, a group dominated by Yale activists whom Lee had been involved with during the 1952 Stevenson campaign for the presidency. The following day, August 27, Lee announced that he was in fact going to run, and that he would try to do something "more forward-looking, more idealistic, if you will." Preoccupied for the first weeks of September with wrestling the nomination from a Democratic opponent, Lee made no political statements to the general electorate that were reported in the *Journal-Courier* until October 5. Before that time several developments occurred on the urban renewal front. They are most economically presented in terms of newspaper headlines, occasionally supplemented with a brief summary of the story:

August 27  MAYOR MEETS WITH OFFICIALS TO DISCUSS SLUM CLEARANCE   The story reported that the mayor would shortly receive reports from city planner Andrews and redevelopment director Spielvogel for submission to Washington.

September 8  MAYOR EXPLAINS HIGHWAY PROBLEMS   The story explained how the Oak Street slum clearance project was being held up by the fight with the highway department over location of the connector and the question of who would pay for it. The mayor reported writing to the highway commissioner for a meeting with him in the week of September 21.

September 10  HOUSING CODE READY FOR CITY ALDERMEN   In this story we learn that the director of the Bureau of Environmental Sanitation had completed a housing code which showed what New Haven was doing to prevent slums. "It is a matter of coincidence," the story noted, "that [Eric] Mood has completed the housing code at the time the Federal Housing and Home Finance Agency issued an order that no funds will be released until information is sent to Washington giving plans of slum prevention."

September 17  MAYOR TO ASK STATE AID ON HIGHWAY LINK

September 21 HOUSING CODE GETS SUPPORT OF LEADERS

September 23 STATE STUDIES CITY PLAN FOR HIGHWAY
LINK This story reported the state had agreed that the Oak
Street extension was necessary for the "revival of the retail
business center in terms of traffic service."

October 3 MAYOR SENDS SLUM REPORTS TO WASHINGTON

One other event of interest occurred before Lee released his
platform on October 5. The executive director of the Chamber of
Commerce sent Lee a copy of the chamber's ten-point program
sometime in mid-September. Lee replied as follows on September
21:

Dear Bill:

In haste, thanks for such prompt action on Bill Wilson.
Thanks, also, for those 10 points. I think they are corkers and I
plan to use them, very frankly.[95]

Whether or not this note to chamber executive Johnson should be
taken at face value I do not know, but it does make it clear that Lee
was at least familiar with the chamber program. Lee released his
campaign platform on October 5. It was presented in detail in the
*Journal-Courier* under the front-page headline "Lee Calls for Group
to Conduct Survey." In the story Lee said he would revitalize all
aspects of the city, appointing within sixty days of his election a
special commission to help him with the task. The platform set out
four general concerns which were not dissimilar to those of the
business leaders: (1) why New Haven had stopped growing; (2) why
trade was declining in the city; (3) overhaul of the city charter; (4)
the need to study the idea of New Haven as part of a metropolitan
area.

Lee then launched a vigorous and skillful campaign on a variety
of fronts. Once again, the flavor can be captured best and most
economically through the newspaper headlines over stories which
discuss programs:

October 8 LEE OUTLINES PROPOSAL FOR PARKS PROGRAM
(p. 1)

October 13 LEE ADVANCES PLAN TO SAVE ON CITY CARS
(p. 1)

October 14 LEE ADVANCES PLAN FOR NEW CITY HALL (p. 1)

October 15 LEE SAYS COMMISSION "TAKING SHAPE" (p. 4)

October 20   LEE ADVOCATES CHARTER STUDY (p. 4)

October 21   LEE CRITICIZES CITY SCHOOLS (p. 4)

October 22   LEE CRITICIZES CITY BUDGET (p. 1)

October 26   LEE ATTACKS OPPONENT FOR CITY SPENDING (p. 4)

October 27   LEE HITS BONDING POLICIES (p. 4)

October 28   LEE SAYS SCHOOL CONDITIONS "CHAOTIC" (p. 4)

October 29   LEE CHARGES INACTION IN TRADE SCHOOL PLANS (p. 4)

October 31   LEE HITS VETS HOUSING (p. 4)

November 2   LEE PLEDGES CLEARANCE OF SLUM AREAS IN CITY (p. 2)

There is little emphasis on urban redevelopment in these headlines, and I could find no indication in any of the stories underneath them that the "smells" in the Oak Street area which supposedly made him "sick as a puppy" in his 1951 campaign (see *Who Governs?*, p. 120) were a central point in this campaign. The emphasis on slums gained a headline on page 2 of the newspaper only on the day before the election, and even here the future mayor was in part concerned with the slum conditions of the temporary veterans' housing in the city.

Just as Lee, the challenger, was attacking and criticizing, so the incumbent was defending and fighting back. When Celentano began his campaign on October 7, several days after Lee was off and running, he tried to take the wind out of Lee's call for a big study by saying that "our ideas have taken such deep root that even the Democratic candidate appears to have been converted." He also pledged that "we will assist and support the Urban Redevelopment Agency in its outlined program of municipal projects." On October 19, again in reaction to Lee's well-planned campaign, the mayor tried to counter by saying that he would shortly put forth his "master plan," a plan which he had not intended to "make a political issue." Indeed, he probably had not planned to make it a political issue, for the plan he was claiming as his own was in fact a revised Rotival plan (The Rotival-Reid Short-Term Master Plan) which had been discussed in the *Journal-Courier* the day before in a story having nothing to do with the election! On October 26, the *Journal-Courier* ran a lengthy story on this new "master plan," which the mayor was now using as evidence that progress was being made in the city. Lee's energetic campaign had forced

Celentano to give greater attention to redevelopment plans which had not interested him greatly in the past.

I do not cite all these headlines and campaign promises to say that urban redevelopment was a burning issue or that Lee won on its basis. The *Journal-Courier*'s final story before the election noted that "today is the last day for pre-election speeches in a mayoralty campaign that has been singularly lacking in excitement." Nor am I claiming that these stories show that Celentano was an active and vigorous mayor and a tireless worker for urban redevelopment. What I do think these stories show is

1. Effort was being put forth by city agencies on urban renewal during September and October, long before Lee was on the scene or making an issue out of the program.

2. The mayor was at least a nominal supporter of these efforts.

3. Lee did not show great interest in urban renewal.

4. Most important, problems with the state were delaying the redevelopment program.

Lee won the election by 3,852 votes, with 86.6 percent of the registered voters taking part in the election. Whether he won as part of the general Democratic upsurge in local Connecticut elections that fall, or because of his very fine campaign, or because of the incumbent's several mistakes, including a disastrous trial balloon on parking automobiles on the hallowed green in the center of the city, is something that need not detain us here, for no analysts of the New Haven scene have claimed that this election was fought over the issue of urban renewal.

### AFTERMATH OF THE CAMPAIGN

Rather than speculating on why he won the election, it is more useful to concentrate instead on the immediate postelection reactions of Rotival and the chamber to Lee's victory, to see if there is any evidence for Dahl's view that business leaders had to be pushed into action on urban renewal by Lee. To the contrary, they were quite eager to get the program moving. If anything, their major concern was that the continuity of the planning not be interrupted by the arrival of a new mayor. This can be seen first of all in the correspondence of Rotival. On November 10, seven days after the election, he wrote a letter to his fellow consultant, Lloyd Reid, in response to Reid's worry that their work might be interrupted as a result of the outcome of the election:

I happen to know Dick Lee, the new mayor, very well, both [from] contacts at Yale, at the Chamber of Commerce and Planning Commission where he served in the early days of our planning. I am sure he is both intelligent and understanding and I look forward to working with him. Regarding our current work, I understand that Norris Andrews is in touch with both the incumbent and Dick Lee, and that the work can proceed without interruption.[96]

On the same day, Rotival wrote a letter to his friend Lee:

Now that the excitement **of** victory has subsided and the era of telegrams has passed, I **want** to tell you how pleased I am, both for you and the City, that **you** have won your battle. . . . I also remember that you have, since the early days, fought for "planning" both at the Chamber of Commerce and the Planning Commission and I am sure that your experience in that respect will have great impact on the future of New Haven. Our planning started, as you remember, in 1941 with Mayor Murphy and it has, except for the war and post-war period, followed since a very straight line. Results begin to show if you go back in mind to the early Master Plan of 1941—we now have arrived at a time of decision, one might even say of decisions as many difficult problems have to be solved in an early future. I would be glad, therefore, to have you call on us, I mean the different planners, Norris Andrews, Sam Spielvogel, Lloyd Reid and even McDougal who has done a lot discreetly, but effectively, for the City, to explain to you how we see the many problems confronting us.[97]

The problems confronting New Haven to which Rotival refers are summarized in a letter he had written to Reid on October 30, four days before the election. The letter reports on a Rotival meeting in Hartford with the State Highway Department and outlines the problems that still remained to be ironed out with the Oak Street connector. It is a highly detailed letter of four pages, mostly concerned with technical matters of highway planning, so I will report only the sociologically and politically relevant highlights.

First, state engineers did not believe that the Oak Street connector would rescue the downtown area: "They believe that New Haven is already moving to the North-East and doubt if we will be successful in the rehabilitation of the South-West, especially between the Railroad Station and the Hospital." [98] Rotival countered this point by saying that the planning commission, the Board of Aldermen, and the Redevelopment Agency are "against the moving of the City in what is nothing but a dead end for New Haven, Whitney Avenue being limited in its development to the North-West by first Peabody Museum, then the playgrounds, then the Hill with its expensive residential areas." He then added a very important second argument, which again shows how critical Yale was to the plans even before Lee became mayor: "I did add, too, that Yale University was interested, at this time, in redeveloping the sector between the Hospital and the University, precisely where our Oak Street scheme is being prepared."

There is evidence available in Yale files for this intriguing comment by Rotival, which is extremely important because it shows Yale involvement in New Haven urban renewal *before* Lee became mayor and many months earlier than other authors have claimed.[99] First, the claim is consistent with the appointment on September 29, 1953, of a special committee to survey the needs of the Yale physical plant. This committee was headed by Provost Stephen Buck. It included Secretary Reuben Holden; Business Manager C. Hamilton Stanford (who was also a Chamber of Commerce director); Bursar F. Spencer Miller; economist John P. Miller; oceanographer Daniel Merriman; Dana Young, chairman of the Department of Civil Engineering; and Benjamin Nangle, professor of English.

Most of the committee's concerns were internal to the campus, but the task of dealing with off-campus housing for graduate and married students was turned over to Secretary Holden at the October 19 meeting after the committee heard an Alumni Council report on the problem. That the focus of the concern with off-campus housing was the Oak Street area is evidenced in the final report of the committee on March 8, 1954. According to this report, "the committee proposes to report on housing for married students and faculty at a later date, when certain plans involving slum clearance and rebuilding may have advanced beyond the present stage." [100]

Rotival's reference to Yale's interest is also consistent with the recommendation contained in the report of the Alumni Council's Committee on Graduate and Professional Schools in the spring of 1953, which was presented to the space committee on October 19. This report says:

A subcommittee on housing has been exploring the possibility of having the University act as the developer of the area which will be released by the City of New Haven when it extends College Street from George Street to Congress Avenue. After two meetings with the Urban Redevelopment Unit of New

Haven the proposition looks promising. The area in question is
ideally located being a twelve acre plot bounded on the north
by George Street, south by Oak Street . . .[101]

The chairman of this special committee, which I believe was
appointed to follow up on the housing concerns expressed in the
*Yale and Her Needs* report of 1950, was New Haven lawyer Morris
Tyler, a director of Union and New Haven Trust and a senior
partner in Gumbart, Corbin, Tyler, and Cooper, one of the two
largest law firms in the city. A member of the Lawn and Graduates
clubs, and a guest at the cotillion ball in 1958-59, he also was the
chairman of the Regional Planning Commission of South Central
Connecticut, an organization formed in 1948 at the urging of the
Chamber of Commerce to coordinate planning of the smaller cities
around New Haven.[102] In addition, Tyler told me he was an intimate
personal friend of Yale professor Griswold, having known him from
Yale student days.[103]

The second major point in Rotival's October 30 letter to Reid
concerns the political situation in New Haven, and it is here that we
find evidence for the Dahl-Wolfinger view that Celentano had not
pressed hard enough with the state: "They all repeatedly mentioned
the fact that, so far, they had never seen evidence of any real
interest from either the Mayor or the Board of Aldermen in any
scheme for New Haven, except in the latter days under pressure of
the election, and they are therefore not convinced that the Board of
Aldermen will be ready, after the election, to back up the plan." [104]
It was on this score that Lee was to play an important role.

That role did not include, as Dahl and Wolfinger believe, selling
the program to reluctant businessmen. We have seen evidence for
this point throughout the detailed narrative of New Haven planning
history, but we see it even more dramatically in the minutes of the
chamber's Steering Committee for Redevelopment in the weeks and
months after the election. We also see in these minutes the basic
reasons for delays in the program.

The first relevant meeting was held on November 9 at the
Quinnipiac Club, a downtown club which serves as an important
focal point for formal and informal discussions among business
leaders. Present for the chamber were Herman R. Giese, vice-
president of Sargent and Company, and president of the Chamber of
Commerce; Willis Thompson, an engineer-architect with the firm of
Wescott and Mapes and chairman of the chamber's Industrial
Development Committee; Charles H. Costello, president of C.
Cowles and Company and chairman of the chamber's Highway
Committee; and W. Adam Johnson, chamber executive director. A

special guest was planning director Andrews. The minutes speak for themselves as far as the chamber's eagerness, and also reveal the problems that the program faced:

> Mr. Giese, Mr. Thompson, Mr. Costello, and Mr. Johnson met with Mr. Andrews to see if they could determine what pressure could be brought on the State Highway Commissioner to make decisions regarding U.S. Route 1 and the Oak Street extension. Mr. Andrews said there were many roadblocks. One of them is a Supreme Court decision regarding the constitutionality of the Urban Redevelopment Act. To obtain a decision, a friendly suit has been brought by the advocates of urban redevelopment against the City of Hartford.

> Mr. Andrews indicated that the Urban Redevelopment Agency had full knowledge of the exact location of the Oak Street Extension. However, it was his impression that the Federal Government would not give full approval to proceeding with Number Three Project [ie., Oak Street] until it is determined whether the City or the State will pay for developing the Oak Street Extension.

> Considering the great amount of confusion about the entire program, President Giese felt we should get the chairmen of the affected committees together on the following day for a discussion of what procedure to follow.

The meeting the next day was relatively straightforward, with most of the same people in attendance except for Andrews. The main concern was to make sure that there were no "outstanding complications between the program proposed by the consultants and the Chamber Ten Point Program." The most interesting decision of the day, from our vantage point, was setting up a meeting with mayor-elect Lee for November 19, a meeting at which "the entire program would be explained to him and he would be urged to get action started on the program." These words are highly significant. Seven days after the election, too soon for the mayor-elect to sell anybody anything, we see the supposedly-reluctant business leaders making plans to meet with him in order to urge him to get action started on a program which they saw as essentially synonymous with their own ten-point program. Even if this evidence does not prove that chamber people made the program happen, it does show conclusively that they were anything but hesitant.

The November 19 meeting with Lee, held over lunch at the New Haven Lawn Club, included the aforementioned Giese, Costello,

Thompson, and Johnson, as well as retailer Harry Barnett, chairman of the chamber's Parking Committee and a member of the Redevelopment Agency since 1952, when he replaced one of the original members. The minutes report that "the entire program was explained to Mr. Lee" and that "Mr. Lee said he was in entire agreement with a program for action." Lee then went on to give his own ideas on the topic, and especially his idea for a large committee of citizens to oversee the program.

During the rest of the meeting several names were suggested to Lee to head his citizens committee, at least one of which he later approached. He was also "presented with a copy of the Chamber's redevelopment map on which was inscribed—'Presented to Richard C. Lee Mayor-elect, November 19, 1953.' " The final words in the minutes, which were certainly not written to impress future researchers, also reveal the chamber's eagerness: "In bringing the meeting to a close, Mr. Giese promised Mr. Lee the full cooperation of all those present and assured him the Chamber is willing to do anything possible to get action started and to get a steamshovel starting work on the redevelopment program."

The next meeting of the chamber steering committee, on November 24, was a particularly happy one for the chamber, for it was held in conjunction with the City Plan Commission and the Redevelopment Agency. The three groups heard a report from the highway commissioner announcing that he had accepted the city's suggestions about the location of Route 1 and that he was willing to build the Oak Street connector at least as far as the railroad cut. This was not as far as the city and the chamber wanted him to extend the connector, but he added a further statement that has significance because it shows that Lee's subsequent selling job on the further extension had a solid basis in previous work: "I am further willing to consider extending it as far west as is deemed necessary if this department, as a state agency, is to provide reasonable traffic service to the central area of the city." In other words, it was just a matter of time—and money. (As Andrews was to remark at a Redevelopment Agency meeting in 1954, the dispute could have been settled in a minute if the city had agreed to pay part of the costs.) [105] The minutes of the November 24, 1953, meeting conclude: "Everyone was enthusiastic about the very favorable action taken by the Commissioner in conforming with the wishes of the City and the Chamber."

On December 4, the highway commissioner spoke at the monthly meeting of the chamber itself, making "further announcements regarding decisions which the Chamber had been [a]waiting for many years." In particular, he said that sixty acres of land near the new Route 1 would be made available for private use. Six days later, on December 10, chamber officials met with Mayor Celentano and the City Plan Commission, and "urged that the city take an option on the land which Mr. Hill had reported as being available for private use." In turn, the New Haven Market said that it would be willing to take an option on the land "providing the Urban Redevelopment Agency will guarantee that the land on which the market is now located will be condemned for redevelopment."

With these decisions about the placement of highways and the acquisition of land for the market, the main concerns of the chamber's ten-point plan were well under way. There remained the problem of arresting growth toward the east side of the city, which could only be dealt with through redevelopment of the Oak Street area on the west side and eventually part of the downtown itself. From the point of view of the chamber, as expressed by its incoming president at the annual meeting on February 10, 1954, there were only two decisions standing in the way of this final step. One concerned an opinion on the constitutionality of the Urban Renewal Act by the Connecticut Supreme Court of Errors, a decision that was expected shortly and was in fact handed down in the following month. The second problem concerned continuing negotiations between "our city and Commissioner Hill as to the extent of the state's responsibility in carrying the Oak Street connector as far as Howe Street," a street that was slightly beyond the downtown area and the hospital.[106] In other words, the city and the chamber wanted the state to pay for the Oak Street connector for an even longer distance than the state had agreed to reluctantly in November. It was this demand, for which there was no real traffic justification from the state point of view, that was to be in good part responsible for planning delays throughout 1954. The problem took so long, and so much of Lee's patience and energy, because the city wanted something for nothing.

The new chamber president did not conclude his presidential address without a statement showing a clear recognition of the need for political leadership to carry out the businessmen's plans. That is, there is room for Dahl's executive-centered coalition in the scheme of things in America, and businessmen are well aware of how important politicians are if business-oriented plans are to be enacted:

> We would also like to say to the Mayor that we believe he has the greatest opportunity for action, on plans which have been formulated and developed over several years, that has been offered to any Mayor in a like period. The plans have been

carefully drawn. New Haven is due for a great renaissance and all that is needed is action and leadership.[107]

And yet the new mayor experienced difficulties in getting his Citizens Action Commission appointed. What happened? It is to the claims about the Citizens Action Commission made by Dahl that I now turn.

## DELAY IN APPOINTING THE CITIZENS ACTION COMMISSION

One of Lee's major campaign promises was that he would appoint a special commission within sixty days of taking office, a commission that would be charged with taking a careful look at the needs of the city. He had major problems in finding a chairman for this commission, and it is this difficulty which is put forth by Dahl—and just about every other commentator on New Haven—as evidence for the claim that local businessmen were reluctant about urban renewal. But a careful consideration of the difficulties shows that the hesitance of the business community, as represented by the chamber, was not the real problem at all. If anything, the businessmen were *too* eager. This conclusion, which stands the conventional wisdom on its head, can be anticipated in the comments made to Dahl by one of Lee's redevelopment aides:

*Informant:* [The informant is explaining that after the election Lee] quickly decided that to get a meaningful Citizens Action Commission, he shouldn't try to meet the sixty-day deadline and, therefore, didn't seriously try to; but instead initiated conversations with the Chamber of Commerce people who were *very anxious* [my emphasis] to start their own CAC under their sponsorship independently at least of the mayor.

*Dahl:* Oh, is that so.

*Informant:* Yes. And there were many meetings. I can remember at least two in the Quinnipiac Club with Bill Johnson [chamber executive director] and Willis Thompson of Wescott and Mapes, one or two others with Bill Falsey of the Board of Finance and Scranton & Co.

From my several interviews on this question, along with a rereading of Dahl's interviews, I think there were four interrelated reasons for Lee's difficulties in obtaining a chairman for CAC. None of them has anything to do with businessmen's reluctance about urban renewal:

1. He asked the wrong people to begin with, people who declined on personal grounds.

2. After suffering these rebuffs, he decided to wait before asking anyone else.

3. He may have had some conflict with the Chamber of Commerce people about what the scope of CAC's charge should be. More specifically, the chamber was perhaps reluctant to include a consideration of the schools of New Haven, preferring to focus on its own project, the urban renewal program.

4. He was hesitant to give too much control to the chamber because of its conservative inclinations.

Each of these points deserves further elaboration.

*1. Wrong choice of people.* In one of Dahl's interviews with a redevelopment aide, he asked about the problem of CAC chairmanship. The interviewee replied that Lee originally asked three people—a banker who excused himself on the grounds of a recent heart attack, an important industrialist very friendly to the project who said that he was far too old for the job, and another prominent but aging industrialist who declined because he thought the job "too political." All of these are perfectly human reasons for declining what might turn out to be a demanding and time-consuming position, and it should not be surprising that members of the ruling class are as human as the rest of us. Those who see resistance to taking on yet another task as evidence against a ruling-class view, fail to take into consideration that even in the lives of ruling-class people there are some of the trials and tribulations that come to everyone.

Refusal by the third person, who allegedly said the program was too political, was used by Lee to show dramatically to Dahl how much resistance he was receiving. According to Lee, the man said the project was too ambitious, that Lee was too young, that he had not voted for Lee, and that "he was too old to get tagged with a project that was so ethereal as to be doomed before it got off the ground." [108] Unfortunately, this man is now dead, so I could not obtain his version of the conversation, and there is no indication that Dahl interviewed this elderly man about the matter. However, I did learn from then–chamber executive director W. Adam Johnson that this man—born in 1880—was so inactive in the business community by that time that Johnson himself barely knew him. Perhaps, then, his major emphasis was on his last point in refusing Lee—his own advanced age. [109]

In any event, these three rejections are not evidence for the reluctance of the business community in general, for Lee was able to turn to the business community when he decided to appoint a committee to help him find a CAC chairman. The three members of that committee were Harry White, manager of the New Haven Dairy and president of the Chamber of Commerce; William J. Falsey, the oft-mentioned municipal bond specialist at Scranton and Company, who also happened to be a chamber director; and Reuben Holden, the aforementioned secretary of Yale University.

After a series of meetings among different principals, the committee found Lee a chairman. He was Carl Freese, president of the Connecticut Savings Bank, on whose board committee-member Holden sat. Freese was also a director of First New Haven National Bank, Security Insurance Company of New Haven, New Haven Gas Company, and Southern New England Telephone Company. In short, Freese touched just about every base there was to touch in New Haven, including the Lawn, Graduates, and Quinnipiac clubs. And he was a former Chamber of Commerce president who was very familiar with the chamber's ten-point program.

*2. Decision to wait.* As a luncheon conversation with the amiable and very impressive Richard C. Lee makes clear, he is a proud and sensitive man. He told me, as he has told others, that he was taken aback by these three rejections, and that he decided to accomplish some things before asking anyone else. Whether this strategy was really necessary or not, his own hesitance after three refusals may account for some of the delay.

*3. Conflicts with Chamber of Commerce people.* So far I have emphasized the great degree of consensus between Lee and members of the Chamber of Commerce. But there may have been some significant differences between them on one or two issues. I say *may* because they are not recalled by former executive director Johnson. However, there is evidence for these difficulties in two different Dahl interviews, one with a politician, one with a redevelopment aide. Both suggest that chamber leaders may have been reluctant to include the schools of New Haven and other matters not directly connected with the renewal program as part of CAC's concern. According to the politician, "a substantial block of them was opposed to including education on the grounds that education was not indigenous or not a part, properly, of the planning for the future." According to the redevelopment aide:

> We were concerned from the outset that it [CAC] be broader in representation and responsibilities in its charge than the Chamber thought it should be—or to be perfectly accurate, the Chamber did not think [he means about larger matters]. In the

beginning they had to be persuaded that such things as education, housing, health, welfare, recreation, human relations were properly a part of this operation at all. They believed in harbor development, industrial development, the metropolitan approach, and Dick [Lee], I think very forcefully argued with them from the beginning ... [The rest of the sentence loses much of its coherence in transcript form due to the interruption of a telephone call.]

Given what I have shown about chamber eagerness for urban renewal, and given what we know about the narrow conservatism of chambers in general, this explanation for the delay makes much greater sense to me than Dahl's. It is an explanation in terms of the tensions between liberals and conservatives. However, it may also be that these tensions were not solely the product of conservatives' recalcitrance. An even subtler point may be involved.

4. *Reservations concerning the Chamber of Commerce.* Evidence that the delay involved slight differences between liberals and conservatives is also found in one of Dahl's interviews with a Yale official who was an adviser to the mayor, only this time the interview suggests that delays may have been due to the liberals' desire to keep a certain distance from chamber conservatives. That is, the major cause of the delay was not the chamber's reluctance to embrace Lee, educational focus and all, but the reluctance of Lee and his Yale advisers to be too closely identified with the chamber. Surprisingly enough, this decision to keep the chamber at arm's length may have been encouraged by the suggestions of the very person—Pittsburgh lawyer Arthur Van Buskirk—whom the chamber invited to speak on urban renewal at its annual meeting in February 1954. According to one Dahl informant:

He [Van Buskirk] came to Dick and I brought him in and he said, "Look, there's one very important thing to learn from this process." This was a surprising thing to come from him: "Never lose control of this, never let the Chamber of Commerce take control of it. This is a political act. In Pittsburgh we found that we were playing the Governor against the national administration and constantly at the mayor, and constantly utilizing our political weapons."

After relating this sophisticated advice that Van Buskirk gave to Lee—and remember the earlier quote from Van Buskirk about how it was better for the mayor to be out in front instead of U.S. Steel or the Mellon interests when it came to condemning people's property—the informant continues by telling Dahl how he and others close to Lee had viewed the local Chamber of Commerce:

Now the Chamber of Commerce was very eager to get in and take over, and a very deliberate decision was made that the Chamber of Commerce would be given a role that would not be an instrument through which [the] business community would be mobilized. It did not have the strength, it had its own ideas, it had certain other tendencies in all communities which would have been dangerous, especially its political relations.

Here again, in Van Buskirk and this Yale official, we see the ideological and political sophistication of the leaders in corporate America. These men did not want the program overly identified with the right-wing image of the chamber, with its penchant for alienating labor and liberals. This sophistication also comes through later in the interview when the Yale official is assessing the roles of the various members of CAC. Speaking of the two labor leaders on the commission, he first says they have been "relatively inactive," but then goes on to say:

Of course they represent the labor view, and they can help to allay any suspicions. They could do something. Their presence is one of the elements which makes this an infinitely more viable instrument for carrying out this program than the Chamber of Commerce ever could have been.[110]

The delay in appointing CAC, then, does not reveal the slightest hesitation or reluctance on the part of New Haven business leaders. If anything, as both this Yale adviser and an earlier-cited Lee appointee told Dahl, business leaders were too eager, a fact which causes considerable difficulties for the conventional account of the origins of urban renewal, a conventional account that is reported in every one of the more than half-dozen books I read on the topic.

## PASSIVE ROLE OF CAC
Dahl also makes much of the fact that CAC took very little initiative in the urban renewal program (pp. 130-33). There are two answers to his claim that it was Lee and his aides, and not CAC, who initiated the major decisions: *First,* all the key decisions, from the point of view of the business leaders, had been made by the Chamber of Commerce and its planning allies before CAC was appointed. Thus there was little for CAC to "initiate" in terms of major decisions.

Since I have made the case for the role of the chamber with new evidence throughout this narrative, let me only add evidence here from Dahl's own interviews. Here is what was said about the importance of the Chamber of Commerce by the utilities executive Dahl quoted (p. 132) as saying that he could not "recall" any cases where CAC modified any proposals brought before it. This comment was in response to a question earlier in the interview about the initiative for the urban renewal program in general: "I think a lot of it came through the New Haven Chamber of Commerce, I would suspect, who had a ten-point program here, you know ..." The utilities executive is a former chamber director.

Here is what another businessman told Dahl when asked about the origins of the program:

*Dahl:* One way to sort of break the ice is to get your conception of what you would regard as the really important and critical decisions that have been made on urban redevelopment since its inception, or if you think they were really made before it officially started.

*Informant:* Well, I think they were made before it started, but I don't think the public realized that they were being made. [He goes on to tell about the role of the Chamber of Commerce.]

*Second,* CAC was meant from the start to be an ideological organization with no initiatory function, and was so understood by the businessmen. Evidence for this point is provided most directly at the meeting chamber leaders held with Lee at the Lawn Club on November 19, 1953, shortly after his election. After telling chamber officials he agreed with their program, the chamber minutes go on to report Lee believed that "the best way to bring it about was through a large committee of citizens. The chief purpose of the committee would be to act as a *public relations media to sell the program"* [my italics]. Since the chamber leaders raised no protest about setting up a public relations committee, and since they supplied Lee with his CAC chairman and numerous CAC members, it must be concluded that they understood and concurred in this strategy.

Another direct piece of evidence for the relatively passive role planned for CAC can be found in the Rotival papers in a letter written by Nicholas de Katzenbach, then a Yale law professor who had been put on the Rotival staff in 1954 to serve as one of the liaisons between Yale and the Redevelopment Agency. The letter, dated October 4, 1954, is to Carl Freese, the banker who chaired CAC: "Owing to its technical nature, *initiative* [my italics] at the planning stage should remain firmly with the Consultant (in collaboration with technical agencies of the City), and independent action should be avoided." [111] Given this strategy, it seems neither unlikely nor surprising that Dahl would find that CAC took no major initiatives when it was never planned that it would take any.[112]

## COMPLETION OF THE OAK STREET PLANNING, 1954-1956

While problems attendant upon the formation and functions of CAC are of importance to social scientists concerned with the structure of power in New Haven and the United States, they were not the major reason for further delays in the Oak Street project. The real problems concerned the argument over the extension and financing of the Oak Street connector, bureaucratic delays in dealing with the federal government, and last-minute changes in the plan.

None of these problems take away from the notion that the Chamber of Commerce and Yale University were the institutions most active in the program. If anything, people from the chamber and Yale became even more prominent during 1954-56. Chamber leaders continued to hold numerous meetings with planners Spielvogel, Rotival, and Andrews, and directors of the Redevelopment Agency; former chamber president Carl Freese was chairman of CAC and very active in the details of the program; and ten of the eighteen original members of the CAC leadership were part of the Chamber of Commerce group.

As for Yale, its participation increased. Not only did lawyer Morris Tyler and university secretary Reuben Holden continue as important liaisons, but President Griswold and law school dean Eugene Rostow became members of CAC. Griswold also offered Yale's intellectual and planning resources to the city.[113] Yale's involvement in the program was enhanced by the election of Yale employee Lee as mayor, for he was on an intimate basis with many of his former employers, including Griswold, with whom he often discussed problems of the program over the telephone. Then too, Lee's 1953 platform—according to several reliable sources, including two Dahl interviewees—had been shaped in good part by three Yale friends: Eugene Rostow, who also headed "Independents for Lee" during the campaign; Chester Kerr, director of Yale University Press; and Edward Logue, a Yale Law School graduate married to the daughter of William DeVane, dean of Yale College since 1938. Following the election, Logue gradually became Lee's right-hand man on most administrative matters, and especially on urban renewal, where his appointment in February 1955 as development administrator put him in charge of all city departments related to that program.

Problems between the State Highway Department and the City Plan Commission over financing and planning the Oak Street connector led to tensions between the Redevelopment Agency and the Lee-Logue team. Spielvogel's repeated requests for clarification on the width, grading, and exit sites for the Oak Street connector, which were necessary if he was to enter into a firm contract with the Housing and Home Finance Agency of the federal government, led the mayor and Logue to conclude that "the incumbent director lacked the drive and zeal they wanted" (Who Governs?, p. 129). Wolfinger's account expands on this point, reducing interagency problems to a personalistic basis by claiming that "Spielvogel and Norris Andrews did not get along," and that Spielvogel "responded to pressure for action by dwelling on obstacles and depicting arcane mysteries which had to be mastered before success could be assured." [114] Finally, in February 1955, Spielvogel resigned and Lee hired as a consultant Carl Feiss, a planner who had worked for the Housing and Home Finance Agency until early 1954.

Feiss's task was to see what needed to be done to solve problems which were delaying submission of a project application. Feiss surveyed the situation and recommended that the agency start all over in terms of its applications. Shortly thereafter, Ralph Taylor, a slightly more experienced director from another city, was hired at the suggestion of Feiss, and the program began to function more smoothly. This series of events, rooted in good part in interagency conflicts, provides the basis for the claim of a highly placed city official of the Lee era that, as he put it in an interview with Dahl: "Redevelopment in New Haven began in February of '55. We had to start from scratch and assemble a team and start to file all the papers and get the whole program launched."

This claim about starting from scratch, reflected in the accounts of Dahl and Wolfinger, is extremely misleading if looked at from the perspective of the program's basic objectives. In fact, the Rotival-Chamber of Commerce plans were basically unchanged. What changed were the applications and justifications sent to Washington. Also changed were the exact structures to be placed in the project. These changes led to more commercial development, rewards for friendly small businessmen and politicians, and an addition to the Grace-New Haven Hospital.

The problem of what structures were to be built once the Oak Street area was cleared had always been uncertain, aside from the commitment to some type of apartment housing and institutional use in part of the area. It was obvious that the new Oak Street connector would cut a wide path in the area, but there was uncertainty about other aspects of the plan. An opportunity for a major building in the Oak Street project arose when the telephone company, whose executives had been extremely active in aiding Lee and the program, decided to erect new headquarters in the general area. After a minimum of negotiations, this building became a cornerpiece of the renewal plan, along with the apartment buildings planned for the use of Yale and hospital families.

Changes in plans necessitated by inclusion of the telephone building and an extension of the hospital are reflected in a letter dated March 21, 1955, from Albert Cole, administrator of the Housing and Home Finance Agency, to Senator Prescott Bush, in response to a Bush inquiry about the status of the New Haven application. The letter also refers to another reason for last-minute changes, the need to add two extra blocks in the northern area of the project in order to compensate for the large amount of land the highway department insisted upon for the connector:

> Two questions have been the subjects of recent discussions with officials of New Haven. One, the submission and approval of a loan and grant application containing these two additional blocks. Under the agreed conditions, the New Haven delegation was informed that it was legally possible to proceed in this manner. Secondly, the question of land disposal policy was discussed. There seemed to be no obstacle for specific purpose use in the proposed redevelopment as concerned Yale University Faculty Housing, New England Telephone Company Building and New Haven Hospital extension.[115]

With approval of the final change in plans, the Oak Street project was set. However, there were further delays because of problems with developers. None of these problems is theoretically significant except one, Yale's failure to obtain the land on which apartments were to be built, despite months of planning and negotiations. I will not attempt to deal with this question in depth, for I could not pursue it in the detailed way such a problem needs to be researched in order to reach a definitive resolution. This is because Yale files were only available to me through March 1955, due to a university rule that a twenty-year period must elapse before papers are available to researchers. All I want to do here is call into question the idea that Lee forced Yale into open bidding for the land, instead of selling it outright to the university, because he feared the reaction of voters to a "giveaway" to Yale.[116]

Contrary to this interpretation, I think Lee was forced to accept open bidding because other potential developers forced his hand.

Using the Dahl files, I would piece the story together as follows. A New York developer approached an important New Haven businessman and Democratic party leader about the possibility of buying land in the Oak Street area for apartment housing. The businessman-Democrat went to Lee and Logue with the proposal, but was turned down. This led to conflict within the party, and charges by the Democratic businessman and his friends that Lee and Logue were "giving" the land to Yale. The developers then put pressure on the Housing and Home Finance Agency office in New York to put the land up for bid. The Housing and Home Finance Agency, in turn, put pressure on Mayor Lee, a fact which Lee confirmed in my interview with him. New Haven officials then tried to work out a compromise whereby those who made lower bids in an open auction could, if they wished, match the highest bid after the bidding was completed. The outside developers protested, claiming this would allow Lee and his associates to pick among the matched bidders, and once again claims of "sellout" to Yale were raised. Wolfinger acknowledges this point when he writes:

> Indeed, this seemed to be the point of the initial ground rules for the auction, which provided that after the high bid had been ascertained any other bidder could match this price, in which event the city could choose among them. One out-of-town group felt this would let the city choose Yale no matter how the bidding came out, and, it is likely, *made use of its political connections to get the federal government to force the city to drop this provision* [emphasis mine].[117]

The result of all this maneuvering was that Yale lost out in the public auction because it did not want to bid beyond $1,150,000, a figure it did not know was only $100,000 below the top price which the eventual winner was willing to offer. Yale officials were at first irritated because they had wasted considerable time in negotiations with city officials, but were not overly concerned because they knew the apartments were to be built anyway. One high Yale official explained it to Dahl as follows in October 1957, six months after the auction. His words are of considerable theoretical significance, for they show how major power centers get what they want even when they "lose" a specific "decision":

> I don't feel the least bit sorry that we're out of it. It was so complex, the arrangement was so complex, we were just involved in so much red tape of all kinds. . . . I don't care what the University Towers is or who it is if it gets some decent

apartment houses over there. . . . In this I think we've won two-thirds of the battle anyway and we don't have any of the headache and no responsibility and nobody can accuse us of taking more prime land off the tax roll.

Of more lasting importance was the extremely bad blood that developed within the Democratic party among very important leaders, one or two of whom resigned from key positions shortly thereafter, and have not worked with Lee since that time. It was this conflict, not a rejection by voters, that Lee was trying to avoid.

My interpretation of these events suggests the problem was a conflict rooted in competition over business profits and political favors, which is not a major issue between pluralist and ruling-class perspectives because we all agree that there is sometimes competition over business deals. There was also a conflict within the Democratic party machine that is at issue, over whose friends would be favored with the newly cleared land. While this is an interesting problem common to machine politics, it is not the same thing as saying Lee was restrained from selling the land to Yale by his fears of an electorate that had given him a 65-35 percent landslide victory in 1955 despite a Republican campaign based in good part on the charge that Lee was a "little boy blue" who was "selling out" to his old friends at Yale.[118] Business pressure on the Housing and Home Finance Agency, and conflict within the local Democratic party machine, seem to be more important in this case than fears of the electorate.

## ORIGINS OF THE CHURCH STREET PROJECT, 1955-1957

While the origins of the Oak Street project are of primary importance in understanding urban renewal in New Haven, it is also necessary to briefly consider the origin of the second New Haven renewal project, the Church Street project, which made dramatic changes in the downtown business district. Such a consideration reveals once again that it was business leaders, and in particular those at the First New Haven National Bank, who made the project possible, and not Lee and his aides, as Dahl has claimed. Consideration of the Church Street project also shows how Yale's resources were an essential ingredient in the urban renewal program.

As the Oak Street plans were finalizing, the Lee-Logue team began to think about the next step in the revitalization of the downtown, namely, a renewal of several blocks of the downtown area itself. This large and drawn-out project was to suffer interminable delays due to personality clashes, conflicts among major owners, nervousness on the part of the Housing and Home Finance Agency, and

legal challenges by the small businessmen of ethnic origins who
were being displaced.[119]

The first thoughts on downtown urban renewal involved a
completely private project by a multimillionaire developer, Roger
Stevens, known to Logue and Lee because he was a major
Democratic party fundraiser and contributor. When this plan fell
through because some local businessmen held out for high prices for
their land and structures, local officials began to think in terms of
smaller, federally subsidized projects which would rebuild parts of
the downtown in small parcels at a time. However, when Lee aides
went to the directors at the First New Haven National Bank with
their tentative federal project, they were told to think bigger and to
do it "right." One informant explained it to a Dahl assistant as
follows, as summarized in Dahl's files:

> When Lee and Logue first went to talk to the people at the First
> National Bank with their South Central Project [ie., Church
> Street], they had a rather modest and undeveloped, un-
> thoughtout plan for the South Central Project. The First
> National Bank said they would support the plan if it were
> made into a really big thing. I asked why. [Informant] said it
> was partly because they didn't want to go to the trouble of
> relocating unless the project was really worth it and partly
> because *they wanted to see the town grow* [my emphasis].

Another, even more important, informant put it this way to Dahl
directly:

> Then there was another important thing that happened there
> when we failed [in the private redevelopment scheme]. We had
> another sketch made. By this time the bank was all hot about
> this and all for it and we got with six of them in the president's
> office and they told [us] to go back and tell Dick Lee that they
> were interested only if we did it right, and [if] we didn't widen
> Orange Street. You go back and tell Dick Lee that if he isn't
> doing things right, the bank isn't interested. So [we] said, well,
> you have to understand that we have to go federal completely
> in order to do that—that didn't seem to bother them—and also
> that Dick can't carry this whole thing on his own and he's got
> to have strong business support.

In the light of these accounts, which show that Lee and his aides
had a clear mandate from the ruling class to do it big, it is surprising

that Dahl would give so much credit in his account to the "initiative" of the Development Administrator in drawing up the plans:

> With Church Street, it was the Development Administrator himself who, after months of consideration, discussion, and preliminary planning, sat down late one night and drew on a city map the boundaries he then proposed and the Mayor accepted—boundaries that in their economic and social implications seemed so bold and daring that for months the exact nature of the proposal was kept in secrecy as the Mayor, the Development Administrator, and the Redevelopment Director tested it for feasibility and acceptability (p. 128).

Given the facts about the role of the First New Haven National Bank in the project, this is probably the single most . inaccurate interpretation in *Who Governs?* Nor are comments about secrecy entirely accurate. It may have been secret from the general public and the small businesspeople it was going to uproot, but it was not secret from the most important members of the local ruling class, as Dahl's own interviews show:

*Dahl:* When was your meeting with the bank?

*Informant:* Spring of '56.

*Dahl:* I'm still puzzled as to where your CAC people were in all this.

*Informant:* Well, Freese was thoroughly involved. [Freese was president of Connecticut Savings Bank and a director of First New Haven National Bank, among other business organizations.]

*Dahl assistant:* When did the CAC know? Did Freese tell anyone on the CAC who wasn't in the bank? Or directly involved? I suppose Gumbart told Tyler. [Gumbart was a partner in Gumbart, Corbin, Tyler, and Cooper and a director of the First New Haven National Bank. Tyler was Gumbart's law partner and a director of Union and New Haven Trust Company.]

*Informant:* Oh yes, Tyler knew about it. Gene Rostow [Yale law school dean] knew about it. Frank O'Brion [Tradesmen's National Bank], although he wasn't on the CAC ... Bill Hook [chairman of United Illuminating and a major figure in the New Haven community until his death in 1958] knew about it and was instrumental in getting Welch to go along with this arrangement.

*Dahl:* What did he do?

*Informant:* He persuaded Welch that if he didn't go along with this arrangement, he was not entitled and could not get any particular sympathy in the business community for his sad plight. And I think Falsey [municipal bonds specialist, member of city finance board] knew about it. And Golden [local Democratic leader and insurance broker] knew about it.

*Dahl assistant:* Isn't Welch tied up with one of the banks?

*Informant:* Yes, Welch is senior vice president of New Haven which is now merged with the First National.

The dialogue goes on to name several other people, including some nonbusiness members of CAC, but I think the point has been made. The Church Street project was worked out privately in conjunction with several major figures in New Haven, and in particular those with connections to the First New Haven National Bank and Yale University.

Beyond the fact that the mayor and his aides were functioning as part of a group which was primarily big businessmen and their lawyers, the basic problem in Dahl's interpretation of the origins of the Church Street project is his failure to see the structure of the situation within which the "initiative" of the Development Administrator occurred, a structure which makes what the development administrator did "obvious" and "natural," given past planning by Rotival, Andrews, and the chamber, and the needs of major business leaders. This point is made clearly in another dialogue with a redevelopment official about the origins of the Church Street project:

*Dahl assistant:* You decided you had to have another one. Now when did you decide that other one was going to be Church Street?

*Informant:* Well, when you're familiar with the planning program, it's a very easy decision to make. In fact, it would have been a very wrong decision to have decided against it, except possibly for Wooster Square.

*Dahl:* What do you mean, "when you're familiar with the planning program?"

*Dahl assistant:* The planning program said that Church Street was going to be next, is that it?

*Informant:* Oh no, there wasn't—I shouldn't say the planning program because there wasn't an action planning program, but if you're familiar with the planning of the city of New Haven as it stood in January or February or March of '55, you know that you want to include the area bounded by the railroad station and George Street.

*Dahl assistant:* Because it's adjacent to the Oak Street area, is that it?

*Informant:* Yes. And because the market is there and you've got to build in [the area] to get rid of the market, and you've got to be able to redevelop the market or otherwise the market operators will not [words unintelligible]. And it's all meshed together.

I would only add that it is all meshed together by the needs and desires of the big business community of New Haven, and it is these needs and desires which created the context within which the Lee administration had to operate. Lee and his aides could do nothing without the backing of the most powerful business elements in the community. This point is made in an interview by Dahl with another key redevelopment official, in which he asked why certain people were consulted on the Church Street project:

*Informant:* Obviously, the United Illuminating Company is a very powerful organization. Mr. Hook has for many years been a dean of business administration in New England. He's one of the finest men around. His properties and his interests are adjacent to the Church Street project area. If Mr. William C. Bell [of United Illuminating] and Mr. Bill Hook go along with something, you've got powerful backing. They're one of the elements in this picture that we've got to have if we're going to succeed. . . . In putting together the potential for this, we go to the people, let's say, that we want on our side and perhaps that we're not absolutely sure of having on our side in a given project and work on them.

*Dahl assistant:* Weren't you sure of Mr. Hook? Or was there perhaps another reason?

*Informant:* Well, here again, what we needed particularly in this Church Street thing, and this is a case in point, we needed the backing of the financial, industrial, public utility, and banking powers. If they were with it, we knew that other people are all for it. . . . But, in other words, a group of earnest people is not going to get very far in urban renewal, in my opinion. I know of only one way to do it, which is to get the most powerful people in the community.

*Dahl:* I agree, and that's one reason why we're interested in it—that here, presumably, are the more powerful people in the community and we're trying to find out who they are.

*Informant:* Well, I can give you a list of those.

As already noted, there is a long and arduous story that goes with the Church Street project due to the maneuverings for greater advantage among three or four businessmen and the anguished protests of store owners and shopkeepers who did not even know they were going to be displaced until they read it in the newspapers. The success of these smaller businesspeople in delaying the project and forcing the city into more generous relocation treatment, evidence for the fact that ruling classes do not get everything at the snap of a finger, led to one of the more theoretically interesting aspects of the Church Street project, the involvement of Yale. As delays in the project continued, the developer wearied of having his money tied up in an unprofitable situation. Lee and Logue had to look elsewhere for help in financing, and the result was a $4.5 million loan from Yale in 1962. Wolfinger describes this as a "fortuitous event." [120] I would suggest, to the contrary, that this was only the latest in a series of events stretching back at least to Yale's willingness to buy land in the Oak Street area, which shows that Yale was one of the essential backbones of the project.[121]

Negotiations over the loan between Lee and Yale also led to the involvement of R. H. Macy and Company in the project, which became a major factor in ensuring its success:

> In the course of negotiating the loan, Lee had met with a member of the Yale Corporation who was also a director of R. H. Macy and Company. Through him the mayor renewed relations with the Macy management that spring and by the end of the summer Lee had negotiated an agreement for Macy's to build a $5 million department store in the project area.[122]

And, as Wolfinger notes, the loan from Yale and the contract with Macy's "started to project on its way at last." [123] He also reports that Mayor Lee's electoral fortunes recovered in 1963 after he won by only 4,000 votes in 1961 due to project delays.

In considering the nature and scope of the Church Street project from beginning to end, we find the same two critical factors as in the Oak Street project—major business leaders and Yale University.

Planners and administrators drew the designs that business people accepted or rejected, and politicians skillfully orchestrated the complex proceedings and dealings with the general public, but the goals and benefits were in the hands of the local ruling elite, representing the general interest of the New Haven branch of the national ruling class in maintaining Yale University as a leading educational institution and in ensuring high profitability and values for downtown land.

## SUMMARY

This chapter shows that *Who Governs?* is seriously deficient in its interpretation of urban renewal in New Haven. Theoretically, the book did not impress upon the reader that ruling-class power at the national and state levels created the crucial ideological context and governmental structures which encased local decision making, and that big businessmen and Yale officials were the major connections to those levels. Methodologically, it did not develop a complete picture of the power network in New Haven, did not present the variety of agency and personal documents necessary to fully understand the history and background of the decision, and relied too heavily and uncritically on interviews with people who had a great stake in interpreting the origins of urban renewal to their own advantage. Empirically, the book is factually wrong in many instances, such as the role of Yale and the Chamber of Commerce, because of its theoretical and methodological shortcomings.

At the same time as we have shown that ruling-class leaders were central to urban renewal in New Haven, we have seen that difficulties in coordinating various levels of government and bureaucracy, and conflicts with small businessmen, led to delays and adjustments in the program. We have also seen that the need for legitimacy and pliable politicians was essential to the success of the program. Such realities are sometimes taken as evidence for "pluralism" in social science literature, but they do not really contradict a ruling-class view, which does not deny that the ruling class must often struggle in order to implement its policies and realize its goals. But whether we look at the origins of the local urban renewal program (in the Chamber of Commerce and Yale) or its eventual outcome (land for the expansion of Yale, the hospital, and the downtown business community), we must conclude, contrary to *Who Governs?*, that there is a power structure in New Haven, with Yale, the First New Haven National Bank, and the Chamber of Commerce at its heart, as we suspected they would be on the basis of the social and economic networks developed in the previous chapter.

Now that we have seen through the empirical work in chapters 2 and 3 who really rules in New Haven, it is time to turn our attention in the final chapters to more general methodological and theoretical points that can be developed from this study of one small city.

## NOTES

1. *The President's Advisory Committee on Government Housing Policies and Programs,* December 1953, p. 2. The committee also said that "It is especially important to develop in at least a few cities in the United States pilot projects of effective local action at all stages of the slum-prevention process. The experience of cities in connection with such demonstration projects will be tremendously useful in guiding citizens and local officials in other cities."

2. "ACTION to Fight Slums and Neighborhood Blight," *American City* (December 1954): 23.

3. "Action on Slums," *The New York Times,* November 19, 1954, p. 39. The way in which the Advertising Council functions as an ideological arm of the ruling class has been described in detail and with case examples by Glenn Hirsch, "Only You Can Prevent Ideological Hegemony: The Advertising Council and Its Place in the American Power Structure," *The Insurgent Sociologist* (Spring 1975).

4. "The Red Cross of Housing," *Urban Land* (July-August 1954): 2.

5. Jeanne Lowe, *Cities in a Race with Time* (Random House, 1967), p. 41.

6. Jeanne Lowe, "Lee of New Haven and His Political Jackpot," *Harper's Magazine* (October 1957): 36. A copy of the manuscript for this article was sent by *Harper's* to a Lee aide for his comments. Lee obtained 20,000 copies of the article, distributing 10,000 in New Haven for his reelection campaign that fall, saving the other 10,000 for his projected campaign for higher office. (I obtained this information from Dahl's files.)

7. "ACTION Urban Renewal Clinic," *American City* (February 1957): 113.

8. Daniel Ellsberg, *Papers on the War* (Pocket Books, 1972), pp. 78-79.

9. Raymond Wolfinger, *The Politics of Progress* (Prentice-Hall, 1974), in his more detailed accounting of the urban renewal program, does give recognition to Bush's role, but apparently was unaware of Bush's earlier involvement in formulating Yale's growth plans.

10. Nathaniel Keith, *Politics and the Housing Crisis Since 1930* (Universe Books, 1973), pp. 53-54, 68.

11. Nathan Straus, *Seven Myths of Public Housing* (Knopf, 1944), pp. 59-60. For a full demonstration of Straus's argument see pp. 50-53, 60-61, 68-69, 70-75, 91-93.

12. Lowe, p. 28. For a parallel and more recent account based on historical archives, see Mark I. Gelfand, *A Nation of Cities* (Oxford University Press, 1975), p. 112 ff.

13. "New York Men Aid in Urban Planning," *The New York Times,* March 10, 1940, sec. 13-14, p. 1. One of the first projects of the revitalized institute was a study of downtown parking problems in sixty-two cities in conjunction with the Yale University Bureau for Street Traffic Research. For this story see "Experts to Study Decentralization," *The New York Times,* April 28, 1940, sec. 11, p. 7.

14. For an exceptionally detailed analysis of the role of the Council on Foreign Relations in planning postwar foreign policy, see Laurence H. Shoup, "Shaping the Postwar World: The Council on Foreign Relations and the United States War Aims during World War II," *The Insurgent Sociologist* (Spring 1975).

For evidence on the important role of the Committee for Economic Development in determining postwar economic policy, see Karl Schriftgiesser, *Business Comes of Age* (Harper & Row, 1960). For the role of the National Planning Association as well as further information on the Committee for Economic Development and other big-business policy groups, see David Eakins, "The Development of Corporate Liberal Policy Research in the United States, 1885-1965," Ph.D. diss., University of Wisconsin, 1966.

The major concern of this planning was the avoidance of another Great Depression after the war ended. The work of the Council on Foreign Relations focused on methods of creating international organizations which would allow greater overseas sales and investments by American corporations. The work of the Committee for Economic Development gave more attention to domestic spending programs. Part of the rationale for the Greer-Hansen slum clearance program involved the creation of domestic spending programs to ensure economic prosperity.

Economist Hansen was a central figure in the work of the Council on Foreign Relations at this time, as Shoup shows, but his urban renewal work with Greer was done under the auspices of the National Planning Association and the Federal Reserve Board. The Greer-Hansen pamphlet, *Urban Redevelopment and Housing*, was published as Planning Pamphlet no. 10 by the National Planning Association in December 1941, and also privately for institute members by the Urban Land Institute.

15. Lowe, p. 30.

16. Ibid. In the words of Greer and Hansen, pg. 7: "Under such conditions, there would appear to be no alternative to having the Federal Government shoulder whatever the burden may turn out to be, as the cost of a job of civic sanitation—of cleaning up the social and economic mess left by past generations, for which only society as a whole can be held mainly to blame."

17. Straus, p. 81. As a member of a wealthy financial family, and as a man who had made money in real estate in his own right, Straus knew whereof he spoke.

18. Guy Greer, "A New Start for the Cities," *Fortune* (September 1944): 153. Greer had joined the board of the Urban Land Institute in 1943, but was more sympathetic to public housing than most of its members.

19. For Alvin Hansen's appreciation of Bettman, see *Journal of the American Institute of Planners* 11 (Winter 1945): 38-39. For a longer assessment of his role in planning see John Lord O'Brian, "Alfred Bettman," *Journal of the American Institute of Planners* 11 (Autumn 1945), pt. 2: 1-6.

20. "To the Honorable Chairman and Members, Sub-Committee on Housing and Urban Redevelopment, Committee on Post-War Planning," *Journal of the American Institute of Planners* 11 (Spring 1945): 6.

21. Ashley A. Foard and Hilbert Fefferman, "Federal Urban Renewal Legislation," in James Q. Wilson (ed.), *Urban Renewal: The Record and the Controversy* (MIT Press, 1966), p. 104.

22. See Keith, ch. 2, for a good account of the strength of the prohousing group.

23. Lowe, p. 31.

24. Foard and Fefferman, p. 106.

25. Ibid.

26. Ibid., p. 106.

27. Lowe, p. 31.

28. Foard and Fefferman, p. 80.

29. Ibid., p. 83. For a detailed discussion of the political infighting, see Keith, chs. 3, 4. Keith shows how the nature of the fight shifted depending upon the relative strength of Democrats and Republicans in Congress with every two-year election. He also describes the tactics of the conservative coalition, particularly in the House, in delaying the bill.

30. Ibid., p. 85.

31. Ibid., p. 79n.

32. Bettman, "Honorable Chairman and Members," p. 10.

33. Foard and Fefferman, p. 93.

34. Ibid., p. 92.

35. Ibid., pp. 92-93.

36. G. William Domhoff, "Where a Pluralist Goes Wrong," in idem, *The Higher Circles* (Random House, 1970), ch. 9.

37. Ibid., ch. 6; James Weinstein, *The Corporate Ideal in the Liberal State* (Beacon, 1968); Roger Friedland, "Corporate Social Control in the Central City: The Case of Urban Renewal" (unpublished paper, University of Wisconsin, 1974).

38. Wolfinger, p. 148.

39. *Business Action*, May 7, 1948, p. 22.

40. Ibid., May 12, 1950, p. 19.

41. *Creating Better Cities* (U.S. Chamber of Commerce, 1951), pp. 159-60.

42. Ibid., p. 173.

43. Ibid., p. 178.

44. Ibid., p. 181.

45. Ibid., p. 188.

46. Ibid., p. 188.

47. Ibid.

48. Ibid., p. 189.

49. Ibid.

50. Ibid., p. 189.

51. The Urban Land Institute became very concerned that state enabling legislation for urban redevelopment include a provision for redevelopment agencies separate from the local housing authority when it saw federal legislation was likely to put the program under the National Housing Authority. For the clearest statement and rationale of this strategy, see "Discussion of Principles to be Incorporated in State Urban Redevelopment Enabling Acts," *Technical Bulletin*, no. 2 (June 1945), Urban Land Institute.

52. Ibid., pp. 190-91.

53. *City Planning and Urban Development*, U.S. Chamber of Commerce, Construction and Civic Development Department, 1952, p. 20.

54. *Planning Urban Renewal Projects*, U.S. Chamber of Commerce, Construction and Civic Development Department, 1960, pp. 1-2.

55. Keith, p. 156.

56. Lowe, p. 115.

57. Lowe, p. 133.

58. Ibid., p. 134.

59. Ibid., pp. 139-40, 150, 153.

60. Seymour Papers, Box 70, Yale University Library.

61. See Winslow's "Opportunities and Responsibilities of the Health Officer in Connection with the Federal Housing Acts," *Journal of the American Institute of Planners* 5 (1939): 25-29.

62. Rotival Papers, Yale Law School Library. What little order these papers have is due to the work of A. Tappan Wilder. I am indebted to him for telling me about these absolutely invaluable papers, which have received no use except from Wilder and myself.

63. The chamber balked at first about Rotival's suggestion to concentrate industrial development in the Quinnipiac Valley area.

64. Dahl perhaps did not realize that Lee had been a chamber employee at this critical juncture, for he makes no mention of it in his discussion of Lee's background. He only notes that Lee "served as an officer in the Junior Chamber of Commerce" (p. 118). One of Lee's jobs at the chamber was to help organize the Junior Chamber of Commerce. Since much merriment has been made over Floyd Hunter's characterization of Lee as a "businessman" in a review of *Who Governs?* in the *Administrative*

*Science Quarterly* (March 1962), it might be well to note that he was a little closer to the mark than Dahl. Lee was not a businessman, but he was certainly the businessmen's direct employee at one time.

65. Lohmann's papers contain an interesting exchange of letters which reveal how members of the local ruling class viewed Lee in 1947. On March 19, 1947, local business leader H. C. Knight wrote Lohmann praising Lee's work on the Charter Committee of New Haven: "He is still growing in the minds of our citizens as one whom they respect and trust. He knows the score in the operations of municipal government." Lohmann replied on March 20 that "he is a very valuable fellow to us and I am glad to have your comments so that I can pass them around among the university officers." Lohmann Papers, Box 342, Yale University Library.

66. Maurice Rotival, *Report to the New Haven Redevelopment Agency: Selection of Redevelopment Areas According to the Master Plan*, July 1951, pp. 26-28. This draft is in the Rotival Papers.

67. "The Postwar Council of the New Haven Chamber of Commerce," p. 2. This four-page document is in the pamphlet file of the Free Public Library, New Haven, Connecticut.

68. "Report to the Housing Authority of the City of New Haven," from the office of Douglas Orr, August 1944, p. 4.

69. Ibid., pp. 39-40.

70. That Orr was a member of the New Haven upper class is suggested by the fact that he was a member of the Lawn Club and the Graduates Club. He was the architect for the Lawn Club as well as for many expensive homes in the city. Among the business directorships he held at one time or another during the 1940s and 1950s were the First New Haven National Bank, the Security Insurance Company of New Haven, the New Haven Savings Bank, and the New Haven Gas Company.

71. "Guide to City Planning in New Haven, 1955," *Journal of the Union & New Haven Trust Company* 20, no. 5 (June 1955): 1. This "journal" is merely a large brochure.

72. Lowe, p. 34.

73. A new provision allowing projects to encompass deteriorating areas that were not yet slums also aided the program by allowing planners to develop bigger and more expansive plans.

74. Lowe, p. 86.

75. Walter H. Plosilz, "A Reconsideration of Community Power Structure and Urban Redevelopment: A Case Study of New Haven, Connecticut," M.A. thesis, Political Science Department, Pennsylvania State University, December 1968, p. 79.

76. Friedland, p. 14. The amount of public housing increased in the 1960s under the Democrats and with pressure from urban uprisings.

77. Scott Greer, *Urban Renewal and American Cities* (Bobbs-Merrill, 1965), p. 32.

78. For a summary of federal urban redevelopment and urban renewal activities from the point of view of housing, a summary which shows the many ways in which public housing was consistently thwarted, see *Housing a Nation* (Congressional Quarterly Service, 1966). Keith, p. 14, reveals much about this thwarting when he says: "The liberals of both parties have tended to cluster in the legislative committees and have been largely responsible for the major housing and community development legislation which has been enacted. On the other hand, the conservatives have tended to cluster in the Appropriations Committees of the two Houses where control over the purse-strings has largely determined what can actually be accomplished under the legislative mandates."

79. Celentano's chief aide, Stanley Venoit, served on the chamber's Industrial Development Committee at the time. He recalls that Celentano was basically sympathetic to urban redevelopment, but not notably active in the matter.

80. Minutes of the New Haven Chamber of Commerce, July 21, 1950. Copies of these minutes, which A. Tappan Wilder obtained from the chamber itself, were made available to me through his kindness. I will not footnote them in each case hereafter, but instead note their dates in the main text.

81. Dahl had an assistant staked out in the mayor's office in 1957 and 1958, but he did not have anyone at the Chamber of Commerce, the First New Haven National Bank, major law firms, or social clubs. This reflects a considerable theoretical bias which affects the results of his investigation.

82. "Chamber Urges Quick Action on Urban Redevelopment," Newsletter, August 30, 1950, p. 2.

83. Wells, on the other hand, left Yale for a year in Puerto Rico, and showed no further interest in New Haven politics when he returned to the city.

84. The book for which they shared primary responsibility was The Case for Regional Planning, with Special Reference to New England, Directive Committee on Regional Planning (Yale University Press, 1947).

85. Newsletter, June 8, 1951, p. 3.

86. Rotival, pp. 17-18.

87. Yale and Her Needs, prepublication draft, Office of University Development, p. 20.

88. Minutes of the Redevelopment Agency, November 1, 1951. Thanks to A. Tappan Wilder, I was able to find these minutes on the seventh floor of the Redevelopment Agency located at 157 Church Street in New Haven.

89. Ibid., January 17, 1952.

90. For purposes of simplicity, I will not deal with another aspect of Rotival's second 1951 report, the exact placement of a highway on the other side of the city, a highway to Hartford. This problem involved the fact that the state's plan would cut through the Wooster Square residential neighborhood, perhaps dooming that area to further decline. After much struggle, but less than in the case of the Oak Street connector, the alignment was moved in conformity to the city's wishes.

91. Rotival Papers. The papers are not ordered enough to be more specific.

92. Ibid.

93. Ross's statement that "they educated us" suggests a proper assessment of the role of planners and other experts in the United States. They do not have a function independent of the framework and goals set by big businessmen and other leaders within the ruling class, but they do make a significant contribution in terms of developing and carrying out solutions to problems set for them by the business leaders. They "think" for the ruling class, often in special institutes, programs, or university departments funded by major businesses and foundations.

94. Newsletter (July 1953): 3, for a presentation of the program.

95. This letter was found in Chamber of Commerce files and made available to me by A. Tappan Wilder.

96. Rotival Papers.

97. Ibid. McDougal, it will be recalled, is the Yale law professor who was a member of the Redevelopment Agency.

98. Ibid.

99. Wolfinger, p. 291, with his usual emphasis on the initiatory role of the city government, believes that "these needs [Yale housing needs] suggested to Lee and Logue [my italics] that Yale would be the ideal customer for the redevelopment land on its doorstep. At the same time there was scarcely any interest [my italics] in New Haven affairs at Yale."

100. "The Building Requirements of Yale University," Space Committee Report, March 8, 1954, p. 42.

101. Provost Office Papers, Box IV, Yale University Library.

102. City planner Andrews later became director of this agency.

103. It is possible to find evidence for Yale interest in redevelopment land as early as August 1952, when then secretary Carl Lohmann queried architect Douglas Orr about the possibility of placing a new medical school dorm on redevelopment land. Orr disagreed with the idea in a lengthy memo dated August 14, citing acquisition problems and a likely two-year lag among several reasons for his disagreement. The new dormitory was subsequently built on land already owned by the university. Lohmann Papers, Box 363, Yale University Library.

104. Rotival Papers.

105. Redevelopment Agency minutes, February 26, 1954.

106. *Newsletter* (January-February 1954): 2.

107. Ibid.

108. Wolfinger, p. 229.

109. The example of Robert Woodward and Carl Bernstein is apropos to this point. In their book about the Watergate investigations, *All the President's Men* (Simon & Schuster, 1974), they write that they never published a controversial claim unless they could verify it with at least two sources. Social scientists doing decisional analyses would do well to adopt the critical stance of investigative journalists and detectives, instinctively doubting everything told to them and constantly checking and cross-checking their findings against the claims of other interviewees and the written record.

110. Just as the Pentagon Papers, the Watergate tapes, and the revelations about CIA and FBI activities confirm our worst suspicions about the heavy-handedness and immorality of American rulers, whether of the Kennedy, Johnson, or Nixon variety, so too do statements such as I have just quoted suggest that the leading thinkers, planners, and apologists for the American ruling class are as sophisticated in their understanding of the need for ideological legitimacy as we thought they were. For further evidence of this sophistication, see Shoup and Weinstein.

111. Rotival Papers. The quote is from page 2 of the letter to Freese.

112. Dahl and Wolfinger both recognize and document the major functions of CAC: the ideological one of selling the program to the public, and the pragmatic one of having the most important businessmen on CAC deal with any dissidents within the business community. Since there is no disagreement among us on these points, I will not belabor them here.

113. For evidence on this point, see the letter from Spencer Toll to Edward Logue, September 11, 1954, in the Rotival Papers. See also the letter from Edward Logue to Maurice Rotival, July 20, 1954, in the same collection. The role envisaged for Yale by these people was a relatively minor one—building models of the new plans, providing space for the Rotival staff, and permitting use of the Yale library.

114. Wolfinger, p. 273. Neither Dahl nor Wolfinger ever interviewed Spielvogel about his role even though he has had an office one block from the New Haven green since he left the Redevelopment Agency. They relied on accounts by members of the Lee-Logue administration. Nor did they unearth interagency memos which reveal the substantive problems which bedeviled Rotival, Andrews, and Spielvogel until the Oak Street connector conflict was resolved just at the time when Logue and his "team" took over to perform alleged wonders with their aggressive and often secretive tactics.

115. Rotival Papers. Perhaps the major gap in this study is the unavailability of Prescott Bush's letters and personal papers, the whereabouts of which are not known to any members of his family.

116. Wolfinger, pp. 290-94, adopts this interpretation. At the same time, he gives an accurate account of the conflict which led to open bidding.

117. Ibid., p. 293. The words I have italicized in the above quote show that Lee's major problem was with the federal government, not with "public sentiment."

118. Ibid., ch. 4, contains the best discussion I have read on the nature and persistence of machine politics in New Haven and other major cities. But Wolfinger does not use this discussion as part of his explanation for why Lee was forced to auction the apartment land. Here the problem is not one of evidence, but of the interpretation of evidence within the confining perspective of the pluralist framework.

119. The facts of this project are told in great detail by Wolfinger, ch. 10.

120. Ibid., p. 345.

121. A change in federal urban renewal laws in 1959 permitting cities to count new university construction as part of their one-third cost also allowed Yale to benefit New Haven urban renewal. Two new colleges being built by Yale were gerrymandered into an urban renewal project in the Dixwell area, reducing the city's share to zero and even providing "credits" toward the next renewal project.

122. Wolfinger, pp. 343-44. Wolfinger does not name this person, but he is J. Richardson Dilworth, who has managed the Rockefeller family fortune since 1958 as head of Rockefeller Family and Associates. He also is a director of Chase Manhattan Bank and Chrysler Motors, among others. For information on Dilworth, see G. William Domhoff, "Rockefeller Economic Power: An Overview"; Charles L. Schwartz, "What the Rockefeller Family Owns," *International Socialist Review* (January 1975). These papers were the basis for testimony before the House Judiciary Committee hearings on the nomination of Nelson Rockefeller for the vice-presidency, testimony which brought a lengthy response from Dilworth, including commentary on his role in Yale investments. See *Nomination of Nelson A. Rockefeller to Be Vice President of the United States,* Committee on the Judiciary, House of Representatives, 93rd Congress (Washington, D.C.: U.S. Government Printing Office, 1974).

123. Ibid., p. 344.

# 4
# METHODOLOGY OF POWER STRUCTURE RESEARCH

Aside from a few theoretical and methodological comments, the focus of my concern to this point has been primarily empirical. I have tried to show the several ways in which *Who Governs?* and its companion volumes were factually wrong about the structure of power and its operation in New Haven. In making this empirical refutation, I have tried to demonstrate the nature of power structure research by the process of doing it, but I have not presented a systematic discussion of the rationale of the research process itself.

This chapter will present the methodological framework which has informed the previous empirical efforts, a framework that can be considered a basis for power structure research in general. This framework will be contrasted with that underlying the research presented in *Who Governs?* Hopefully these more general and abstract comments will make more sense to the reader in light of what has been demonstrated in the case of New Haven.

Discussions of power structure research center around critical analysis of the three "methods" assumed to be basic in such research—the "reputational," wherein people supposedly in a position to know are asked to name the "top leaders" in a community or nation; the "decisional," wherein those who initiate or veto policy proposals are studied in an effort to determine if the same few people dominate in a wide variety of "issue areas"; and the "positional," wherein the social and economic connections of those holding key leadership positions in major institutions of the community or nation are studied to determine if any one group or class is significantly overrepresented in the leadership hierarchy. Books which exemplify each method are noted, such as Floyd Hunter's *Community Power Structure* for the reputational, Dahl's *Who Governs?* for the decisional, and C. Wright Mills's *The Power Elite* for the positional. The discussion then proceeds to recount the pros and cons of each method, often suggesting that it would be best to use a combination of the three in future studies. But there is much more to studying power structures than any of these discussions imply. Moreover, despite the different theoretical biases said to be implicit in each of the three methods, they are in some ways more similar than they are different. In terms of the data they generate, they can be seen as variations on one basic technique—developing lists of names and searching out connections among them.[1]

Power structure methodology does not fall into the traditional categories used to organize discussions of methodology within sociology and political science. Most practitioners of these disciplines think of methodology in terms of experimental methods, survey methods, case study methods, and field studies. However, power structure methodology is not really any of these, although surveys, case studies, and field studies are occasionally useful techniques in mapping a power structure or learning about some of its major characteristics. Rather, power structure research in its most general form is a species of "network analysis," and as such it is foreign to social scientists trained in terms of traditional methodological rubrics. Its closest cousin within the social sciences, methodologically speaking, is sociometry, which has been rightly described as "curiously peripheral—invisible, really—in sociological theory."[2]

Before presenting a methodological framework based on network analysis, it is important to outline the alternative view developed by Dahl in 1958 in a famous and oft-cited article entitled "A Critique of the Ruling Elite Model." In that article Dahl concluded that "I do not see how anyone can suppose that he has established the dominance of a specific group in a community or a nation without basing his analysis on the careful examination of a series of concrete decisions."[3] With this statement, Dahl insisted that the decisional method was the only one of any real use in power structure studies. The other methods that had been used up to that time, the reputational and positional, were dismissed by Dahl when he followed the sentence quoted above with the assertion that he found it "a remarkable and indeed astounding fact that neither Professor Mills [who used the positional method] nor Professor Hunter [who relied heavily on the reputational method] has seriously attempted to examine an array of specific cases to test his major hypothesis." [4]

What Dahl thought to be an "astounding fact" was interpreted as something even worse—as downright taboo—by many young social scientists, and that was that as far as power structure methodology was concerned, even though Dahl later used the positional method in showing how control of the mayor's office in New Haven had shifted from the patricians to the entrepreneurs to the "ex-plebes" in the course of New Haven history (Who Governs?, chs. 2-4). The 1958 paper and the subsequent discussion in Who Governs? became the received wisdom of power structure methodology, and it was many years before social scientists in any number began to rethink the problem. The formal language of Dahl's final formulation was as follows:

> To sum up: The hypothesis of the existence of a ruling elite can be strictly tested only if:
> 1. The hypothetical ruling elite is a well-defined group.
> 2. There is a fair sample of cases involving key political decisions in which the preferences of the hypothetical ruling elite run counter to those of any other likely group that might be suggested.
> 3. In such cases, the preferences of the elite regularly prevail.[5]

I would be exaggerating slightly if I left the impression that Dahl's view was adhered to by everyone. There were people who continued to use the reputational and positional methods, or who did studies suggesting that findings from the different methods sometimes overlapped or complemented each other. However, no one successfully challenged Dahl's general formulation of the problem, and it is in this context that it will be taken as representative of the dominant social science viewpoint and used as a counterpoint for the discussion to be presented here.

## QUESTIONS IN POWER STRUCTURE RESEARCH

Since methods are designed in order to answer questions, it seems best to begin by considering the basic questions posed in power structure studies. In a general sense, it is obvious what interests power structure researchers: the distribution of power within the social system under scrutiny. But those who study power structures do not really begin from such a disinterested vantage point. Almost certainly they will be trying to determine whether or not some social class, economic group, ethnic group, or religious group is the dominant force within a given community or nation. They will be attempting to determine if there is a ruling class or if there is a less concentrated, more pluralistic distribution of power wherein several or many groups partake in the disposition of rewards and issues.

Concern with discovering the existence of a ruling group—or with testing the hypothesis that a given group is the ruling one—has been the main focus of power structure research. This concern leads to the more specific questions found in the power structure literature. These questions can be presented in two groups. The two questions in the first group are methodological in nature, and are basic to any power structure studies. The four questions in the second group are substantive in nature, and may or may not be of interest to researchers, depending upon their particular theoretical bent.

### Basic Methods Questions

1. What are the indicators or evidence that can be used to demonstrate that the group or class in question is in fact "powerful" or "dominant"?

2. What are the indicators that allow the researcher to specify which individuals and/or organizations are part of the class or group whose "power" is being investigated?

### Substantive Questions

1. How do we know if a class or group is "cohesive" enough to exercise its collective will?

2. How does the alleged power group under scrutiny formulate the policies and politics it wishes to impress upon the rest of society?

3. How does the alleged power group brings its policies to bear upon economic, governmental, and other important institutions of society?

4. How does the alleged power group maintain its dominance over other groups in society?

Although the four questions in the substantive category are in an order that builds from the most basic to the most general, this does not mean that each and every one of them must be answered in every power structure investigation. Rather, I am only saying that these questions encompass the range of concerns found in past and present power structure studies. These concerns, in turn, reflect the interests of specific disciplines and theories.

Most political scientists, for example, are especially interested in the question of how an alleged power group dominates government because the processes of government are of substantive interest to them. While I will shortly argue that it is not "necessary" to show how a ruling group dominates government in order to demonstrate satisfactorily that a ruling group exists, the question is certainly legitimate. The same point could be made about all the substantive questions posited above. We study them because they are of inherent interest to power structure researchers or because they are related to a more general body of theory in which the investigator is interested.

In the case of empirically oriented Marxists, to take another example, they not only have a concern with demonstrating that there is a ruling class in a given society—a concern which soon involves them in the development of power indicators and class-membership criteria—but they also wish to show how this ruling class controls economic institutions and maintains its dominance over other groups in society. Marxists have often been critical of certain aspects of power structure research because many of its practitioners do not formulate their questions in terms of how the capital-owning ruling class defines itself and develops its policies on the basis of its need to dominate the nonowning workers and to make profits from their work. On the other hand, social scientists of a non-ruling class or pluralist persuasion are usually more interested in the process by which a potential ruling group or class formulates politicies and has them carried out by government. These concerns follow from their theoretical focus, which has different concerns than those generated by a Marxist framework.

To a certain degree, definitions and methods are inextricably imbedded in the theoretical assumptions within which we operate. No method can be entirely free of value-based assumptions. Nevertheless, in the next few sections I will attempt to formulate a methodological statement general enough to encompass the concerns of all theoretical perspectives without doing any of them injustice. Hopefully it will be specific enough to allow researchers of varying theoretical orientations to carry out empirical studies that shed light on the theory in question.

## POWER INDICATORS AND THE MEANING OF POWER
Every power structure researcher sooner or later confronts the

problem of defining *power*, for it must be shown that a group or class has power if it is to be considered a ruling class or elite. However, his or her heart usually does not warm to the topic, for definitions of *power* may seem far removed from the empirical work at hand. Thus discussion usually begins by noting that philosophers and theoreticians have provided a multitude of definitions of this slippery term, as indeed they have. After the reader is properly overwhelmed by the welter of words contained in the various definitions, the author rescues him or her by pointing out that there are certain points in common to all the definitions, or that they can be reduced to one or two basic types. Thus, Dahl suggests, in his paper on "The Concept of Power"—a theoretical preliminary to the more methodological "A Critique of the Ruling Elite Model" and the more empirical *Who Governs?*—that an emphasis on power as a "relationship" is inherent in most definitions, and that most definitions rest on the "intuitive idea" that "A has power over B to the extent that he can get B to do something that B would not otherwise do." [6] Sociologist Steven Lukes claims that there are two major traditions within the social sciences in conceptualizing *power*. The first, of which Dahl and most power structure researchers are members, defines *power* in terms of conflicts among groups or individuals. Differences within this general framework for defining *power* concern the degree to which the researcher focuses on decision making in the public arena or on the suppression of conflict in direct and indirect ways. The second tradition, exemplified by the work of Talcott Parsons, defines power as a resource of the society or community, emphasizing its benefits to the whole society rather than conflict between groups or classes. [7]

Once the researcher has defined *power* to his or her satisfaction, the discussion is usually ignored in research operations. This is because, as Dahl notes, a "formal definition" of *power* "is not easy to apply in concrete research problems; and therefore, operational equivalents of the formal definition, designed to meet the needs of a particular research problem are likely to diverge from one another in important ways." [8] Dahl does not reach out to narrow this gap between formal and operational definitions of *power*. He instead writes that the separation might be necessary for some time to come, and that we should learn to live with different definitions of *power*:

> Thus we are not likely to produce—certainly not for some considerable time to come—anything like a single, consistent, coherent "Theory of Power." We are much more likely to produce a variety of theories of limited scope, each of which employs some definition of power that is useful in the context

of the particular piece of research or theory but different in important respects from the definitions of other studies.[9]

Although this *may* be a useful perspective if we think in terms of a theory of power which must encompass experimental dyads and small groups in social psychology laboratories as well as national power structures and relationships among nations, it is not a satisfactory resolution of the problem within the context of power structure research. Power structure research needs a way of thinking about *group* or *class* power which leads to a generalized conception rather than a variety of theories of limited scope.

At the most general level, *power* is best defined for purposes of power structure research within the conflict tradition embraced by pluralists and Marxists. As Lukes summarizes in critiquing the functional view held by Parsons, functional, nonconflictual definitions of power

> are out of line with the central meanings of "power" as traditionally understood and with the concerns that have always centrally preoccupied students of power. They focus on the locution "power to," ignoring "power over." Thus power indicates a "capacity," a "facility," an "ability," not a relationship. Accordingly, the conflictual aspect of power—the fact that it is exercised *over* people—disappears altogether from this view. And along with it there disappears the central interest of studying power relations in the first place—an interest in the (attempted or successful) securing of people's compliance by overcoming or averting their opposition.[10]

*Social power* in its most general meaning has to do with the domination of one group or class by another, and it can be inferred from who benefits the most from the functioning of the social system under examination.[11] In this conception, the power of a group or class can be inferred from the distribution of values people seek, such as wealth, income, good education, and good health. This emphasis on distributions of values people seek—benefits—as indicators of power does not contradict the conceptual emphasis on power as a relationship, for these distributions can be seen as outcomes of power relations or struggles among groups or classes. Nor does it conflict with the Marxist view of class as a relationship, for the value distributions can be seen as indicators of exploitation of one class by another.[12]

Dahl does not reject this conception of power directly in *Who Governs?* However, he does so by implication by regarding wealth and income as "resources" that can be brought to bear in the struggle for political influence (pp. 239-45).[13] Although Dahl does not reject "who benefits" in a direct fashion, Polsby does so in *Community Power and Political Theory*, suggesting several reasons why "knowing value·distributions is insufficient and perhaps misleading in discovering who rules":

> (1) value distributions occur without explicit decisions taking place, hence may tell us nothing about decision-making; (2) values within the community may be distributed in important ways as a by-product of decisions and nondecisions made outside the community; (3) there are many irrationalities in decision-making, which may lead to the distribution of values in unpredictable, unintended ways; (4) the powerful may intentionally distribute values to the nonpowerful.[14]

None of these reasons amounts to an insurmountable objection. When Polsby says that value distributions can occur without explicit decisions taking place, he is equating *power* with *decision making*, and thus defining away the more general conception of power. When he objects that irrationalities may lead to the distribution of values in unpredictable and unintended ways, he is raising an objection that may be a problem if we look at the beneficiaries of one or two decisions or policy outcomes, but it is hardly likely that the general picture of power in a community or nation is a result of unintended consequences. When he objects that the powerful may intentionally distribute values to the nonpowerful, he is suggesting a possibility hardly likely to be a regular occurrence of any magnitude, and which in any case would only serve to decrease disparities, not remove them. As to his point that value distributions within a community may be affected by decisions outside the community, he is raising an objection that only holds for communities, and is not an argument against using value distributions in studying larger power structures.

As political scientist William C. Mitchell wrote in the late 1960s, when doubt began to grow about the pluralist view of power: "Let us try defining power not as one who makes decisions but as who gets how much from the system. Those who acquire the most goods, services, and opportunities are those who have the most power." [15] This focus on who benefits certainly fits our "intuitive idea" of what power is all about, for most of us believe that most people seek wealth, high income, low taxes, good health, long life, happiness, nice homes, and long vacations. However, an emphasis on who benefits, or indeed, on who determines what a benefit is, involves us at the level of what Alford and Friedland call "systemic or class power." It is a definition imbedded in the assumption that power has to do with domination of one group or class by another, and not only with domination of government or successful involvement in specific decisions. It does not focus on who will fill the seats of formal authority within the key institutions of the social system, nor does it concern itself with who will "win" in a specific situation or decision-making process. We need to be aware that there are other levels or kinds of power—the structural and situational—that must be considered.[16]

The differentiation of systemic, structural, and situational types of power within the overall conception of power helps to explain the failure of rival theoretical schools to directly confront each other. It also helps us to make our power indicators more explicit. Work on power and power indicators by Marxists, as will be demonstrated in a later section of this chapter, has been concerned with systemic and structural levels of power, using who benefits and overrepresentation in important positions of formal authority (in corporations, foundations, and the executive branch of the federal government) as indicators of power. Elite theorists such as C. Wright Mills have tended to concentrate on the positional or structural level, using who sits atop key institutions as their indicator of power, while pluralists have tended to concentrate on the situational level, using "who wins" as their primary indicator of power.[17]

Each of these indicators of power is to a certain degree imbedded in a set of theoretical biases. Due to their respective underlying assumptions, Marxists see class domination as the major problem, elitists regard institutional command as a primary concern, and pluralists view decision-making victories in the political arena as the important focus of attention. However, this differentiation of levels and indicators can be pushed too far, for each can be intimately related to the other. For example, critics of the decision-making focus would be likely to agree that an unbroken series of true victories in the political arena for an insurgent group or class would be very likely to lead to changes in who benefits. Similarly, successful attempts to gain seats of formal authority in the important institutions of society are likely to affect the distribution of values in favor of the group or class gaining the seats.

Power indicators, then, are of three general types—who benefits from the system, who directs or governs important institutions, and who wins on important decisions. To a certain degree, each of these indicators reflects a theoretical bias, and to a certain degree each type of indicator may point to different groups of people as "powerful." Those who are wealthy and well educated may not hold government positions (as in New Haven), and those who win on specific decisions may not be wealthy or hold important positions. In the final analysis, the overall power of a group or class must be inferred from the distribution of values or benefits, on the assumption that those who command institutions or win in the decision-making process will try to do so in order to increase benefits to their group or class.

A merely theoretical resolution of the meaning of power and the nature of power indicators is not the final goal of this chapter, which is focused upon the methodology of power structure research. This discussion should have research consequences. The idea of different levels of power brings us to the notion that the researcher should try to plan his or her investigation in such a way that it can be shown that who benefits, who governs, and who wins are one and the same class or group, *or else present the historical and sociological explanation for any disparities that may appear among the three levels of power or types of indicators of power.*

For example, in the present study I have to tried to show how the people in New Haven who *benefit* the most from the social system—the wealthy upper class—were able to *win* on the question of urban renewal even though they held few formal seats of governmental authority. Put another way, who benefits, who governs, and who wins did not point to one and the same group or class in New Haven, as Dahl reports they did in its earlier history, and it therefore became necessary to explain how and why the positional level can be by-passed in this city.

In conclusion to this general discussion of power, I have tried to suggest a relational, conflict-based definition of power that can be operationalized by indicators that point to systemic (class), structural (institutional), and situational (decisional) levels of power operation. This view is less than a "single, consistent, coherent 'Theory of Power,'" and I thus agree with Dahl that such a theory would be difficult to achieve at this time.[18] However, I am also arguing that it is possible to attain more than "a variety of theories of limited scope, each of which employs some definition of power that is useful in the context of the particular research or theory." [19]

## MEMBERSHIP INDICATORS

A second methodological problem basic to all power structure research—criteria which indicate class or group membership—has not generated the concern attendant upon the definition of power and the development of power indicators. It seems to be a more straightforward and less emotionally charged question because the inference of class or group membership from a set of indicators has common agreement among a variety of theoretical perspectives.

If we are testing the hypothesis that a given class or group is a ruling or dominant one, there is no doubt that Dahl is right to insist that the membership or boundaries of the group in question must be clearly specified in advance: "And a proponent must specify what group he has in mind as his ruling elite. Once the group is specified, then the test I have suggested is, at least in principle, valid." [20]

For general purposes, the philosophy of science implied in Dahl's statement is too constricting.[21] It limits research to hypothesis testing, ruling out purely empirical studies that begin with no other assumption than the notion that power in a community or nation may be organized into specific cliques, groups, or classes. It does not allow for the fact that the reputational and positional techniques for mapping power structures, when utilized in the fashion to be presented in a later section, do not of necessity have to begin by specifying the group under study, but by their very nature end up demonstrating that the allegedly powerful people located by the technique are in fact members of a group or class.

Being able to specify who is and who is not a member of the alleged ruling group is essential to power structure research. This is because relationships among individuals are the basic elements with which power structure research begins, even though the basic conceptual tool of the researcher may be *class, group, institution,* or even society as a whole. For example, we cannot establish the cohesion of a group unless we can identify its individual members and determine their degree of interaction; nor can we demonstrate how an alleged ruling group dominates government unless we can show that the individuals and institutions receiving tax favors, government positions, or enactment of policy suggestions are disproportionately drawn from the group or class under consideration.

This emphasis on relationships among people as the elements of any collectivity or organization that we analyze is also made from a social-systems perspective by Bertram M. Gross:

> The basic element of system structure in any nation is the people of the country. They are the basis of the entire social system. Land, minerals, and man-made facilities are "resources" only because the people find them useful. Groups exist only because of the interrelations between individual human beings. Social power is exerted by, with, on and for people individually, and by people acting together in groups. External relations are relations among people. Social and

cultural values are never disembodied; they exist only because people hold them. Thus, all the other five elements of system structure are merely ways of elaborating on certain stable characteristics of, and interrelations among, people.[22]

The necessity for membership indicators and the study of individuals and their relationships will become more obvious when I consider the several techniques utilized in mapping power structures. For now, the point can be summarized by saying that group or class indicators are ultimately necessary in a power structure study, but they need not be present at the beginning of the investigation unless a specific hypothesis is being tested.

## ANALYZING POWER STRUCTURES

All power structure studies, whether exploratory or hypothesis-testing in nature, must deal with the problems of power indicators and membership indicators. But what does it mean to *analyze a power structure*? And how do we do it? Let me begin by defining *structure* and *analyze*, and then move on to what becomes the straightforward meaning of the phrase *analyzing power structures*.

*Structure* is a term referring to relationships or patterns of relationships among the constituent elements of the phenomenon under consideration. We can speak of the structure of international relations, the structure of the coal industry, the structure of a small group, or the structure of a person's ideas and attitudes. For power structure research, however, the relationships implied by the term *structure* are best conceptualized in terms of *networks*. Networks are specific sets of linkages among given groups of persons and organizations. They have the important property that "the characteristics of these linkages as a whole may be used to interpret the social behavior of the persons involved."[23] Networks concretely describe the structure of relationships that characterize a group, community, or class. The linkages that make up the structure of relationships in a network can include such relationships as friendship, common group membership, partnership, common corporate directorships, employeeship, discipleship, and many other relationships. Some networks will be characterized by numerous kinds of linkages or relationships among members, others may be based upon only one type of relationship. For example, the networks which unite a ruling social class may include linkages of kinship, friendship, and common property ownership; indeed, it is these linkages which lead us to describe that network as a social class. On the other hand, the networks that connect the ruling social class to other social groups and classes may involve only the relationship employer-employee, as in the relationship to the working class, or may be mediated through white-collar professionals who work for institutions controlled by ruling-class directors, as in the case of relationships with the poor and oppressed.[24]

*Analyze* is a term implying the discovery of patterns and relationships. We analyze some entity to find out its constituent parts and how they relate to each other to form the given entity. The techniques for discovering these relations are many and varied, ranging from detective-type work in field settings to mathematical manipulations in the computer center.

Having defined *structure* and *analyze*, it is now possible to give a precise explanation of the phrase *analyzing power structures*, which I have been able to use throughout the book because of our shared intuitive understanding of what the phrase means. Formally speaking, to *analyze a power structure* is to discover a network of people and institutions who differentially benefit from the functioning of the social system and to determine how this network dominates the structural and situational levels of power operation. Whether the power structure involves cliques, institutions, interest groups, or social classes depends upon the type of problem being investigated and the theoretical focus of the investigator, but the generic term *power structure* encompasses all these conceptions if thought of in network terms.

Conceptualizing power structure research as a form of network analysis is a methodological strategy which does not favor or preclude any of the theoretical frameworks for interpreting and guiding power structure research. It is not meant to be a substitute for theory, as it tends to become in social anthropology, the discipline that has made the greatest use of network analysis to date.[25] Rather, through its careful specification of the people and organizations in a given group or class and its emphasis upon the exact nature of the linkages among them, it makes possible a clearer understanding of what it is to do research within any of the theoretical paradigms that have been used by power structure researchers. Moreover, because it can take advantage of developments in graph theory, matrix algebra, and various lattice algebras, it provides the possibility for more quantitative research than has been possible heretofore.

Network analysis, as conceived for purposes of power structure research, has "crucial sociological and mathematical differences" from the approach of conventional sociometry.[26] These differences involve the fact that conventional sociometry focuses primarily on social relations among people in a network, conceiving of the *points* or *nodes* of the network as people, and linkages among points as social relationships (e.g., liking, hating, owing). This usual approach does not give full play to the other basic type of social tie discussed by social scientists—membership. We not only relate to people and institutions, but we are members of groups and organizations, a fact which tends to be put aside, conceptually speaking, in sociometry. In the important conceptualization of network analysis suggested by Ronald L. Breiger, there are two kinds of networks, relational and membership, and they must be understood as distinctive. People are linked to other people by specified relationships, groups are linked to each other by common memberships. In other words, a network of corporation directors linked together by their common corporate board memberships is in actuality two networks. One is a network of boards, which is the institutional level, linked together by their members. The other is a network of members, which is the group or class level, linked together by common boards. "Either or both of these networks may be substantively important, and certain information about either network may be derived from the other." [27] Breiger's point is important because it makes explicit the rationale for tracing names and organizations and overlapping memberships in power structure studies. Then too, it leads to mathematical techniques that are "useful in the study of director interlocks, clique structures, organizations within communities and national power structures, and other collectivities which share members." [28]

## DOING A POWER STRUCTURE ANALYSIS

Now that the analysis of power structures has been cast in terms of networks, it is possible to be more specific about how to do the research itself. The first step of a power structure study involves mapping (tracing, developing) the connections of people and institutions comprising the alleged power network. The mapping can utilize a variety of connections which range from kinship ties among leading families, to social connections among leaders with a reputation for power, to the interlocking directorships among leaders of the business community. The discovery of connections the researcher wishes to utilize can be done by positional, decisional, or reputational methods. Arguments persist over the strengths and weaknesses of each of these techniques for mapping a power structure, but the important point is what they have in common—they all generate lists of names and seek out selected kinds of connections among those names.

The second step in a complete power structure study involves an analysis of money flows into and out of the alleged power network. An analysis of money flows is really only another way of establishing connections among people and institutions, except the linkage is some type of money transaction rather than kinship, friendship, common institutional membership, or any of the other traditional linkages used to establish a network. In terms of the networks of people and institutions mapped in the first phase of a power structure study, there are four kinds of money flows in the network, any one of which may be helpful on a specific research problem:

1. people to people (e.g., campaign donations, gifts, loans);

2. people to institutions (e.g., taxes, donations to foundations by wealthy individuals);

3. institutions to people (e.g., corporate stock dividends, foundation grants to professors);

4. institutions to institutions (e.g., foundation grants to policy groups, corporate donations to foundations).

The third step in a power structure study, a step which is implicit in many studies but treated systematically in few, involves content analysis of communications (e.g., speeches, position papers, books, memos, letters) of people and institutions at central or critical junctures in the power network. Whether they conceptualize it in this way or not, content analysis is what researchers do whenever they draw inferences about policy positions, plans, ideology, or class consciousness from any spoken or written statement. Such content analyses can range from the casual interpretation of a speech or statement, to systematic qualitative treatment of several speeches or articles in terms of one or another theoretical perspective, to detailed quantitative treatment of hundreds of written messages. In the latter case, computer programs are often used to read the texts and sort specified phrases into empirically derived categories or the researcher's theoretical categories.[29]

The final aspect of a power structure study involves articulation of the power indicators which qualify the network under study as a power network. In practice, evidence that the network ranks high on various power indicators of a systemic nature is often collected as the investigation proceeds (e.g., wealth and health statistics). With structural or situational indicators the power of the network cannot be determined until the investigation is completed, such as in a decisional study, where interventions in the decision-making process by members of the network are the indicators of power, or in a positional study, where overrepresentation of members of the network in government or key decision-making groups is the indicator of power.

Most power structure studies do not go much beyond the initial step of mapping the network of people and institutions by the positional, reputational, or decisional methods. Because social background information on national-level leaders is more readily obtainable than reputational or decisional information, most studies of nationwide power structures have been positional mappings of structural power in which investigators concerned themselves almost exclusively with social and educational connections of business leaders and government officials. They usually find that people of high social status and prestigious university backgrounds are greatly overrepresented in important institutions.[30] With the notable exception of Floyd Hunter's informative study of the national power structure in the late 1950s, reputational studies have been confined by and large to the study of regions, cities, and small towns.[31] Dozens of researchers have ventured into cities and communities all over the United States, usually concluding that upper-middle-class informants of professional and business occupations believe the biggest businessmen and corporate lawyers of the given area are at the center of a cohesive power structure.[32] When a positional study is done in conjunction with the reputational study, there is usually a considerable overlap in the two networks. However, the reputational method seems to discover some members of the power network who are not in visible positions of power. By using the positional method in conjunction with his modification of the original reputational questions, sociologist Charles M. Bonjean has shown that the legitimacy and visibility of local power structures can be determined, and that purely symbolic leaders can be distinguished from visible and concealed leaders.[33]

Positional and reputational mappings, and thus findings based upon them, have been questioned by those social scientists of whom Dahl, Polsby, and Wolfinger are prototypical. Overrepresentation of a group or class in government, as found in positional studies, does not necessarily mean the group or class is powerful, these critics claim, for the position holders may be restrained by the general ideology of the community or society, by regard for the "national interest," by fear of voters, or by policy inputs of other groups or classes not represented directly in the government. Similarly, the reputational method is criticized because a reputation for power may not necessarily mean those with the reputations are in fact powerful. Each informant may have a different understanding of what is meant by *powerful*. The informants chosen may be a biased group. Opinions may be distorted by the media visibility of some individuals. A general reputation for power may be incorrectly inferred by informants from power in one narrow issue-area.[34]

Critics of positional and reputational techniques have advocated the decisional approach, and it has been used for several studies at the local level. When used with the positional or reputational method, it often leads to contradictory findings, with a greater emphasis on governmental leaders as important elements in the power structure. Such was the case for Syracuse and several smaller cities.[35] However, the most famous and oft-cited decisional study which suggests the predominant role of government leaders in community power structures is Dahl's study of New Haven, and it has been one purpose of my restudy of New Haven to demonstrate that a decisional study can be very misleading if the researcher cannot overcome difficulties encountered in obtaining documents, letters, memos, and minutes necessary to make a complete study. Despite the best efforts of researchers, aspects of the situation may remain secret, participants may not be able to correctly assess the roles of various members of decisional circles, and the actual dynamics of the process may be forgotten or distorted shortly after the issue is resolved.[36]

Because all three approaches have their strengths and weaknesses, the mapping step of a power structure study should involve all three whenever possible.[37] In such cases, it is usually best to begin with the positional approach to provide a general context. The researcher should gather from businesses, labor unions, voluntary associations, and government agencies the names of all people in positions of institutional importance. These names should be studied to determine social, economic, and political connections among them. Common neighborhoods, intermarriages, common club memberships, interlocking directorships, campaign donations, or other linkages of interest to the researcher can be used to determine whether or not positional leaders fall into one or more cliques, groups, or classes.[38]

Positional mapping should be followed by a reputational mapping. This can be done in one of three ways: (1) interviewing a cross-section of people, thereby eliminating the criticism that informants or judges selected by the researcher may be biased; (2) obtaining nominations from leaders of all local voluntary associations, and then going directly to those nominated, as Floyd Hunter did in the late 1960s in Oakland, to eliminate the problem of judges; or (3) interviewing positional leaders active in several organizations, as in the study of a Midwestern community by Robert Perrucci and Marc Pilisuk.[39] Once names are obtained from one of these starting points, it is important to interview those most frequently named, in turn obtaining names from each of them. If there is a power structure in the area under investigation, the researcher should quickly begin to receive the same names over and over again. Within three or four rounds, the circle should be essentially "closed." That is, every new person interviewed should be supplying names of people who already have been identified as powerful. When utilized in this way, the reputational method complements positional mapping in three ways—by revealing which leaders are the most active and important, by ascertaining the actual nature of the relationships among specific leaders, and by finding those leaders who do not hold formal positions.[40]

Finally, decisional studies can be undertaken within the context provided by positional and reputational studies. The first problem to be solved in this aspect of the investigation involves the determination of the decisions to be studied, a problem with more difficulties than meets the eye. Dahl tried to deal with this problem by picking issues of apparent community interest, two of which—city schools and urban renewal—involved large governmental expenditures, and one of which—party nominations—involved the electoral process. But all of these issue areas may miss the point as far as a power structure is concerned. Most school decisions are routine and may be of little moment to a power group that lives in suburbs or sends its children to private schools; urban renewal funds come primarily from Washington, thereby costing local groups very little. As for nominations for political office, it would have to be established that who holds local office is of consequence (in terms of benefits) to the power group before it could be said that this was an issue area worth studying. Alford put the matter well as part of a criticism of Dahl for his neglect of structure in his study of New Haven:

> The neglect of structure leads to rather narrow constructions of concepts and data, of which several examples can be given. Dahl calls the party struggle Pattern C ("fighting it out") because there is no possible way to compromise the necessity of one candidate winning an office, and therefore no way to reach consensus on a "policy." But this is an "issue-area" quite different from the others; it is a procedural device to determine which particular individuals will hold particular positions, and it is not at all the same as a struggle over which policies shall be carried out, except insofar as individuals represent different policy positions and different interest groups, and this aspect Dahl doesn't really consider. The electoral struggle is not a "policy" at all, and should not be seen as in the same theoretical plane." [41]

If Dahl's issue selections were arbitrary, so have been those of most other researchers. One empirical way out of this problem has been suggested by Bonjean and Grimes—interviewing leaders and residents at large to ascertain the most salient issues:

Manifest content, cost, participation, the number of individuals affected by the outcome, and other criteria have been used to select those issues that investigators term "important." Polling of leaders themselves is a less common way to assess the importance of issues, yet this type of reputational selection may be preferable to the use of "objective" criteria since it would reflect the extent to which the saliency of issues may differ among communities themselves. That is, the most important issues perceived by leaders or residents at large in Community X may be different from the issues perceived as most important by leaders or residents of community Y.[42]

Bonjean and Grimes then show in the case of six communities in the Southwest that there were large enough differences in the rankings of issue areas that "had the first three issues presented been selected for decisional analysis in all six communities, there would be no community where the three most 'important' issues were investigated." [43] Of particular interest in this approach would be any discrepancies in rankings between leaders on the one hand and members of less powerful groups or classes on the other, for issues seen as unimportant by the powerful and important by the powerless may be those issues kept out of the political arena and mass media, never to become "live" issues. Hunter reports a finding that points in this direction for Atlanta when he shows the great difference in rankings of issue areas between the White and Black reputational leaders in that city. Whites saw the plan of development and traffic control as most important, Blacks focused on improvement of schools and housing.[44]

Because leaders and mass media can play an important role in determining what people regard as an important issue, sociologists Harvey Molotch and Marilyn Lester suggest that another way to select issues is to focus on accidents and scandals.[45] Such issues may momentarily compromise the power group's routine control of events and reveal a great deal about the workings of power. An oil spill in Santa Barbara provided insight into the close relationship between the federal government and the oil companies, Edward Kennedy's accident at Chappaquidick provided a look at how the rich can avoid criminal prosecution, and Watergate gave us an unprecedented view of money in politics and the behind-the-scenes powers of the presidency.[46] Molotch and Lester contrast such accidents and scandals with the kind of routine events selected by political scientist Edward Banfield in his decisional study of Chicago:

> He selects the issues which received the widest coverage in the media and assumes these to be synonymous with "key" political issues, uncritically letting the organized ways in which events get done determine his subjects of study.... Lost in this type of research are the ways in which powerful event makers are able to have their public agendas adopted by the media through their organized promotional activities.... It is certainly not by chance that the kinds of issues to which we typically have access are of the sort which Banfield studies; e.g., where to locate the next branch of the University of Illinois or the next convention center.[47]

There is no easy way to focus on one or two decisions in order to determine the power structure in a community or nation. Similarly, the need for more than one method of mapping a power structure should be apparent. However, when used in various combinations determined by the nature of research questions and constraints of time and budget, the positional, reputational, and decisional techniques can provide us with the basis for more complete investigations of a power structure in terms of its cohesion, ideology, adaptability, and resistance to change.

### DO MARXISTS DO DIFFERENTLY?

Arguments over the value of positional, reputational, and decisional techniques of mapping a power structure have taken place within the mainstream of American social science. They have not tended to involve Marxists, some of whom believe that much of power structure research has a personalistic and instrumentalist perspective incompatible with or irrelevant to their structuralist perspective.[48] However, an analysis of the books and articles on the ruling class most often cited by Marxists shows that they employ the same methods and power indicators as many non-Marxist power structure studies. In fact, the best of the Marxist books is one of the few studies available which includes all major aspects of a good power structure study.

The most general Marxist work on power in Western societies is Ralph Miliband's *The State in Capitalist Society*. Written primarily for the purpose of showing that "the pluralist-democratic view of society, of politics and of the state in regard to the countries of advanced capitalism is in all essentials wrong," it brings together a vast amount of information purporting to show capitalist domination of government in the United States, Western Europe, and Japan.[49] After defining the ruling class as "that class which owns and controls the means of production and which is able, by virtue of the economic power conferred upon it, to use the state as its instrument for the domination of society," Miliband proceeds to support his case by relying almost exclusively on the positional approach, showing that businessmen, and members of the upper and middle classes generally, are "predominantly, not to say overwhelmingly, the source from which the state elite are drawn." [50]

As for the political and governmental figures who are not of the higher classes in background, Miliband claims they are ideologically committed to the basic principles of capitalism, which makes it difficult, if not impossible, for them to act in opposition to the general nature of the social order. This leaves the task of showing how this ideological commitment is brought about, and Miliband responds by adducing evidence to show big business's domination of mass media, education, and the symbols of nationalism and (to some extent) religion. He concludes that "control over 'the means of mental production' has been of great importance in legitimating capitalist rule." [51]

Miliband also has a chapter in which he recounts the numerous instances in which governments have helped capitalists through subsidies, tax favors, strike breaking, suppression of anticapitalists, and aid to overseas sales and investments. He is thus using as power indicators various value distributions which are the outcomes of governmental decision-making processes. Finally, Miliband cites a variety of economic statistics which he sees as indicators of power, a point summed up late in the book when he says:

> Unequal economic power, on the scale and of the kind encountered in advanced capitalist societies, inherently produces political inequality, on a more or less commensurate scale, whatever the constitution may say. Similarly, it is the capitalist context of generalized inequality in which the state operates which basically determines its policies and actions.[52]

Miliband's effort contains nothing that is outside the general framework necessary for power structure research. It provides membership indicators for its hypothesized ruling class—owners and controllers of the means of production—and indicators of power to support its claims—greater benefit from governmental decisions, higher standing on wealth and income statistics, and overrepresentation in government. That is, it uses a mixture of systemic and structural power indicators.

Marxist books and articles focused exclusively on the United States are of a similar nature. For example economist Victor Perlo in *The Empire of High Finance* asserts that big capitalists are the dominant group—"a few hundred or at most a few thousand men of wealth determine the destinies of the nation." [53] In the first of three sections in the book, utilizing data on interlocking directorships, joint ownerships, partnerships, and bank loans, he shows that the men of wealth are tied together into what he calls a "giant network of corporate monopoly," a "power network," a "financial oligarchy," and a "spider web." [54] The second section presents details on post-World War II gains, losses, shared ownerships, and rivalries of the eight major financial empires Perlo believes to exist within the overall financial oligarchy.

Section 3 presents his evidence that the financial oligarchy dominates government. It is of three types—governmental favors to big business, positional overrepresentation in the executive branch, and financial domination of political parties. As to governmental favors, he points to a variety of loans, subsidies, and tax breaks which allegedly go disproportionately to big business. As to positional evidence, he enumerates connections suggesting that "Washington, Incorporated, has become the alter ego of Wall Street—with a common board of directors." [55] He documents this most systematically in the case of the first Eisenhower administration, reporting on the backgrounds of 272 men in policy making and top executive positions: "At least 150, a clear majority, were active capitalists or wealthy men through inheritance or former business activity. Moreover, most of the 122 not classified as capitalists had a lifetime of intimate connection with and service to capitalists." [56]

After asking why such men would be appointed to government positions, he answers his own question by saying they have an "iron grip on the political parties," an iron grip that "involves long-standing connections with the local political machines, control of publicity media, and possession of the income needed to finance national campaigns, now generally estimated to cost about $150 million." [57] In Perlo's work, then, power is being inferred primarily from governmentally determined value distributions, positional overrepresentation, and disproportionate campaign finance donations. There is nothing in Perlo's work that does not fit in our general framework.

Another Marxist account of the American ruling class can be

found in an article written by economist Paul M. Sweezy in response to a sociology graduate student who challenged him, as an editor of the independent Marxist journal *Monthly Review,* to justify with a "probing analysis" his repeated use of the term *ruling class.* Sweezy deemed the challenge "an eminently fair one," and the result was a succinct overview of the American ruling class which would need little modification if it were being written today.[58]

Sweezy begins by discussing certain basic features of social classes and by establishing the fact of their existence in everyday life, then moves on to one of the questions I have claimed to be basic to power structure research—membership criteria. As far as the ruling class, core members are defined as "big capitalists" or "big property holders," with a "fringe" category which includes smaller property owners, government and business executives, and some professionals.[59] After presenting evidence for the cohesiveness of the ruling class—in a section on "the structure of the national ruling class"—Sweezy turns to the problem of "how the ruling class rules," which encompasses the second question basic to power structure research—power indicators.

In terms of the economy, Sweezy believes the ruling class has power because "its members either directly occupy the positions in the economy where key decisions are made or, if they do not occupy the positions themselves, they hire and fire those who do." [60] That is, we should find a disproportionate number of big capitalists and big property holders running corporations and serving on boards of directors—positional criteria of structural power—or intervening in economic decisions which researchers agree to be "key decisions"— obviously a decision-making indicator of power in the economic realm. In terms of the government, Sweezy calls on two familiar power indicators, overrepresentation in governmental positions and disproportionate campaign contributions to the political parties:

> The ruling class rules the government (using the term as a short-hand expression for all levels of government) in the sense that its members either directly occupy the key positions (largely true in the higher judiciary and the more honorific legislative jobs, increasingly true in the higher administrative jobs), or they finance *and thus indirectly control* the political parties which are responsible for staffing and managing the routine business of government.[61]

Sweezy's article touches on many other problems, including

ruling-class ideology (which he implies can be studied through what I have called "content analysis" of certain newspapers, magazines, and newsletters) and ruling-class conflicts, but the most important issues are contained in the material I have quoted or paraphrased. Once again, the questions considered pertinent in an oft-cited Marxist analysis of the American ruling class are readily encompassed within the methodological framework presented in this chapter.

The best Marxist book on the American power structure, historian James Weinstein's *The Corporate Ideal in the Liberal State,* is a study in political ideology which attempts "to show that liberalism in the Progressive Era—and since—was the product, consciously created, of the leaders of the giant corporations and financial institutions that emerged astride American society in the last years of the nineteenth century and the early years of the twentieth." [62] To document his thesis, Weinstein has to take all the steps inherent in a thorough power structure study.

First, Weinstein establishes the big-business nature of the National Civic Federation, the organization whose "corporate liberal" political ideology he intends to analyze. He does so by means of a network study of individual members which showed that "by 1903 there were representatives in the NCF of almost one-third of the 376 corporations with a capitalization of more than $10,000,000 and representatives of sixteen of the sixty-seven largest railroads in the United States." [63] He also enumerates the names and connections of many of the most prominent business and public members in order to make his point. Having established the nature of the NCF, he analyzes the memos, minutes, and model bills it produced, as well as private correspondence of its leaders which pertains to the federation and its activities. This content analysis established that the NCF frequently used such concepts as "business responsibility," "social cooperation," and "partnership with government" in a favorable context, rejecting the nineteenth-century shibboleths of laissez faire and unrestrained competition. Content analysis also revealed the specific programs which the federation evolved to put its "corporate liberal" ideas into action. These programs concerned capital-labor relations, workmen's compensation, and regulatory commissions, among other things.[64]

The political ideology and programs of the NCF established, Weinstein traces the networks through which the ideology and policies were disseminated to other social groups and the government. In the area of ideology, he shows the way in which the NCF's various departments worked with corporations to set up programs in recreation, religion, and education for workers. In the area of policies, he traces the network of cabinet-level and legislative-committee contacts through which the NCF was connected to government by means of overlapping memberships, business relationships, and friendships. The book ends with a chapter in which Weinstein shows that many of the principles formulated by the NCF between 1900 and 1915 were implemented by the federal government when NCF members and friends went to Washington to serve by appointment in the government during World War I.

Weinstein's argument is subtle and detailed, and it represents a major advance in Marxist thinking about power in America, but it is built on the same foundations as any other power structure analysis, Marxist or otherwise. It defines its ruling or power group—big capitalists. It establishes the networks through which they operate—corporations, policy-planning groups, special commissions, and general conferences. It analyzes the output of a central point in the network—NFC—in order to infer the ideology and programs of big capitalists. It establishes their networks to government and other social classes. And it shows they have the "power" to have their programs enacted by government (decisional criterion of power).

## CONCLUSION

The analysis of power structures has certain basic methodological components whether it is done by a pluralistic political scientist such as Dahl looking at decision making in New Haven or a Marxist historian such as Weinstein looking at political ideology. Power structure research involves mapping networks of people, institutions, and money flows, and then doing content analyses of the verbal and written outputs of those networks. This is the case whether the researcher builds his or her network with no preconceptions by use of reputational interviews with a random sample of citizens, or begins with a positional analysis of the directors of major banks and corporations because he or she is testing the hypothesis that big businesspeople dominate a given city or nation. It is the case if the researcher thinks in terms of social classes, groups and institutions, or individuals and coalitions. Sooner or later, the researcher will have to demonstrate the existence of a class, group, or coalition, and will have to show that it has power, whether by pointing to value distributions, positional overrepresentation, or the networks of people and institutions through which it directly or indirectly dominates governmental decisions.

Methodologically speaking, what differentiates various studies is the accuracy of their membership indicators, the completeness of their networks, and the type of power indicators they utilize. Dahl, in his study of New Haven, had only a partial picture of membership in the social and economic notables, an incomplete decisional network that he did not follow to its institutional bases in corporations, banks, law firms, and business associations, and only a situational indicator of power—successful intervention in the governmental decision-making process. Given the incompleteness of his network analysis and his theoretical neglect of systemic and structural power, this decisional indicator of power led him astray.

Different theoretical perspectives lead to inevitable differences in the types of questions asked and interpretations made. It might be possible to reduce some of the areas of disagreement if the methodology of power structure research was further developed and more widely utilized in its totality.

## NOTES

1. See the fine paper by Charles Kadushin, "Power, Influence, and Social Circles: A New Methodology for Studying Opinion Makers," *American Sociological Review* (October 1968), for an analysis which shows the basic similarity of the three traditional methods.

2. Mark S. Granovetter, "The Strength of Weak Ties," *American Journal of Sociology* (May 1973): 1360. Granovetter describes sociometry as the "precursor of network analysis."

3. Robert A. Dahl, "A Critique of the Ruling Elite Model," *American Political Science Review* (June 1958), as reprinted in G. William Domhoff and Hoyt B. Ballard (eds.), *C. Wright Mills and The Power Elite* (Beacon Press, 1968), p. 31.

4. Ibid. In writing this paper, Dahl was clearly reacting to the debate which had been generated in social science circles by Floyd Hunter's *Community Power Structure* (University of North Carolina Press, 1953) and C. Wright Mills's *The Power Elite* (Oxford University Press, 1956).

5. Dahl, "A Critique of the Ruling Elite Model," p. 31.

6. Robert A. Dahl, "The Concept of Power," *Behavioral Science* (July 1957). Within the social sciences this type of definition of power is usually traced back to Max Weber.

7. Steven Lukes, *Power: A Radical View* (Macmillan Press, 1974). This brief book, with a good annotated bibliography, presents a clear and insightful critique of recent conceptions of power within the social sciences.

8. Dahl, "The Concept of Power," p. 202.

9. Ibid.

10. Lukes, p. 31.

11. Robert R. Alford and Roger Friedland, "Political Participation and Public Policy," *Annual Review of Sociology* 1 (1975): 431, make the most recent social science argument for this general definition, concluding that "power is held by those who benefit over time from the operation of social, economic, and political structures."

12. James Stolzman and Herbert Gamberg, "Marxist Class Analysis versus Stratification Analysis as General Approaches to Social Inequality," *Berkeley Journal of Sociology* (1973-74): 111, make this point when they note that "this disparity [income inequality] was in Marx's estimation but one symptom of a more total and thoroughgoing relation of exploitation." I agree with Stolzman and Gamberg that income inequality and other power indicators are only rough approximations for an "index of exploitation."

13. This perfectly reasonable way of thinking about wealth within the political arena is not incompatible with conceiving of wealth as an indicator of group or class power.

14. Nelson Polsby, *Community Power and Political Theory* (Yale University Press, 1963), p. 132.

15. William C. Mitchell, "The Shape of Political Theory to Come: From Political Sociology to Political Economy," in Seymour M. Lipset (ed.), *Politics and the Social Sciences* (Oxford University Press, 1969), p. 114.

16. See Alford and Friedland for a more detailed presentation of this view of power.

17. Hunter uses *status* or *reputation* for power as one of his power indicators. This is a useful indicator which taps people's perceptions on "who benefits" and "who wins" in their community.

18. Dahl, "The Concept of Power," p. 202.

19. Ibid.

20. Dahl, "A Critique of the Ruling Elite Model," p. 32.

21. For a philosophical critique of Dahl's work from the point of view of a sophisticated political theorist, see Peter Euben, "Political Science and Political Silence," in Philip Green and Sanford Levinson (eds.), *Power and Community* (Vintage Books, 1970).

22. Bertram M. Gross, "Social Systems Accounting," in Raymond Bauer (ed.), *Social Indicators* (MIT Press, 1966), p. 187.

23. J. Clyde Mitchell, "The Concept and Use of Social Networks," in J. Clyde Mitchell (ed.), *Social Networks in Urban Situations* (University of Manchester Press, 1969), p. 2.

24. Hunter, *Community Power Structure*, pp. 130-34, gives a good example of this latter point when he shows that the White power network in Atlanta was connected to the small and less affluent Black power network through secondary figures and White politicians. By way of contrast, his more recent work on Atlanta shows that the White power network and the increasingly affluent Black power group now have more direct relationships through interlocking directorships and monthly meetings to discuss general city problems (Hunter, personal communication). If the links between the two power networks were to come to include *friendship, social intermingling,* and *intermarriage,* we could speak of them as an integrated social upper class.

25. The ways in which social anthropology substitutes network analysis for larger social theory are most forcefully pointed out by Edward Robbins, "Ethnicity, Networks, and Class: Current Trends in Anthropology," Meetings of the American Anthropological Association, December 1974, a paper in which he also points out that networks can be used to develop a class view of society in the Marxist sense.

26. Ronald L. Breiger, "The Duality of Persons and Groups," *Social Forces* (December 1974): 71.

27. Ronald L. Breiger, personal communication, October 21, 1975.

28. Breiger, "The Duality of Persons and Groups," p. 70. For examples of power structure research utilizing network conceptions and a variety of quantitative techniques, see Joel Levine, "The Sphere of Influence," *American Sociological Review* (February 1972); Edmund W. McLaughlin, "The Power Network in Phoenix: An Application of Smallest Space Analysis," *The Insurgent Sociologist* (Spring 1975); John Sonquist and Thomas Koenig, "Interlocking Directorships in the Top U.S. Corporations: A Graph Theory Approach," *The Insurgent Sociologist* (Spring 1975).

29. For an introduction to content analysis, see Ithiel de Sola Pool (ed.), *Trends in Content Analysis* (University of Illinois Press, 1959). For a sourcebook with numerous content analysis methods developed in the study of politics, poetry, mass media, and dreams, see George Gerbner et al. (eds.), *The Analysis of Communication Content*

(Wiley, 1969). An example of elementary content analysis relating to power structure research in the United States is Francis X. Sutton et al., *The American Business Creed* (Harvard University Press, 1956).

30. For summaries of pre-1960 positional studies on the United States, see Mills; Suzanne Keller, *Beyond The Ruling Class* (Random House, 1963). For more recent information, see G. William Domhoff, *Who Rules America?* (Prentice-Hall, 1967); Elizabeth Mintz, "The President's Cabinet, 1897-1972: A Contribution to the Power Structure Debate," *The Insurgent Sociologist* (Spring 1975); Richard Zweigenhaft, "Who Represents America?" *The Insurgent Sociologist* (Spring 1975); Michael Merlie and Edward Silva, "The First Family: Presidential Kinship and Its Theoretical Implications," *The Insurgent Sociologist* (Spring 1975). Positional mappings also predominate in the study of other countries. For a summary of these studies on Western Europe and Japan, see Ralph Miliband, *The State in Capitalist Society* (Basic Books, 1969).

31. Floyd Hunter, *Top Leadership USA* (University of North Carolina Press, 1959).

32. E.g., Carol E. Thometz, *The Decision Makers: The Power Structure of Dallas* (Southern Methodist University Press, 1963); William V. D'Antonio and William H. Form, *Influentials in Two Border Cities: A Study in Community Decision Making* (University of Notre Dame Press, 1965); Delbert C. Miller, *International Community Power Structures: Comparative Studies of Four World Cities* (Indiana University Press, 1970). The D'Antonio-Form and Miller books also show that businessmen are not as prominent in the reputational power structures found in cities in other countries.

33. For a convenient summary of earlier work and recent findings, see Charles M. Bonjean and Michael D. Grimes, "Community Power: Issues and Findings," in Joseph Lopreato and Lionel S. Lewis (eds.), *Social Stratification* (Harper & Row, 1974), pp. 381-83.

34. Polsby; Raymond Wolfinger, "Reputation and Reality in the Study of Community Power," *American Sociological Review* (October 1960).

35. Linton Freeman, Thomas J. Fararo, Warner Bloomberg, and Morris C. Sunshine, "Locating Leaders in Local Communities: A Comparison of Some Alternative Approaches," *American Sociological Review* (October 1963); Douglas M. Fox, "The Identification of Community Leaders by the Reputational and Decisional Methods," *Sociology and Social Research* (October 1969). For studies which do show overlap of decisional findings with those of the positional and/or reputational approaches, see James D. Preston, "Identification of Community Leaders," *Sociology and Social Research* (January 1969); William J. Conway, "Economic Dominants and Community Power: A Reputational and Decisional Analysis," *The American Journal of Economics and Sociology* (July 1973).

36. Raymond Bauer, "Social Psychology and the Study of Policy Formation," *American Psychologist* 21 (1966); Domhoff, *Who Rules America?* pp. 6-7, 144-46.

37. For somewhat similar orientations, see Delbert C. Miller, "Power, Complementarity, and the Cutting Edge of Research," *Sociological Focus* (Summer 1968): 11-13; Kadushin, pp. 693-96.

38. Methods for obtaining such information at the local level were outlined in 1952 in a paper reprinted as a research guide in the 1960s by Students for a Democratic Society and widely used in the civil rights and antiwar movements. See Robert K. Lamb, "How to Study Your Own Home Town," *Human Organization* (Summer 1952). Methods for obtaining such information on the national level from biographical references, business directories, law firm directories, and federal government directories can be found in the numerous articles in the *NACLA Research Guide* (NACLA, Box 226, Berkeley, Calif.). Other excellent starting points are *Open the*

*Books,* a guide to the study of corporations, and *People Before Property,* a guide to researching property ownership, both obtainable from Urban Planning Aid, 639 Massachusetts Avenue, Cambridge, Mass.

39. Not all informants will be equally useful if a cross-section of the community is interviewed. Howard J. Ehrlich, "The Social Psychology of Reputations for a Community Leadership, *Sociological Quarterly* (Fall 1967), presents new information and summarizes previous studies which show that only informants with high socioeconomic level, residential stability, participation in voluntary associations, and knowledge of community issues are able to provide more than one or two names. Only 48 percent of the people in Ehrlich's sample could give even one name, and only 18 percent could give four. A mere eighty people received a majority of the 2,299 nominations made in a county of 425,000 people, and only 705 names were produced in all.

For a brief account of the Hunter study of Oakland, see Floyd Hunter, "The Application of Computers to Community Power Study," in Frederick M. Wirt (ed.), *Future Directions in Community Power Research* (Institute of Governmental Studies, University of California, Berkeley, 1971).

For the Perrucci and Pilisuk study, see "Leaders and Ruling Elites: The Inter-organizational Bases of Community Power," *American Sociological Review* (December 1970).

40. For the questions that are usually asked to obtain this kind of information, see Hunter, *Community Power Structure;* Thometz; or Miller, *International Community Power Structures.*

41. Robert R. Alford, "New Haven: A Test of Stratification Theory?" unpublished manuscript, p. 44.

42. Bonjean and Grimes, p. 383.

43. Ibid., p. 384.

44. Hunter, *Community Power Structure,* pp. 214-15, 222-23.

45. Harvey Molotch and Marilyn Lester, "Accidents, Scandals, and Routines: Resources for Insurgent Methodology," *The Insurgent Sociologist* (Summer 1973).

46. Harvey Molotch, "Oil in Santa Barbara and Power in America," *Sociological Inquiry* (Winter 1970); Robert Sherrill, *The Last Kennedy* (Dial, 1976).

47. Molotch and Lester, pp. 3-4. The book by Banfield to which they refer *(Political Influence,* Free Press, 1962) is one of the most frequently cited evidences of pluralism aside from Dahl's *Who Governs?* The "pluralism" it reveals involves minor conflicts within a large power structure that has to coordinate with the top levels of an entrenched Democratic party organization.

48. Nicos Poulantzas, *Political Power and Social Classes* (New Left Books, 1973) is the fountainhead of this line of thought as it applies to power structure studies. For a statement of this view by the American Marxist who popularized it in the United States, see James O'Connor, *The Fiscal Crisis of the State* (St. Martin's Press, 1973), pp. 68-69, wherein it is said that "monopoly capitalist class interests (as a social force rather than as an abstraction) are not the aggregate of the particular interest of this class but rather emerge within the state administration 'unintentionally.' In this important sense, the capitalist state is not an 'instrument' but a 'structure.'"

49. Ralph Miliband, *The State in Capitalist Society,* p. 4.

50. Ibid., pp. 23, 59. Miliband concludes his third chapter with the claim that "what the evidence conclusively suggests is that in terms of social origin, education and class situation, the men who have manned *all* command positions in the state system have largely, and in many cases overwhelmingly, been drawn from the world of business and property, or from the professional middle classes" (p. 66).

51. Ibid., p. 262. After dozens of pages on control of the processes of political

socialization, Miliband gives over only one page to what he recognizes may be an even more important point, the subtle way in which "subordinate status" in itself tends to produce "qualified acceptance rather than its total rejection" (p. 263).

52. Ibid., p. 265.

53. (International Press, 1957), p. 13. Perlo is a leading theoretician of the Communist party in the United States.

54. Ibid., pp. 16, 17, 42, 61. Perlo says that the term *spider web* is an "excellent one to characterize the complex network of financial institutions through which the oligarchy runs the economic life of America," but that it oversimplifies the complexity of the network" (p. 61).

55. Ibid., p. 15.

56. Ibid., p. 280.

57. Ibid., p. 277.

58. Paul Sweezy, "The American Ruling Class," *Monthly Review* (May-June 1951). Reprinted in Paul M. Sweezy, *The Present as History* (Monthly Review Press, 1953), p. 120.

59. Ibid., p. 128. In a detailed empirical study, the amount of capital or property defining *big* would have to be specified, and more exact criteria would have to be developed for determining which small property-holders, executives, officials, and professionals should be included. Sweezy recognizes this point, and implies that interaction as social equals would be his criteria for membership in the ruling social class (e.g., pp. 124, 127).

60. Ibid., p. 134.

61. Ibid. I italicized *and thus indirectly control* in the quotation because it makes explicit the inference on which the power indicator is based. Sweezy is assuming that with most politicians there is usually "ready access" or a "quid pro quo" involved in large financial contributions. That is, campaign contributions are a means of influencing "who wins" in specific decision-making situations.

62. (Beacon, 1968), p. xv.

63. Ibid., p. 8. In presenting this network information, Weinstein is relying on the work of Gordon M. Jensen, "The National Civic Federation: American Business in an Age of Change and Reform, 1900-1910" (Ph.D. diss., Princeton University, 1956).

64. In content analysis terms, Weinstein does a qualitative content analysis using theoretical categories derived from Marxist theory.

# 5

# COMMUNITY POWER STRUCTURES AND THE NATIONAL RULING CLASS

Throughout the chapters devoted specifically to New Haven I suggested that the economic and social notables in that city were but one small part of a national ruling class, and that community power structures cannot be understood unless studied in relation to national power. It is now time to be more systematic about these points. In this final chapter I will describe the nature and functioning of the national ruling class, emphasizing the ways in which leading businessmen, bankers, and lawyers in New Haven are intertwined with it. I will also describe the networks of people and institutions through which the national ruling class dominates local government in the United States—shaping its structure, on the one hand, and facilitating federal-local governmental relations on the other. As noted in the Preface, it is hoped that this chapter will suggest a more fruitful departure point for community power studies.

By the mid-1970s there were over 300 journal articles and books dealing with community power structures, most of them written between 1955 and 1968. And yet, as several social scientists have pointed out, the findings from these studies are at great variance and do not add up to a systematic body of knowledge.[1] Analyses of these studies show that the mapping technique used—reputational or decisional—and the disciplinary background of the investigator—sociologist or political scientist—predict much of the variation in findings, hardly an encouraging revelation, but one which helps to explain why most social science textbooks on local government still end up rehashing the classic works of Hunter and Dahl, and then report in dismay that the distribution of power in communities remains an unsolved question.[2]

From my theoretical point of view, the major problem with the community power structure literature, for all its methodological difficulties, is its failure to consider local power in relationship to the national ruling class and the needs of the national corporate economy. Community power studies can be rescued from their dead end only if they focus on how the local community and its leadership group function within the national corporate structure, and on how that structure limits possible policy options of local governments. In the apt phrase of sociologist Harvey Molotch, the city must be seen as a "growth machine," one of the primary engines of a national capitalist system geared to capital accumulation and ever-increasing profits.[3] Cities often develop specialized functions in order to maximize their profit-making capacity. Some become commercial and retail centers, others become financial centers, still others educational or recreational centers, a point that is obvious when we think of such cases as Detroit (automobiles), Hartford (insurance), Las Vegas (recreation), or New Haven (education).

While mainstream social scientists now emphasize that community power structures do not function in a vacuum, the vertical linkages they search for are primarily to the federal government, which has come to play an increasing role in communities over the past two or three decades through programs in public works, housing, urban renewal, transportation, and welfare. Thus, sociologist Terry Clark begins his brief overview book on *Community Power and Policy Outputs* by noting that "community studies have too often assumed the community to be a closed system," that "the problem has become recognized as fundamental," and that "efforts are underway to provide answers." [4] However, ongoing research by himself and others he reviews contains no consideration of linkages to the national ruling class, large corporations, and urban policy-planning institutions, but only a consideration of ties to state and national government. The closest any of the studies come to considering the corporation-based national ruling class is with the variables "economic diversification," "absentee ownership," and "industrialization." [5]

## NEW HAVEN AND THE NATIONAL RULING CLASS

The goal in this section is to present a brief description of the national ruling class based upon previous research, and to demonstrate that the social and economic notables of New Haven are part of this ruling class. This can be accomplished by organizing the information into four basic assertions.

1. *The American ruling class is a social upper class nationwide in scope.* Comprising at most .5 to 1 percent of the population, the social upper class in the United States is made up of wealthy businesspeople and their descendants. Although businesspeople are the core of the class, many of its members have become corporate lawyers, architects, professors, artists, physicians, and jet setters. The continuity of the upper class is very great, with many core families which go back several generations or more. At the same time, there are new families joining each generation, families where the breadwinner has struck it rich, slowly climbed a corporation hierarchy, or accumulated stock and other wealth while earning a high salary as a foundation executive, university president, legal adviser, or consultant. New members also come into the upper class through intermarriage, with wealthy young women marrying academically successful law and graduate students, and wealthy young men marrying the more attractive and educated of middle-class women.[6] The social standards of this class are maintained by a variety of mechanisms, including common schooling, common club memberships, and the use of social secretaries to arrange debutante balls and other social gatherings. There is a great deal of intermingling of old and new rich, despite some gossip about the "age" of a family's money; this intermingling is especially great among their children. Interaction in a variety of settings—schools, country clubs, resorts, parties, and charitable events—leads to a considerable amount of intermarriage, the sine qua non of a social class.[7]

The social and economic notables of New Haven are tied in to this national upper class in two ways. First, the most prominent families and business leaders in New Haven go to the same schools, vacation in many of the same resorts, and belong to many of the same clubs as their wealthy counterparts in larger cities around the country.[8] Second, many upper-class people from other cities are members of New Haven social clubs, in good part because so many wealthy leaders graduated from Yale, to which they often return for alumni gatherings and sporting events.[9]

The social connections of New Haven notables to the rest of the upper class can be shown most directly in the case of club memberships. Twenty-four of the sixty-four locally-based economic notables listed in biographical sources which contain club information are in social clubs in other parts of the country. By far the most frequent of these nonlocal connections is the Yale Club of New York, with ten. There are also two memberships in the Hartford Club in Hartford, the Century Association in New York, and the Farmington Country Club in Virginia. Of the forty-seven nonlocals among New Haven economic notables on whom club information could be located, twenty-seven are in exclusive clubs in other cities. Seven are in the Hartford Club, seven in the Algonquin Club in Boston, and four are in the Links Club in New York, a club which sociologist E. Digby Baltzell characterizes as "the New York rendezvous of the national corporate establishment." [10] From one to three are in elite clubs in Providence, Baltimore, Pittsburgh, and Chicago.

2. *The American ruling class provides basic leadership for top banks and corporations in the United States.* Through interlocking directorships, common stock ownership, holding companies, and other mechanisms, the big-business community is a complex network that encompasses all regions of the country. While the network is comprised of city-based and regional cliques at its densest points, there are multimillionaires, highly paid corporate executives, and university-based experts who serve as bridges from one clique to another, tying the network into one large whole. Companies such as American Telephone and Telegraph, General Electric, Security Pacific Bank, Morgan Guaranty Trust, and Chase Manhattan Bank serve as key focal points.[11]

The predominance of upper-class people in this corporate network was shown in detail by Baltzell for the city of Philadelphia. Using the Philadelphia *Social Register,* Eastern private schools, and exclusive Philadelphia clubs as his upper-class referents, he demonstrated that the officers and directors of major banks, insurance companies, and manufacturing concerns in the city were part of the upper class.[12] Expanding on Baltzell's work, I showed in 1967 that 53 percent of the 884 men directing the largest fifteen banks, fifteen insurance companies, and twenty industrials met one or more indicators of upper-class standing, a very high percentage for a segment of the population that accounts for less than 1 percent of the total.[13]

More recently, I found that 673 of the largest 797 corporations for 1969 had at least one connection to an interlocking social network of 11 upper-class clubs and four policy-planning groups. Even more impressive, virtually all of the top 25 corporations in each business category were related to this network—25 of 25 for industrials, 25 of 25 for banks, 23 of 25 for insurance companies, 24 of 25 for transportation companies, 24 of 25 for utilities, 19 of 25 for retails, and 18 of 25 for conglomerates.[14] Many corporations had more than one connection to the club-policy network. General Motors, the largest industrial company at the time, had 29 connections via its 23-man board of directors—9 ties to the Links Club of New York; 5 to the Detroit Club; 1 each to the Century Association in New York, the Somerset Club in Boston, the Bohemian Club in San Francisco, and 12 to three policy-planning groups. Bank of America, the largest bank, had 29 connections; AT&T, the largest utility, had 40; and Sears, Roebuck, the largest retail, had 19. The company with the most connections to the network was Chase Manhattan Bank with 47. The findings of this study can also be analyzed in terms of the corporate ties of specific clubs, which more directly shows upper-class involvement in corporations. The Links Club, for example, had 113 connections to the largest 25 banks and 79 connections to the largest 25 industrials, while the Pacific Union Club in San Francisco had 53 connections to the largest 25 banks and 24 to the biggest industrials.

The economic notables in New Haven are part of this nationwide corporate network. Through these men, New Haven-based corporations are only one or two steps removed from most major corporations on the Eastern seaboard, and even from several large businesses based in Chicago and Los Angeles. These linkages are accomplished in two ways—by the outside directorships maintained by economic leaders who live in New Haven, and by the New Haven directorships of economic leaders who live in other cities. Local New Haven business leaders are directors of eighteen corporations in other cities. Most of these corporations are rather small or regional in nature, but two or three, such as Canada Dry Corporation and Monroe Calculating Machines, are well known nationally. By far the more important economic ties of the New Haven business community to the national corporate network are those of outsiders who sit on New Haven boards, a finding which reflects the secondary nature of the New Haven business community within the national structure. Seventy-one directors from outside New Haven link New Haven corporations to well over one hundred businesses, dozens of which are of nationwide stature. The most frequent of these ties are to nearby Bridgeport and Hartford through a number of businesses, but there are also numerous connections to companies in Boston and New York. The presence of Sears, Roebuck executives on the boards of both Safety Industries and High Standard Manufacturing provides a connection to Chicago, and the fact that Seamless Rubber Company (at the time period under consideration, the 1950s) was a subsidiary of Rexall Drugs provides a link to Los Angeles.

A handful of companies are responsible for bringing the most prominent of these men to New Haven—Sargents and Company; Safety Industries; New York, New Haven, and Hartford Railroad; and Southern New England Telephone. The most central of these is Southern New England Telephone, with men on its board who also sit on New York Trust Company, Chase Manhattan Bank, First National City Bank of New York, Travelers Insurance, United Aircraft, and Burlington Industries, among many. Economically speaking, it is the board meetings of Southern New England Telephone wherein national business leaders "interface" with top leaders from New Haven, for the five New Haveners on the board are also directors of First New Haven National Bank (three); Connecticut Savings (two); and New Haven Savings Bank, Berger Brothers, New Haven Gas, and Security Insurance.

3. *The American ruling class is the major repository of corporate legal advice in the country.* The largest law firms in each city, dominated by partners with impeccable social credentials, are linked to each other through active involvement in such nationwide organizations as the American Bar Association, the American Law Institute, and the American Judicature Society, and through local services they provide for each other's major corporation and bank clients.[15] New Haven is no exception. Its major law firms, which already have been shown to serve the largest businesses in New Haven, also provide local counsel for several non–New Haven corporations. Thus, Wiggin and Dana, which has such important local clients as Yale University, First New Haven National Bank, Union and New Haven Trust, and United Illuminating, also has working relations with Metropolitan Life, Prudential, Liberty Mutual, Detroit Steel, and Western Union. Gumbart, Corbin, Tyler, and Cooper, counsel for numerous large firms in New Haven, is local counsel for such national giants as Equitable Life, New York Life, Mutual Life Insurance Company of New York, and Aetna. Biggest of the outside clients for Morgan, Morse, Well and Murphy is General Motors Acceptance Corporation, followed by General Ice Cream Corporation and Fidelity and Casualty Company of New York. Stoddard, Persky, Eagen and Cokey take care of local legal problems for Interstate Department Stores and John Hancock Mutual Life.

4. *The American ruling class dominates government and public debate in the United States through a variety of policy-planning organizations.* Funded by corporate dues, foundation grants, and personal donations, policy organizations—the best known of which are the Council on Foreign Relations and the Committee for Economic Development—provide a setting wherein bankers, busi-

nesspeople, and lawyers from every part of the United States join together to discuss common problems, iron out differences, groom new spokespeople, hear the advice of hired experts from universities and think tanks, and formulate policies and programs to cope with changing economic and political realities. The policy-planning groups are also connected to major corporations through common directors. The Committee for Economic Development, for example, had 46 connections to the top 25 industrials during the late 1960s and early 1970s; it also had 63 among the biggest 25 banks. The Council on Foreign Relations had 58 and 53 connections, respectively, to these two sectors of the corporate community for the same time period. A detailed study of 154 Business Council members for 1970 found that its members had 730 directorships in 435 corporations, including 176 of the top 797.[16]

Policy-planning groups connect to government through a variety of methods:

1. members of these groups are often appointed to important government positions;

2. members of these groups are often appointed to special presidential commissions which suggest new policy;

3. members and employees of these groups often testify before Congress or consult with agencies of the executive branch;

4. the organizations publish books, pamphlets, journals, and position papers which are widely read in government circles;

5. members of these organizations often start ad hoc groups to influence government and public opinion on specific issues of concern to them.[17]

As might be expected in the case of these relatively small leadership groups, which recruit on a nationwide basis, only a few locally-based economic notables in New Haven are members of the major policy-planning groups. James W. Hook, whom Dahl describes as one of the leading businessmen in New Haven (p. 116), was a member of the Business Council until his death in 1958, as was Fred R. Fairchild, an emeritus Yale professor who turned eighty in 1957 while serving as a director of United Illuminating and Connecticut Savings Bank. Similarly, only a few of the nonlocal economic notables are members of these exclusive leadership groups, one of the more prominent being New Yorker Richard C. Patterson, Jr., a director of the New York, New Haven, and Hartford Railroad, who was in both the Business Council and the Council on

Foreign Relations. In the case of policy groups, by far the most important ties between the national ruling class and New Haven are provided by Yale. Yale's board of trustees for the late 1950s included several men who were members of these organizations, among them former secretary of state Dean Acheson (Council on Foreign Relations), J. P. Morgan and Company executive Charles D. Dickey (Business Council), Pan American World Airways president Juan Trippe (Business Council, Council on Foreign Relations, Committee for Economic Development), and Standard Oil heir John Hay Whitney (Business Council, Council on Foreign Relations). In addition, Yale academics were advisors to many of these groups. Significantly, two of Mayor Lee's most ardent Yale supporters on urban renewal, president A. Whitney Griswold and law school dean Eugene V. Rostow, were active in the Council on Foreign Relations. Indeed, the numerous roles—local, regional, and national—played by Griswold and Rostow are symbolic of the complex relationships which unite leaders of specific institutions and cities into a nationwide ruling structure.

It is through one of the policy-planning networks linking corporations, foundations, policy groups, and government that the American ruling class dominates local governments, and it is to that network that we will turn in the next section as the starting point of a discussion of how the national ruling class dominates local government.

Hopefully, the previous few pages have provided an overview of the national upper class and an adequate summary of the kind of social, economic, legal, and policy-group linkages which provide the evidence for the claim that social and economic notables of New Haven can be considered part of this national upper class. In presenting this evidence for New Haven involvement in a national upper class, I am not asserting that each and every one of the local social and economic notables qualify on national-level criteria as members of the national upper class. However, I am asserting that there is enough overlap for New Haven social and economic notables to be considered a "local branch" of the national upper class.

This claim is clearly a matter of judgement, and it implies criteria for ascertaining whether or not a local elite is part of a national social grouping. These criteria include the degree of involvement in, or overlap with, the nationwide upper class. However, because so few studies of this question have been done, the judgement remains qualitative, guided by the most general categories for characterizing local upper classes. On one extreme, there is considerable overlap and interaction—in schools, clubs, resorts, and corporations—among the very wealthiest families and businesspeople in the largest cities all over the country, and they are the focal points of the national upper class. At the other extreme, as community studies of social stratification have shown, there are small cities and towns with few or no members of the local elite who qualify as members of the national upper class. In such cases it might be more appropriate to talk of a "local upper class" rather than of a "local branch" of the national upper class.

New Haven falls in neither of these obvious categories. However, the extent of local elite overlap with elites in larger cities is considerable and impressive. Due to the age and location of New Haven, and the presence of Yale University and several major corporate headquarters, local notables maintain a degree of interaction with wealthy business families from neighboring large cities that is likely to prove greater than that for cities of comparable size in other parts of the nation. The secondary nature of New Haven within the national structure can be made somewhat precise by noting that more big businessmen from outside New Haven come to that city for corporate board meetings than there are New Haven businessmen who go to other cities for major board meetings. Similarly, there are more outsiders with national-level social connections who belong to New Haven social clubs (in good part because of their ties to Yale) than there are New Haveners who belong to prestigious social clubs outside the city.

In terms of social interaction, it is possible to conceptualize local upper classes as levels within a national upper class, with the level assigned a given city depending upon the degree of overlap with elites in other cities in the network. This would be the kind of empirical solution to the problem suggested by clique-detection methods based on algebras which uncover hierarchies among complex matrices of overlapping memberships.[18] Whatever label we put on a local upper class which had little or no overlap with the national upper class, there would still remain the question of how the more isolated or strictly localized elites related to the national-level structures of class and power. In terms of that question, the problem would be to determine if isolated elites had more difficulty in gaining access to the federal government and/or had more conflict with their less localized counterparts in other cities.

In summary, New Haven's social and economic notables are a branch of the national ruling class, albeit a secondary branch. At the same time, this may be in good part a matter of labeling. The important question of how local elites relate to the national-level ruling class and the federal government still remains whatever designation is given to a local upper class in a city like New Haven.

It is to this question of how the national ruling class relates to local government in general that we now turn.

## THE URBAN POLICY-PLANNING NETWORK

The American ruling class began as a series of separate, local ruling classes. Only gradually in the eighteenth century, and especially in the years before and after the Revolutionary War, did the ruling class become somewhat united and national in scope.[19] During that century, and throughout the nineteenth as well, these local branches of the ruling class dominated their home cities directly by serving on the city council and in the mayor's office. In this regard the history of New Haven as traced by Dahl in *Who Governs?* is quite typical. From 1784 to 1842, the mayors of New Haven were from the patrician group of "established" families that had founded the city. For the next fifty-eight years, most of the mayors were from the rising group of businessmen who pushed their way into the higher circles through success in industrial and financial enterprises. As Dahl says (p. 11), there is no question about who dominated the city during this long period.

The situation became less clear in the twentieth century, not only in New Haven, but in other cities as well. Industrialization, massive immigration, and urbanization of the rural population were filling the cities with a working class that increasingly wrestled the ruling class for power in the city, sometimes through the Democratic party political machine, sometimes (in 1900-17) through the Socialist party. Many members of the upper and upper-middle classes were moving into the suburbs, making it even more difficult for big property owners to maintain direct control of the city government. These changes, as Dahl shows, were reflected in the changing backgrounds of mayors. "Ex-plebes," most of whom had attained middle-class status, were replacing the big businessmen in the mayor's office *(Who Governs?,* ch. 4).

As these several changes in the city were taking place around the turn of the century, there appeared the beginnings of the policy-planning network which would later develop the programs, techniques, and rationales for domination of local governments by a suburbanized ruling class facing insurgency from both the working class and rising small businessmen of ethnic origins. That is, as political challenges in the local governmental arena began to raise the possibility of a systemic and structural challenge to ruling-class domination, leading members of the ruling class, with the advice and help of urban experts, reacted by creating a new set of private and governmental structures which would absorb and deflect this growing challenge.[20] The new ruling-class network which created these structures operated under the ideology of "good government," which meant "efficient," "businesslike" government by experts and technicians, as opposed to the "corrupt," "machine-dominated," and "political" government alleged to exist in a growing number of cities. The new movement claimed to make government more democratic and less boss-dominated, although the actual effects of the reforms were to increase the centralization of decision making, remove more governmental functions from electoral control, and decrease the percentage of workers and socialists elected to city councils.

It was not merely disagreements with political machines and socialists which motivated the "good government" forces. Especially in its earliest stages, the movement was concerned to provide more efficient and less costly government. Formerly content to make deals with machine politicians, businessmen were coming to need better city government in order to develop the infrastructure necessary to attract still greater capital investment and capital accumulation:

> Aversion to graft, alone, was not enough to move businessmen to sponsor reform. Though costly, business had accepted and lived with graft for many years. What converted these men into civic reformers was the increased importance of the public functions in the twentieth-century city. Streets had to be paved for newly developed motor vehicles; harbors had to be deepened and wharves improved for big, new freighters. In addition, electric lighting systems, street railways, sewage disposal plants, water supplies, and fire departments had to be installed or drastically improved to meet the needs of inhabitants, human and commercial, of hundreds of rapidly growing industrial centers.[21]

The origin of a nationwide "good government" movement, a movement which is called "middle class" in many social science textbooks, is best symbolized by the meeting in 1894 of local reformers from twenty-one cities in thirteen states. This National Conference for Good City Government brought together about 150 delegates and invited guests, many of whom were leading businessmen, lawyers, journalists, and academics from their respective locales. The connections—social and economic—of these delegates show that a great many were hardly middle class except in the European sense of the term (capitalists, as opposed to feudal aristocrats).[22]

The conference led to the formation of a permanent National Municipal League three months later. It was this organization which was to carry the general ideology and formulate the specific plans of the ruling class in the local arena for three decades, as well as to encourage the later organizations with which it joined to form the urban policy network. Three years after its formation, the National Municipal League, through a special committee made up of businessmen, lawyers, and university professors, began work on a municipal program which would put into practice what the league saw as the essential principles that must underlie successful city government. The committee report, which became a model for charter discussions around the country, called for nonpartisan citywide elections, no salary for city council members, and elections at times other than when state and national elections were being held.[23] As many critics at the time objected, the proposals would make it much harder for workers and Socialists, usually based in specific wards and without the name identification needed in nonpartisan elections, to be elected.

The National Municipal League continued to develop and promote its suggestions for municipal government over the years. By far its most successful modification was in 1915, when it began a campaign for the establishment of what is called the "council-manager" form of government. Under this plan, created by one of the league's members in 1910, the city is seen as a corporation which should be run like any other business. A city council elected at large serves as the board of directors, and a city manager hired by the council functions as chief executive officer in charge of implementing policies and controlling administrative staff. In theory, there was said to be a separation between politics and administration, but subsequent studies have shown that the city manager often becomes an important political figure in the policymaking process.[24]

The council-manager form of government, in conjunction with citywide nonpartisan elections and other league reforms, served to depoliticize city government and turn the city over to businessmen and their hired city managers.[25] Not surprisingly, local chambers of commerce usually pushed for the council-manager form of government. Local businessmen adopted the mantle of reformers in their respective home towns: "The initiative for commission [council] and manager government came consistently from chambers of commerce and other organized business groups; they were the decisive element, in coalition with civic reformers, which made the movement a sweeping success." [26]

The Socialist party and the Democrats fought the city manager form of government favored by the National Municipal League and the chambers of commerce. They were successful in this fight in many large cities, but lost in smaller ones. By 1919, 130 cities had adopted the new plan, and hundreds more were to follow in the next few years. By 1965, over half the cities between 25,000 and 250,000 in population were functioning under council-manager government. The figure was 40 percent for all cities with more than 5,000 citizens, and the plan was especially popular in suburbs.[27]

The National Municipal League did not function in isolation. The good-government forces also created other organizations to cope with businessmen's city problems. One of the most important was the municipal research bureau, an organization to provide the facts and figures in each city, and to provide advice to city officials in drafting legislation and creating administrative structures. Municipal research bureaus sprang up in the first ten years of the century, reaching into dozens of cities by 1940. Their most important successes came in the 1920s and 1930s. They disappeared from the scene after World War II, except in a few cities where they were especially prominent.[28]

Municipal bureaus died in good part because of their success, for many of their suggestions were adopted and many of their functions were taken over by city agencies. They were also eclipsed by the centralization of their functions into a group of national organizations developed in the late 1920s and early 1930s. A prototype of these national organizations was the Bureau of Municipal Research in New York, transformed into a national Institute for Public Administration. It remains today one of the central organizations in the urban network, providing advice to the National Municipal League, the Committee for Economic Development, and other policy-planning groups.

The New York bureau was the first municipal research bureau to be created. Founded by prominent New Yorkers of great wealth, it received a significant minority of its money from men of even greater wealth, such as John D. Rockefeller and Andrew Carnegie: "By 1914 the New York Bureau had spent $950,000, of which $125,000 was contributed by John D. Rockefeller, $117,000 by R. Fulton Cutting, $55,000 by Andrew Carnegie, and $52,000 from Mrs. Edward H. Harriman."[29] Within a short time the bureau was working closely with New York City government. The historian of the movement claims that "for several city administrations the Bureau became virtually an official agency."[30] It was the success of the New York bureau which encouraged the creation of bureaus elsewhere, and it was in part the need for researchers and administrators in these new bureaus that led the New York bureau into the development of a Training School for Public Service in 1911 and its eventual evolution into the Institute for Public Administration.

By 1916 the good-government forces were working through several organizations which some leaders wanted to amalgamate into one large organization. According to this idea, the National Municipal League, the National Civil Service Reform League, the National Voters League, and the Short Ballot Organization would be merged into a single unit. One of the people arguing against this plan was Raymond B. Fosdick of the Rockefeller Foundation. Fosdick's comments are of special interest because Rockefeller money was coming to have considerable influence on political science and public administration, and was to have an even greater impact in the next twenty years. Fosdick argued that "progress is not achieved in the fashion that [is here] implied. Reform is never accepted wholesale. Civic ideals never advance in a uniform line. A little progress in this direction is followed by a little progress in another direction, or from another angle." [31]

Fosdick then suggested the organizational form which was later adopted, in good part because of Rockefeller funding: "our many organizations [would] club together to support a common selling agency or clearinghouse, whose business it would be to take the well established results of study and investigations, and by temperate, sure-footed, and dignified publicity put them before the entire country." [32] This strategy, which took many years until it reached fruition, was carried out by another Rockefeller employee, Beardsley Ruml, working through another Rockefeller foundation, the Laura Spelman Rockefeller Memorial Fund. (Spelman was the maiden name of Mrs. John D. Rockefeller.) In conjunction with political scientist Charles Merriam of the University of Chicago, Ruml encouraged the creation of the Public Administration Clearing House at the University of Chicago. Founded in 1930, PACH's organizers were Richard S. Childs, president of the National Municipal League; Luther Gulick, head of the Institute of Public Administration in New York; and Louis M. Brownlow, a former city manager who had come to know Ruml and Merriam.[33]

PACH was only the first step in the overall organization of the urban policy network. As Brownlow recalls it, PACH was to be at the center of a group of organizations. Ruml and one of his assistants, Guy Moffett, had drawn up a chart which outlined the projected urban policy-planning network in straightforward terms:

That chart consisted essentially of a circle in the middle of a page labeled, "Central Clearing of Information." From it radiated lines which led to circles at the top of the page labeled with the names of organizations such as the Assembly of Civil Service Commissions, the City Managers' Association, the Governors' Conference, the Legislators' Association, and one other labeled "other organizations of public officials." Under these was the note: "Secretariats of the above organizations to be located as far as possible at the same place as the central clearing house of information." At the right of the center circle, one line ran to a circle labeled "Coordination of Publication Activities." On the lower part of the page the lines ran from the center to circles designating existing research organizations such as the Institute of Public Administration, The Brookings Institution, private consulting organizations, universities, and other technical groups. Underneath these was a note: "Activities correlated to some extent to Social Science Research Council." [34]

Among the organizations brought to Chicago by PACH was the Municipal Administration Service, a research department of the National Municipal League which had been created in 1926 with an ongoing grant from the Spelman Fund. Renamed the Public Administration Service, it became one of the most important members of the group. Also brought to Chicago in the late 1920s and early 1930s were such groups as the American Public Welfare Association, the American Municipal League (now called the National League of Cities), the United States Conference of Mayors, the Municipal Finance Officers' Association, and the International City Managers' Association.

Typical of these organizations in its development and functioning was the International City Manager's Association, whose history has been traced in some detail.[35] The organization was founded in 1914, three years after the first council-manager government was adopted. Although it received considerable help from the U.S. Chamber of Commerce in its early years, ICMA did not become an organization of any significance until it came under the financial wing of the Spelman Fund and the Rosenwald Fund of Chicago in 1928. Merriam, Ruml, and Brownlow were the central figures in arranging this new funding relationship. The association was then moved to Chicago, and by 1935 was receiving two-thirds of its operating revenue from the Rockefeller Foundation, which had absorbed the Spelman Fund within its general structure. This financial tie did not end until 1947, when the organization was solidly on its own two feet.

ICMA served several functions. Most importantly, it created national standards and guidelines for the new city manager profession, and promoted the implementation of these guidelines in the training of young city managers. Many universities, encouraged by the grants that foundations close to ICMA were willing to provide, developed courses or programs to carry out the training. ICMA also became a placement center for aspiring city managers, creating a national job market in the field; this further encouraged city managers towards a national and professional orientation. Finally, ICMA provided policy suggestions, research, and a forum for the exchange of ideas among practicing city managers. Taken together, these functions have led to the structuring of a profession which does not have to take specific directions from ruling-class leaders on each and every issue. ICMA "institutionalized" the efficiency and business-oriented mentality which the ruling class wished to have in city administrators.[36]

One of the last groups to join the associations around PACH was the American Society for Public Administration (ASPA), a group which grew to be of great significance by the 1960s. It was founded in 1940 by such public administration leaders at Brownlow, William E. Mosher, dean of the Maxwell School of Citizenship and Public Affairs at Syracuse, and Donald C. Stone, a former Brownlow employee. After an attempt to induce either The Brookings Institution or the Institute of Public Administration to support the fledgling organization, PACH became its major financial underwriter. Finally, in 1956, it was decided that the society could become self-supporting with a special effort to attract members and increase earnings, so a five-year development grant was obtained from the Ford Foundation.[37]

At the same time as Ford was making the grant to ASPA, PACH was disbanded because the foundations thought it had outlived its usefulness. Many of PACH's functions in the area of personnel and publicity were taken over by ASPA. Liaison tasks with administrative agencies of the United Nations and nongovernmental organizations of administrators in Europe were taken over by the Institute of Public Administration with a grant from the Ford Foundation.

These urban organizations, which came to be known as the "1313" group in academic circles because of their common address at 1313 East 60th Street in Chicago, have shaped thinking on urban government since they were brought together in the early 1930s to form a loosely knit unit and create nationwide professional standards and policy guidelines. As Brownlow acknowledged, by the 1950s all of these organizations were "integral and important parts of the American governmental (albeit not official) structure." [38]

Because the federal government has taken an increasing role in urban affairs since the 1960s, many organizations have moved to

Washington, where they have become an urban lobby as well as a policy-planning network. In addition, the groups have been joined by a new policy-discussion organization, the Urban Coalition, which was formed in response to the ghetto uprisings of the 1960s, and by the Urban Institute, which was created in 1968 as a "RAND Corporation" to help the federal government solve urban problems.[39] Then too, the nationally oriented Committee for Economic Development has come to focus more of its attention on local government through specific subcommittees, providing another direct link between the corporate community and the urban policy network. CED committees, which bring together business leaders with experts and administrators from the urban policy-planning groups, have issued four reports on improving and modernizing local government. The reports are meant to serve as guidelines for local businessmen responding to urban problems; they usually call for consolidation of government units, greater centralization of administrative authority, and the creation of superagencies.[40]

Although the U.S. Chamber of Commerce disagrees with some organizations within the urban policy network on specific legislative issues, it works closely with members of the network in helping to shape the structure of local government. Its 1967 pamphlet on *Modernizing Local Government* acknowledges coordination with the National League of Cities, the National Municipal League, and the International City Manager's Association, among others. For basic information on urban reform, the chamber suggests that local businessmen obtain booklets put out by CED, the NML, the National League of Cities, the American Bar Association, the International City Managers' Association, and other organizations which link into the urban policy network.[41]

Despite institutionalization of professional administrative associations and CED's increasing interest in municipal problems, the National Municipal League remains an integral part of the business-dominated urban policy network. Serving on its executive council in the 1970s were business figures from every region of the country, including the president of a leading bank in Atlanta, a partner in a major law firm in St. Louis, and top executives from Ford Motor Company, Pittsburgh Plate Glass, and Aetna Life and Casualty Company. Through these men, the NML helps link the urban policy network to policy-planning groups in other issue area, in particular the Council on Foreign Relations, The Brookings Institution, and the American Assembly.[42]

The urban policy network is tightly knit in personnel and financing, but it is not united on each and every issue. Tensions between the "housers" and the "real estate lobby" described in chapter 3 highlight this point. Generally speaking, these conflicts reflect long-standing differences within the business community between corporate liberals (as embodied in the Committee for Economic Development and large international corporations) and the old-fashioned conservatives (as personified by the U.S. Chamber of Commerce and more local businesses).[43]

## THE METRO GOVERNMENT MOVEMENT

While the urban policy network had considerable success in maintaining direct business control in smaller cities through such devices as nonpartisan citywide elections and the council-manager form of government, these "reforms" were not successful in most big cities. In larger cities, workers and smaller businessmen, especially when well organized into political machines, were able to defeat proposals for this type of government.[44] Urban policy leaders within the ruling class began to realize that large, heterogenous cities required a "strong-mayor" form of government.[45] This realization provided the basis for compromise with Democratic machines and/or minority groups in many cities.

In accepting the need for a strong-mayor form of government, big-city ruling classes were admitting that they would prefer to reach a better accommodation with political machines rather than risk a potentially more divisive conflict with the working classes of their respective cities by trying to have city charters amended in the state legislatures, whose creatures the cities are in the American system.[46] Such accommodation was by and large achieved, although ruling-class spokespersons continued to inveigh against "corruption," "bossism" and "cronyism" through the public opinion organs of the urban policy network. The mechanisms of this accommodation were several, including introduction of a "chief administrative officer" to help the mayor. Equally important were the continuance of financial contributions to the machine and the placing of legal, insurance, construction, and service contracts with the smaller businessmen and lawyers who are part of the machine.[47] Finally, increasing necessity for federal funding in the city allowed local business leaders the opportunity to offer their services to the mayor in his or her dealings with state and federal governments.[48]

Members of the ruling class did not merely settle for the compromise reform of strong-mayor government in large urban areas. They also pushed very hard, once again through the urban policy network, for "metropolitan government," meaning forms of government which transcend city limits and encompass the whole of the urban-suburban metropolis in one governmental form or another. And once again, these plans were by and large thwarted, except in cities such as Miami where there is no well-organized working class, no strong minority movement, and no political machine. But defeats of metro plans were not merely based upon rejection by working-class Democrats. Suburban Republicans of white-collar status were opposed to incorporation into the cities which they purposely had left behind.[49]

With the failure of metro government schemes, local branches of the ruling class in big cities have had to settle for lesser governmental reforms. Certain of these reforms—greater use of annexation powers, transfer or consolidation of specific municipal functions, and creation of special metropolitan-wide districts to perform specific functions—are fairly commonplace. Voluntary associations of local officials have been organized in many areas to encourage cooperation among all cities in the metropolis. They provide a forum for discussion, issue research reports, and occasionally speak as one voice. But the limits to ruling-class power to create structural changes in the governance of large cities are clearly revealed in the defeats of metropolitan government. The ruling class may be able to keep the urban policy debate within fairly narrow limits, but it cannot implement all of its structural plans.

## FEDERAL-LOCAL RELATIONS

The new local-government structures and the ideology of expertise generated by the urban planning network have given the ruling class considerable leverage over city governments. The contributions of this network are not limited to this scope. It also facilitates ruling-class domination of local governments by interposing itself between the federal government and local communities. The organizations of the urban policy network, by providing information and lobbying services in Washington for city governments, help shape the way in which federal aid and services come to cities. This function of the urban policy network first manifested itself in the early New Deal when Louis Brownlow and the Public Administration Clearing House were called upon to help the federal government set up the Public Works Administration to give grants and loans to cities for construction projects. PACH not only suggested the administrative structure through which the program functioned, but provided many of the experts who ran the program.[50]

The relationship between PACH and the New Deal was initiated by Guy Moffett of the Spelman Fund. Moffett made the contact rather than one of the other members of the policy network around PACH because he was a very close friend of Louis Howe, President Franklin D. Roosevelt's most trusted White House aide: "Mr. Moffett took to Mr. Howe a proposal from Public Administration Clearing

House which suggested the President might possibly decide to make certain specific studies and inquiries for which no existing appropriation was available and that, in such event, upon the written request of a member of the Cabinet, the Clearing House would make available, within limits, a sufficient amount of money to finance these studies." [51] The language is laborious, but what it says is quite clear—foundations and policy groups were penetrating the federal government directly and providing a way for the executive branch of government to bypass Congress and strengthen its administrative capabilities. The proposal was duly accepted by the president, cabinet leaders were notified, and, as Brownlow recounts, "immediately requests began to come in." [52]

An even greater intermediary role in federal-local relations on the part of the urban policy network came with the passage of the urban renewal program. This program was the most significant factor in federal-local relations in the fifteen years following its passage. And, as chapter 3 in this book and the work of Roger Friedland and John Mollenkopf have demonstrated, it was the big-business community which shaped the urban renewal program at the national and local levels and helped determine which cities received the biggest grants.[53] Urban policy groups played a similar role in public housing, transportation, and other national-local programs.

As important as the urban lobby is in shaping local governmental structures and securing federal legislation for urban areas, its influence should not be overstated. It can determine the agenda of discussions and set the limits of what is an acceptable alternative, but its plans for local governments are not always accepted as a guide for action because the needs of specific local ruling elites may vary from the general norm. Political scientists Edward Banfield and James Q. Wilson put the matter well:

> There is a tendency for the activists in local government—especially civic association executives, but many bureaucrats and some newspaper editors as well—to take their general policy lines from the executives of the national foundations, from federal agencies, and from such national bodies as the International City Managers' Association, the National Municipal League, the National Association of Housing and Redevelopment Officials, and the American Institute of Planners. The agenda of city government is being determined more and more by professionals within such bodies and less and less by the needs and problems of the particular city. This is not to say that cities are likely to do all, or even very much, of what the

national "experts" say they should do. It is the subjects to be discussed, not the actions to be taken, that will be decided nationally.[54]

Banfield and Wilson's point is useful, for it reveals the limitations of the national urban policy network. It suggests that branches of the ruling class and localized elites must have mechanisms in their respective cities through which the acceptance, rejection, or adaptation of general principles are determined. Such mechanisms do exist, and we now turn to an overview of the localized branches of the urban policy network.

## RULING-CLASS NETWORKS IN SPECIFIC CITIES

In smaller cities, the Chamber of Commerce is usually the focal point through which the business community adapts national programs and creates local ones to meet specific needs. This point has been demonstrated in great detail in the study of a city of 20,000 by sociologists Albert Schaffer and Ruth Connor Schaffer, who also found that social scientists studying community power structures have done very little investigation of this organization.[55] This lack of attention is all the more surprising because an earlier interview study in a Midwestern industrial city of 45,000 produced similar results.[56]

In larger cities, the chamber often takes a secondary role to a smaller, more elite business group. This has been the case especially since World War II, when big businessmen became interested in having an organization with a more "civic-minded," disinterested image to foster redevelopment and renewal:

> After the Second World War, the leading businessmen of most large cities organized themselves to prepare ambitious plans for the redevelopment of the central business districts. The Central Area Committee of Chicago, Civic Progress in St. Louis, the Allegheny Conference in Pittsburgh, the Civic Conference in Boston, the Greater Philadelphia Movement— these and many more organizations were formed on the same pattern. The business elite of the city met privately, agreed upon more or less comprehensive plans for the redevelopment of the central city, and presented the plans to the press, the politicians, and the public as their contribution to civic welfare.... The new committees were different in that they consisted of a few "big men" whose only concern was with the central business district and who, far from regarding them-

selves as special interests, insisted that they served "the public interest," often at a considerable sacrifice of private, business interests.[57]

However, the ruling class does not operate in specific cities through strictly business organizations. It also works through a variety of civic organizations important in shaping public opinion in the urban area—community foundations, taxpayers' associations, charitable organizations, service groups, and cultural centers. The inability to see that these organizations are as central to big-business control of local governments as chambers of commerce and civic redevelopment groups is one of the major weaknesses in the paradigm of pluralistic social science. Thus, Banfield and Wilson treat "power structure and civic leadership" as a chapter separate from "businessmen in politics," a distinction which follows from pluralist assumptions that downplay a class-based perspective.[58] Contrary to this artificial separation, a network analysis of the leadership and financing of civic associations and cultural groups suggests that they are intimately tied to the business community. In Chicago, for example, half the leaders in dozens of civic organizations studied by sociologist Daniel Hoffman were part of the big-business network he identified earlier in his study.[59] As case studies by radical academicians and investigative stories by independent journalists have suggested, these organizations are sometimes used by the ruling class in containing attempts at social change.[60]

The permanent civic associations within local ruling-class networks are not always the best vehicles for bringing about changes in specific governmental structures or policies. Such associations must be concerned with their overall legitimacy and nonpartisan, fair-minded image. They often do not include in their membership the leaders of other sectors of the community who must be involved if a specific program is to be sold to the general public. It is often necessary to create temporary committees to handle particular programs or problems. Such groups were often formed to deal with urban renewal programs in the 1950s and with urban rebellion problems in the 1960s. New Haven, as we have seen, had its Citizens Action Commission to promote urban renewal because of the limitations in the image and policies of the Chamber of Commerce. The numerous emergency committees formed to cope with ghetto uprisings in the late 1960s even coalesced into a national Urban Coalition that promised dramatic changes in urban areas, only to recede in importance after order had been restored. Banfield and Wilson summarize this point: "The limitations of the permanent association being what they are, it is not surprising that when 'important' (and hence controversial) issues arise the almost invariable practice is to create ad hoc associations to do what the permanent ones cannot, or will not, do." [61]

A final organization usually central to any local power structure is the newspaper. Owned and directed by a local wealthy family that is very much a part of the ruling class, or by a nationally based chain with numerous director links to the rest of the corporate network, the newspaper receives two-third of its revenue from advertising. Most of that two-thirds comes from local business sources, especially department stores. Expansion of advertising means profits for the newspaper, and the newspaper becomes a booster for citywide growth and development. Because it has no particular stake in the nature and direction of this growth, it is often seen as a nonpartisan institution which stands above the fight among special interests.

> The newspaper has no axe to grind, except the one axe which holds the community elite together: growth. It is for this reason that the newspaper tends to achieve a statesman-like attitude in the community and is deferred to as something other than a special interest by the special interests.[62]

Due to the local newspaper's dependence upon the success of other businesses and its acceptance of the ideology of growth, it generally can be counted on to print stories and editorials favorable to the "good government" reformers, to suppress stories critical of the local business community, and to accept uncritically the handouts and press releases of the United Fund, the community foundation, and other organizations in the local civic network.

Local power networks for dealing with city government have many common elements, but the focal point of each network will vary from city to city and decade to decade. In Dallas, for example, the major policy organ of the ruling class is the Citizens' Council, which suggests policies and selects candidates to run for office. In Cleveland, a community foundation is at the center of the power structure's ongoing activities; receiving its monies from the largest banks in the city, and from family foundations closely related to those banks, the foundation created new policies during the 1960s in areas ranging from education to administrative reform. In Atlanta in the 1950s, Hunter found that a behind-the-scenes "49 club" was quite important; today the 28-man Action Forum, half black and half white, has taken its place.[63]

Future researchers may find that institutionalized task forces of business "volunteers" have gained new prominence in ruling-class dominance of urban governments. *Business Week* reported in mid-1976 that many cities and states were using these task forces of nonpaid businessmen to tackle fiscal problems, and in the process to restore "confidence" in the business community as well: "Companies, for their part, concerned with skyrocketing tax bills and antibusiness public opinion, are pouring thousands of man-hours and millions of dollars into volunteer efforts. The results are paying off with well-documented savings to the tax payers." [64] In short, if the changes in Atlanta over the past twenty-five years and the introduction of business task forces in many cities are any indication, there will always be room for future studies of local power structures. Changing conditions bring new leaders, new institutions, and new methods of rule to the forefront in the ongoing struggle for power in the American social structure.

## CONCLUSION

Chambers of commerce, civic improvement associations, community foundations, research bureaus, United Funds, community service organizations, and newspapers—these are likely to be the ingredients making up the local policy-planning and opinion-molding network through which a local power structure connects to the national urban policy network, to city government, and to the rest of the population. The shape and size of the power structure may vary from city to city due to the nature of its economic base, size of the city, function of the city in the national economic structure, the strength of working-class organizations, and several other variables. But it is likely, except in very small towns and dying cities, that the local power structure will be related to or part of the national ruling class.

This perspective suggests that it should be the task of community power structure studies to determine the exact nature of the local power network, the ways that it relates to the national ruling class, and factors which account for variations in these relationships from city to city. Such studies should begin with the assumption that the city is a growth machine, and that ruling-class leaders in different cities have different strategies for growth because of their city's specific functions (e.g., financial, industrial, educational, recreational) in the regional, national, and—increasingly—international political economy of corporate capitalism.[65]

Working within this kind of framework, we have been able to determine—contrary to Dahl, Polsby, and Wolfinger—that the city of New Haven has a power structure which intervenes decisively in local affairs of concern to it and is part of the national ruling class.

We have shown that the connections, resources, and needs of Yale University explain why this relatively minor city was able to attract strong local administrators and receive a large amount of urban renewal money from Washington. By beginning our work with a network analysis of people and institutions, which guided us in a search for relevant memos, minutes, position papers, and private letters, we have established in considerable detail the specifics of a policy-formation process that was only partially uncovered by Dahl due to his reliance upon interviews and observations conducted in the midst of a media promotional campaign several years after many of the key policies had been developed under the guidance of the New Haven Chamber of Commerce, with the largest local banks and Yale University looming in the background.

Since it is generally agreed that *Who Governs?* is the best and most detailed of the decision-making studies claiming to show a pluralistic power structure in a city of any significance, it seems likely that studies similar to ours in other allegedly pluralistic cities would uncover power structures that dominate local government and relate in a variety of ways to the national ruling class. If pluralism lives in America, it is in very small towns with little ruling-class involvement, on issues like metropolitan government where both Democratic machines and Republican suburbanites are adamantly opposed to structural change, and on a few governmental decisions of a situational nature which do not challenge overall systemic and structural domination by the national ruling class.

There is, then, a ruling social class in the United States, and this sociological fact should be the starting point for economic and political analysis at any level. This ruling class includes about .5 to 1 percent of the population, owns about 20-25 percent of all privately held wealth, receives a highly disproportionate share of the yearly national income, controls major banks and corporations, formulates economic and political programs through a series of policy networks, and dominates—at the very least—the federal government in Washington, D.C., and city government in New Haven, Connecticut.

## NOTES
1. For the most recent statement of this point, see Charles M. Bonjean and Michael D. Grimes, "Community Power: Issues and Findings," in Joseph Lopreato and Lionel S. Lewis (eds.), *Social Stratification* (Harper & Row, 1974). Reviewing studies which correlate demographic-ecological and policy-output variables with types of power structures, they report minimal and often contradictory results.

For a similar critique, and an excellent annotated bibliography which provides thorough and accurate abstracts of most community power studies published before 1971, see Willis D. Hawley and James H. Svara, *The Study of Community Power: A Bibliographic Review* (American Bibliographic Center—Clio Press, 1972).

2. For studies which show the role of method and disciplinary background in what the researcher finds, see John Walton, "Substance and Artifact: The Current Status of Research on Community Power Structure," *American Journal of Sociology* (January 1966); idem, "Discipline, Method, and Community Power: A Note on the Sociology of Knowledge," *American Sociological Review* (October 1966); James E. Curtis and John W. Petras, "Community Power, Power Studies, and the Sociology of Knowledge," *Human Organization* (Fall 1970); Claire W. Gilbert, "Communities, Power Structures, and Research Bias," *Polity* (Winter 1971).

3. Harvey Molotch, "The City as a Growth Machine," *American Journal of Sociology* (September 1976). For a similar point in an excellent paper on urban renewal, see John Mollenkopf, "The Post-War Politics of Urban Development," *Politics and Society* (Winter 1976).

4. Terry N. Clark, *Community Power and Policy Outputs* (Sage, 1973), p. 5.

5. For a pathbreaking study which transcends these limitations, see Roger Friedland, "Class Power and the Central City: The Contradictions of Urban Growth" (Ph.D. diss., University of Wisconsin, 1976). Using a variety of indices, Friedland operationalizes *corporate power* and *labor-union power*, then determines how these and other variables—e.g., local governmental structure, percentage of poor people in the central city—relate to the size and type of urban renewal program carried out in the city. In general, corporate power has a significant impact on the structure of urban renewal policy formation—as defined by use of corporate plans and the size of the urban renewal bureaucracy—and on the level of urban renewal activity—as defined by number of projects undertaken and acres cleared. The presence of organized labor and a mayor-council form of government also have positive effects. Friedland's research is unique because it combines quantitative sophistication with a thorough grounding in urban political economy and class structure.

6. On the greater upward mobility of women rated as more attractive, see Glen H. Elder, Jr., "Appearance and Education in Marriage Mobility," *American Sociological Review* (August 1969).

7. For documentation of this portrait of the upper class as a social class, see the evidence and footnotes in Cleveland Amory, *The Proper Bostonians* (Dutton, 1947); E. Digby Baltzell, *Philadelphia Gentlemen: The Making of a National Upper Class* (Free Press, 1958); idem, *The Protestant Establishment* (Random House, 1964); Stephen Birmingham, *The Right People* (Little, Brown, 1968); G. William Domhoff, *Who Rules America?* (Prentice-Hall, 1967), ch. 1; idem, *The Higher Circles* (Random House, 1970), chs. 1-4; idem, *The Bohemian Grove and Other Retreats* (Harper & Row, 1974), ch. 3; Lucy Kavaler, *The Private World of High Society* (Douglas McKay, 1960); Peter Prescott, *A World of Our Own* (Coward-McCann, 1970); Dixon Wecter, *The Saga of American Society* (Scribner's, 1937); Paul M. Blumberg and P.W. Paul, "Continuities and Discontinuities in Upper Class Marriages," *Journal of Marriage and the Family* (February 1975).

8. August B. Hollingshead and Fritz C. Redlich, *Social Class and Mental Illness: A Community Study* (Wiley, 1958), pp. 75-76, 80, provide information on the schooling and vacationing patterns of what they call the "core group" within "Class I" in the New Haven area.

9. George W. Pierson, *The Education of American Leaders* (Praeger, 1969), found that 6 percent of the presidents in the top 500 corporations for 1956 were Yale graduates, second only to Harvard; that 8 percent of the officers in thirty-nine of the top fifty-one banks in 1955 were Yale graduates, second only to Harvard; that 15 percent of the partners in eighty-two large law firms in seventeen cities in 1955 were Yale graduates, second only to Harvard; and that 11 percent of leaders of thirty major foundations in 1957 were Yale graduates, once again second only to Harvard. As Dahl notes (p. 138), "old Blues are famous for their loyalty to Yale."

10. Baltzell, *Protestant Establishment*, p. 371.

11. For detailed studies of this network, with relevant references to previous work, see John Sonquist and Thomas Koenig, "Interlocking Directorates in the Top U.S. Corporations: A Graph Theory Approach," *The Insurgent Sociologist* (Spring 1975); Philip Bonacich and G. William Domhoff, "Overlapping Memberships among Clubs and Policy Groups of the American Ruling Class," American Sociological Association, Chicago, September 1977.

12. Baltzell, *Philadelphia Gentlemen*, esp. ch. 14.

13. Domhoff, *Who Rules America*, p. 51.

14. G. William Domhoff, "Social Clubs, Policy-Planning Groups, and Corporations: A Network Study of Ruling-Class Cohesiveness," *The Insurgent Sociologist* (Spring 1975): 179.

15. For information on corporate lawvers and their role in the American business community, see Spencer Klaw, "The Wall Street Lawyers," *Fortune* (February 1958); Jack Ladinsky, "Careers of Lawyers, Law Practice, and Legal Background," *American Sociological Review* 52 (1963); Erwin O. Smigel, *The Wall Street Lawyer* (Free Press, 1964); Albert P. Melone, "Lawyers and the Republic: The American Bar Association and Public Policy" (Ph.D. diss., University of Iowa, 1972); Joseph Goulden, *The Superlawyers* (Weybright & Talley, 1972); Paul Hoffman, *Lions in the Street* (Saturday Review Press, 1973).

16. G. William Domhoff, *The Bohemian Grove and Other Retreats: A Study in Ruling Class Cohesiveness* (Harper & Row, 1974), pp. 107-8.

17. For information on policy-planning groups, see Domhoff, *Higher Circles*, chs. 5-6; idem, *Fat Cats and Democrats* (Prentice-Hall, 1972), ch. 5; idem, "State and Ruling Class in Corporate America," *The Insurgent Sociologist* (Spring 1974); Laurence Shoup and William Minter, *Imperial Brain Trust: The Council on Foreign Relations and American Foreign Policy* (Monthly Review Press, 1977); Karl Schrifgiesser, *Business and Public Policy: The Role of the Committee for Economic Development, 1942-1967* (Prentice-Hall, 1967).

18. Philip Bonacich, "Using Boolean Algebra to Analyze Overlapping Memberships," in K. Schuessler (ed.), *Sociological Methodology* (Jossey-Bass, 1977).

19. Harry Chotiner, "The Aristocracy of Virtue: The First American Ruling Class, 1733-1801" (Ph.D. diss., University of California, Santa Cruz, 1975); idem, "The American Revolution and the American Left," *Socialist Revolution* (April-June 1976).

20. For an articulation of the general problems of power structure research in terms of the systemic (class), structural (organizational), and situational (decisional) levels, see Robert R. Alford, "Paradigms of Relations between State and Society," in Leon N. Lindberg et al. (eds.), *Stress and Contradiction in Modern Capitalism* (Lexington, 1975); Robert R. Alford and Roger Friedland, "Political Participation and Public Policy," *Annual Review of Sociology* 1 (1975). In what follows in this chapter I will try to show how the ruling class operated at the systemic and structural levels to insure its power at the local level even when it was not directly involved in local decision making.

21. James Weinstein, *The Corporate Ideal in the Liberal State* (Beacon, 1968), p. 95.

22. For evidence on this point, see Frank M. Stewart, *A Half Century of Municipal Reform: The History of the National Municipal League* (University of California Press, 1950), pp. 173-79; Norman N. Gill, *Municipal Research Bureaus* (American Council on Public Affairs, 1944), pp. 107-18; and especially Samuel P. Hays, "The Politics of Reform in Municipal Government in the Progressive Era," *Pacific Northwest Quarterly* (October 1964). Hays summarizes previous studies as well as presenting original data on the upper-class nature of the reform movement in Pittsburgh.

23. For systematic evidence on the effects several of these reforms have in

decreasing voter turnout, see Robert R. Alford and Eugene C. Lee, "Voting Turnout in American Cities," *The American Political Science Review* (September 1968).

24. John C. Bollens and John C. Ries, *The City Manager Profession: Myths and Realities* (Public Administration Service, 1969).

25. Weinstein, ch. 4; Willis D. Hawley, *Nonpartisan Elections and the Case for Party Politics* (Wiley, 1973) provides recent systematic evidence for this point on one of these "reforms," nonpartisan elections.

26. Weinstein, p. 99.

27. Leonard E. Goodall, *The American Metropolis* (Merrill, 1968), pp. 60-61.

28. For a history of these bureaus which shows their business support and orientation, see Gill.

29. Ibid., pp. 16-17.

30. Ibid.

31. Stewart, p. 165.

32. Ibid.

33. Louis Brownlow, *A Passion for Anonymity* (University of Chicago Press, 1958), pp. 254-55. Brownlow, who served as the head of PACH until 1945, tells the story of the origins and functions of the urban policy network as well as anyone before or since, but for a good scholarly account in the context of a larger study, see Barry D. Karl, *Executive Reorganization and Reform in the New Deal* (Harvard University Press, 1963).

34. Ibid., pp. 249-50. For more recent evidence on the existence of this network, see Suzanne Farkas, *Urban Lobbying* (New York University Press, 1971), pp. 80-97. Farkas's book contains much useful information, but it confuses the history of the network by overemphasizing Brownlow and ignoring the systematic role of Rockefeller money in creating it. It also tends to stay at the staff level in its analysis of linkages, thereby downplaying the legitimization and boundary-setting provided by the businessmen, lawyers, and foundation officials who oversee the general operation.

The Social Science Research Council mentioned by Brownlow was put together in 1924 by Ruml and Merriam, and funded by the Rockefellers through their foundations. It became the main organization through which social scientists' efforts were channeled into questions of concern to leaders within the ruling class. There was hardly a development in conventional social science between 1925 and 1955 that was independent of very specific administrative structuring and financial nourishment by the SSRC and the Rockefeller foundations.

For further information on the SSRC, see Benjamin W. Smith, "Some Notes on the Social Science Research Council and the Governing Class Theory of American Politics," American Political Science Association Meetings, Los Angeles, September 1970; Elbridge Sibley, *The Social Science Research Council: The First Fifty Years* (Social Science Research Council, 1975).

35. Richard J. Stillman, *The Rise of the International City Managers' Association* (University of New Mexico Press, 1974).

36. And if, as seems likely, the history of other urban-oriented professions is similar to that of city managers, then we see again the danger of overemphasizing specific decisions at the expense of more general features which ensure ruling-class domination. This point is very relevant to the question of urban renewal, for one of the professional organizations created and maintained in the University of Chicago-PACH-Rockefeller urban complex was the National Association of Housing and Redevelopment Officials.

37. Brownlow, p. 465.

38. Ibid., p. 466. Farkas, p. 23, reports that the unofficial relationships were made official in the 1960s when a presidential executive order decreed that "executive

Community Power Structures and the National Ruling Class **179**

agencies consult with the Conference of Mayors, the Governors' Conference, the National League of Cities, and the National Association of Counties about all major administrative regulations affecting federal urban programs or involving relations among the three levels of government. The effect of this requirement was to give to the inter-governmental lobby a formal position as part of the federal decision-making machinery."

39. The Urban Institute, which receives most of its monies from large foundation and governmental contracts, describes itself as a "nongovernmental, nonprofit research organization" which "cooperates with federal agencies, states, cities, associations of public officials, the academic community and other researchers" (*Search: A Report from the Urban Institute,* Summer 1976, p. 13). This characterization suggests little connection to the leading institutions of the ruling class. However, among the twenty trustees of the institute for 1976 were institute chairman Charles L. Schultze, a Senior Fellow of The Brookings Institution, who became chairman of the Council of Economic Advisors in the Carter administration; Kingman Brewster, Jr., president of Yale University; John H. Filer, chairman of Aetna Life and Casualty Company; Bayless A. Manning, president of the Council on Foreign Relations; Arjay Miller, dean of the Graduate School of Business at Stanford University; and Cyrus R. Vance, a Wall Street lawyer and Yale University trustee who became secretary of state in the Carter administration. Eight of the remaining trustees were businessmen or corporate lawyers, two were professors, two were executives of urban organizations, one was a Rockefeller (John D., IV), and one was the president of the institute itself. The Urban Institute board is symbolic of the kind of leadership which sets the tone and general directions of the urban policy network.

40. The four reports produced by the Committee for Economic Development on urban problems are *Guiding Metropolitan Growth* (1960), *Modernizing Local Government* (1966), *Reshaping Government in Metropolitan Areas* (1970), and *Improving Productivity in State and Local Government* (1976).

For a succinct analysis of how such "reforms" function to protect the interests of the ruling class in urban areas, see Robert R. Alford, "Reform Government and Bureaucracy: American Responses to the Urban 'Crisis,'" International Sociological Association Meetings, Messina (Italy), April 1976.

41. *Modernizing Local Government* (U.S. Chamber of Commerce, Washington, D.C., 1967), pp. 16, 23. I am grateful to one of my former students, Ronald Pomerantz, for his paper on "Local Government and the Ruling Class" (Winter 1972), which brings together information on books and pamphlets of the U.S. Chamber of Commerce, the NML, and several other urban organizations.

42. For a clique-detection analysis based on Boolean algebra which places the NML in a clique with the American Assembly, the National Planning Association, the Council on Foreign Relations, The Brookings Institution, and the Century Association, among others, see Bonacich and Domhoff.

43. For good accounts of this conflict within the business community, see Weinstein; Schriftgiesser.

44. Raymond Wolfinger, *The Politics of Progress* (Prentice-Hall, 1974), ch. 11, shows that the Democratic machine successfully opposed several attempts to change the form of city government in New Haven.

45. Goodall, pp. 34-35; Stewart, p. 68, relates that the NML in its 1941 Model City Charter suggests as an alternative to the council-manager form the strong-mayor plan, "with an elective mayor as chief administrator to have all the administrative powers and control given to the manager in the council-manager form of government."

46. Hays, p. 163, reports that elites in Pittsburgh had the city charter amended in the state legislature, thereby avoiding a vote within the city itself.

47. Michael Royko, *Boss* (Dutton, 1971), provides an excellent account of how the big-business community works with the Democratic machine in Chicago.

48. See Friedland for several good examples of big business aid to cities in obtaining federal monies during the 1960s and 1970s.

49. Goodall, ch. 7, has a good overview of proponents and opponents of metropolitan government.

50. Brownlow, pp. 282-85.

51. Ibid., p. 280.

52. Ibid.

53. Friedland; Mollenkopf.

54. Edward Banfield and James Q. Wilson, *City Politics* (Harvard University Press and MIT Press, 1963), p. 334.

55. Albert Schaffer and Ruth Connor Schaffer, *Woodruff: A Study of Community Decision Making* (University of North Carolina Press, 1970), ch. 6, esp. fn. pp. 144-45 reviewing the sparse literature on the topic. However, there is evidence that the Chamber of Commerce and similar business organizations provide many city council members in small cities. See Kenneth Prewitt, *The Recruitment of Political Leadership* (Bobbs-Merrill, 1970), pp. 84-86, 161-64.

56. Peter Rossi, "The Organizational Structure of an American Community," in Amitai Etzioni (ed.), *Complex Organizations* (Holt, Rinehart, & Winston, 1961).

57. Banfield and Wilson, p. 267. For excellent studies of how these committees have operated, see Theodore Hayes, *Power Structure and Urban Policy: Who Rules in Oakland?* (McGraw-Hill, 1972); Chester Hartman, *Yerba Buena: Land Grab and Community Resistance in San Francisco* (Glide, 1974); Bob Sheak, "Rape of St. Louis: A Study of Corporate Responsibility" (Socialist Caucus and Radical Action for People, Summer 1971).

58. Banfield and Wilson, chs. 17, 18.

59. Daniel R. Hoffman, "The Power Elite of Chicago: The Concepts of Community Power and an Empirical Study" (M.A. thesis, University of California, Santa Barbara, 1971), p. 96.

60. Bob Sheak, "The Center of Power in St. Louis, Interlocking Directorates, and the United Fund" (Radical Action for People, October 1970); Roldo Bartimole, "Torch Now Pressures Legal Aid with Fund Cut," *Point of View*(2150 Rexwood Rd., Cleveland, Ohio), March 27, 1976, p. 1.

61. Banfield and Wilson, p. 257.

62. Molotch, pp. 315-16. Molotch, ibid., also notes that "the papers do tend to support 'good planning principles' in some form because such good planning is a long-term force that makes for even more potential future growth."

63. On Dallas, see Carol E. Thometz, *The Decision-Makers: The Power Structure of Dallas* (Southern Methodist University Press, 1963). On Cleveland, see William C. Barnard, "Foundations: Life Force of the City," *Cleveland Plain Dealer*, June 15, 16, 17, 1969. On Atlanta's "49 club," see Floyd Hunter, *Community Power Structure* (University of North Carolina Press, 1953), pp. 85-86. On the Action Forum in Atlanta, see "Integrating Atlanta's Power Elite," *Business Week*, November 24, 1973.

64. "Business Volunteers: A Boon to Government," *Business Week*, June 7, 1976.

65. For the ways in which the political economy of the Bay Area and the "Pacific Rim" shaped the growth strategies and urban renewal plans of San Francisco business leaders, see Hartman, *Yerba Buena*.

# NAME AND SUBJECT INDEX

party machine, 62, 107, 160, 168, 175
Department of Public Health, 64
Detroit, 152
Detroit Club, 155
De Vane, William, 103
Development Administrator, 109, 110
De Vito, Dominic, 86
Dickey, Charles D., 27, 158
Distillers Limited, 28
Downe, Charles, 65, 67, 69, 85
Dudley, George W., 65, 67, 69
Dudley, Samuel W., 26

Economic notables, 3, 5, 6, 15, 16, 147, 153, 155, 157, 159; Dahl's list, 29; defined, 4; goals of, 7; overlap with social notables, 13, 14, 30-36
Edwards, Charles G., 51
Eisenhower, Dwight D., 41, 43, 56, 75; administration, 142
Electoral process, 138
Electorate, 5, 6
Ellsberg, Daniel, 44-45
*The Empire of High Finance,* 142
Equitable Life, 156
Euston, Andrew F., 86
Executive-Centered coalition, 48, 49

Fairchild, Fred, 27, 157
Falsey, William J., 86, 97, 99, 110
Farmington Club, 154
Fefferman, Hilbert, 55
Feiss, Carl, 104
Fidelity and Casualty Company, 156
Firestone Tire and Rubber Company, 26
First Federal Savings and Loan Association, 26
First National City Bank of New York, 156
First New Haven National Bank, 18, 19, 20, 23, 29, 30, 31, 78, 85, 86, 99, 107, 108, 109, 110, 113, 156
Fletcher, Richard, 78
Foard, Ashley A., 55
Ford Foundation, 166
Forty-Nine Club, 173
Fosdick, Raymond B., 164
Fraser, Angus, 65, 79

Friedland, Roger, 129, 170
Freese, Carl, 99, 102, 103, 109

General Electric, 27, 154
General Ice Cream Corporation, 156
George H. Walker and Company, 28
George Street, 92-93, 111
Giese, Herman R., 93, 94-95
Golden, John, 110
Goldman, Sachs and Company, 52
"Good government," 161, 173
Governor's Conference, 165
Grace–New Haven Hospital, 67, 70, 80, 83, 86, 104; extension, 105
Graduates Club, 16, 17, 26, 27, 30, 67, 78, 93, 99
Graph theory, 133
Greater Philadelphia Movement, 171
"The Green," 65, 70
Greer, Guy, 52, 56
Greer-Hansen, 52, 53, 60
Greer, Scott, 75
Griswold, Whitney A., 93, 103, 158
Gross, Bertram M., 131
Guaranty Trust Bank, 28
Gulick, Luther, 164
Gumbart, William, 109
Gumbart, Corbin, Tyler and Cooper, 20-21, 28, 93, 109, 156

Hardley, Morris, 27
Hamden, 80
Hamilton, Rolland J., 51
Hansen, Alvin, 52, 53, 54, 55, 56
Hansen-Bettman, 54
Hanover Bank, 27
Harbor, 67, 69
*Harpers Magazine,* 43
Harriman, (Mrs.) Edward H., 163
Harrison, Wallace K., 64
Hartford, 17, 48, 91, 152, 154, 155
Hartford Club, 154
Hawkins, Charles W., 57, 58, 59
Healy, Kent, 27
Highways, planning of, 69
High Standard Manufacturing, 155
Hill Area, 80
Hoffman, Daniel, 172
Holden, Ruben A., 26, 28, 92, 99, 103